RADIOHEAD

Tempo
A Rowman & Littlefield Music Series on Rock, Pop, and Culture

Series Editor: Scott Calhoun

Tempo: A Rowman & Littlefield Music Series on Rock, Pop, and Culture offers titles that explore rock and popular music through the lens of social and cultural history, revealing the dynamic relationship between musicians, music, and their milieu. Like other major art forms, rock and pop music comment on their cultural, political, and even economic situation, reflecting the technological advances, psychological concerns, religious feelings, and artistic trends of their times. Contributions to the **Tempo** series are the ideal introduction to major pop and rock artists and genres.

RADIOHEAD

Music for a Global Future

Phil Rose

ROWMAN & LITTLEFIELD
Lanham • Boulder • New York • London

Published by Rowman & Littlefield
A wholly owned subsidiary of The Rowman & Littlefield Publishing Group, Inc.
4501 Forbes Boulevard, Suite 200, Lanham, Maryland 20706
www.rowman.com

6 Tinworth Street, London, SE11 5AL, United Kingdom

British Library Cataloguing in Publication Information Available

Library of Congress Cataloging-in-Publication Data

Names: Rose, Phil, 1969– author.
Title: Radiohead : music for a global future / Phil Rose.
Description: Lanham : Rowman & Littlefield, [2019] | Series: Tempo: a Rowman & Littlefield music series | Includes bibliographical references and index.
Identifiers: LCCN 2018050756 (print) | LCCN 2018051207 (ebook) | ISBN 9781442279308 (Electronic) | ISBN 9781442279292 (cloth : alk. paper)
Subjects: LCSH: Radiohead (Musical group) | Alternative rock music—History and criticism.
Classification: LCC ML421.R25 (ebook) | LCC ML421.R25 R66 2019 (print) | DDC 782.42166092/2—dc23
LC record available at https://lccn.loc.gov/2018050756

∞ ™ The paper used in this publication meets the minimum requirements of American National Standard for Information Sciences Permanence of Paper for Printed Library Materials, ANSI/NISO Z39.48-1992.

Printed in the United States of America

*Dedicated to all human beings
and especially my mother.*

In the dark times
Will there be singing?
There will be singing.
Of the dark times.
—Bertolt Brecht, "Motto to the Svendborg Poems"

The voice in my head first and foremost says that during times when things are bad, people don't want to hear it. There's times when we're open to it as a general population and there's times when we aren't. When things are fucking heavy, we don't want to be reminded. [But] I'm always conscious of the fact that what [Donwood] and I do—what we all do—is to remind them.
—Thom Yorke

CONTENTS

SERIES EDITOR'S FOREWORD

Radiohead might be just too perfect a choice of subject matter for this Tempo series, given its interest in examining rock and popular music as it intersects with its times, taking cues from giving direction to culture. Tempo aims to ultimately give readers a greater appreciation of the fluidity of influence among rock, popular music, and culture, and while Radiohead did not form in 1985 to become a subject of study itself, or to express critical theories of mediated existence, it now sort of feels that it did. It might be more plausible to say Radiohead set out to perform mediated existence itself—not theories about it—and because it has done it so well, there is now this welcomed feeling of inevitability about the band for academics and fans. It is just that kind of band, which makes it a perfect topic for Tempo and a fitting last book for the series as it comes to an end with this study from Phil Rose.

Having written about Radiohead before, as well as about Roger Waters and Pink Floyd, Rose brings his measured blend of learning from deep fandom and scholarship to help readers appreciate what could otherwise feel like a "good-for-you" lecture on the importance of a rock band. Rose's way of applying crucial theories of media, communication, and cultural studies to Radiohead is a great match for Radiohead's way of creating music that theorizes about media, communication, and culture. Rock and roll has become considerably smarter because of Radiohead, Rose points out, but not any less fun. If you want an artist's insight into the malaise, hesitations, cynicisms, and enduring dreams of humans in an internet age at the end of a millennium and into the first decades of a new one, Radiohead is now necessary listening. If you have realized the surest thing one can say about cultural institutions is that they will eventually fail, leaving you hoping for a better iteration of your next mediated existence, Radiohead is there to be your romantic inspiration as you both still hold firmly to the belief in a better future, however much effort it might take to build it.

Scott Calhoun

TIMELINE

Cultural Events	*Radiohead* *Life and Career*
1944 Bretton Woods Agreement; founding of IMF and World Bank 1947 General Agreement on Tariffs and Trade (GATT)	
	1985 Radiohead forms at Abingdon School
	1986 first gig at Jericho Tavern as "On a Friday"
1989 fall of Berlin Wall; rise of digital wireless mobile communication; release of Timothy Berners-Lee's World Wide Web	1987–1991 Radiohead attend university, except for Jonny
1989/1990 Margaret Thatcher's failed introduction of Community Charge (poll tax) 1990, September 11 George H. W. Bush describes "new world order"	

Cultural Events	Radiohead Life and Career
1991 February 13 Amiriyah Shelter Massacre; first Gulf War March reunification of Germany December 26 dissolution of Soviet Union	**1991** Colin Greenwood gives demo recording to Keith Wozencroft of EMI December 21 group signs six-album deal with EMI
1991–1999 Balkans conflict	**1992** name change to Radiohead May *Drill* (EP) released
1993 February 26 first World Trade Center bombing	1993 February *Pablo Honey* released
1994 April 7 to mid-July Rwandan genocide October World Bank/International Monetary Fund demonstration (Madrid)	**1994** Stanley Donwood becomes group's resident album cover artist alongside Yorke September *My Iron Lung* (EP) released
1995 January 1 WTO commences	**1995** March *The Bends* released July–September tour as opener for REM September "Lucky" produced for Warchild
	1996 new recording equipment installed at Canned Applause
1997 February Ralph Nader's group Public Citizen leaks online draft of OECD's proposed Multilateral Agreement on Investment (MAI)	**1997** Donwood creates band's first website June *OK Computer* released December *No Surprises/Running from Demons* released

Cultural Events	Radiohead Life and Career
1998 50th anniversary United Nations Declaration of Human Rights May 16 first "global" day of action, coinciding with WTO in Geneva; international civil society movement against MAI	**1998** Grammy Best Alternative Rock Performance: *OK Computer* April *Airbag/How Am I Driving?* (EP) released May 7 *Television Commercials* (video) released November *Meeting People Is Easy* (Grant Gee) band's first webcast
1999 January Racak "incident" (Kosovo War) June G8 protests, Cologne November "Battle of Seattle"; World Trade Organization protests	**1999** band introduces W.A.S.T.E., online merchandising operation June Yorke's Drop the Debt campaign, Cologne
2000 Y2K breakdown fears September IMF/World Bank protests in Prague November U.S. election: George W. Bush	2000 October *Kid A* released
2001 January iTunes commences July G8 protests in Genoa September 9/11 attacks on United States; "War on Terror" and systematic U.S. torture programs begin October U.S.-led invasion of Afghanistan	**2001** Grammy Best Alternative Rock Performance: *Kid A* June *Amnesiac* released November *I Might Be Wrong: Live Recordings* released
	2002 Grammy Best Recording Package: *Amnesiac* Special Edition

Cultural Events	*Radiohead* *Life and Career*
2003 March Anglo-American invasion of Iraq; false claims of weapons of mass destruction December UN report on climate change	**2003** June *Hail to the Thief* released October *Body Song* released
2004 January Hutton Inquiry into mysterious death of Dr. David Kelly (UK government biological weapons expert, former Iraq weapons inspector, and whistleblower) April leak of graphic photos depicting U.S. soldiers abusing and sexually humiliating Iraq prisoners at Abu Ghraib prison	**2004** Nigel Godrich Grammy for Producer of the Year: *Hail to the Thief* Jonny Greenwood becomes composer in residence for BBC Concert Orchestra April *Com Lag (2plus2isfive)* released December *The Most Gigantic Lying Mouth of All Time* DVD release
2005 July London terror attacks	
2006 October Wikileaks launched	**2006** January–April recording with outside producer Mark "Spike" Stent July *The Eraser* released
2007 São Paulo near total ban on outdoor advertising/billboards April Virginia Tech Massacre	**2007** October 1 *In Rainbows* pay-what-you-want download commences December *There Will Be Blood* released
2008 September 15 global financial meltdown; international banks soon deemed "too big to fail," an	**2008** April W.A.S.T.E. Central serves as social networking service for Radiohead fans

Cultural Events

admission that free enterprise
system is finished
October Congress passes $700
billion "bailout" to stabilize Wall
Street
November Barack Obama elected
as first African American
president

2009
December Copenhagen Climate
Summit

2010
May Bradley Manning arrested for
leaking classified U.S. information

2011
Arab Spring; Occupy Wall Street
October global protests

Radiohead Life and Career

May *The Eraser Rmxs* released
June EMI release *Greatest Hits*
December EMI Radiohead box
set; New Year's Eve hourlong
program *Scotch Mist*

2009
Ed O'Brien becomes founding
director of Featured Artists
Coalition
February Grammy Award for Best
Alternative Music Album: *In
Rainbows*
March first performances in South
America
August first ever appearances in
Austria and Czech Republic;
"Harry Patch (In Memory Of)"
released—proceeds to British
Legion; "These Are My Twisted
Words" uploaded to BitTorrent

2010
Atoms for Peace performances
August *Familial* released
November *Norwegian Wood*
released

2011
February 18 *The King of Limbs*
self-released as download
August *Running Blind* EP
(Selway)
September Jonny Greenwood
performances in Poland with

Cultural Events	*Radiohead* *Life and Career*
	Steve Reich and Krzysztof Penderecki October *TKOL RMX 1234567*; *We Need to Talk About Kevin* released December *The King of Limbs: Live from the Basement*
	2012 Colin Greenwood becomes global ambassador for Children's Radio Foundation; Selway becomes patron of Oxford's Pegasus Theatre; Jonny Greenwood's three-month residency with Australian Chamber Orchestra (Sydney) March Greenwood/Penderecki recording released September *The Master* released
2013 June Edward Snowden leaks regarding extent of U.S. surveillance—flees to Hong Kong and then to Russia	2013 February *Amok* released March Steve Reich debuts Radiohead-inspired piece "Radio Rewrite"
2014 ISIS/ISIL gains global prominence	2014 February Polyfauna app September *Tomorrow's Modern Boxes* released on BitTorrent October *Weatherhouse* released December *Inherent Vice* released
2015 December Paris UN Climate Conference	2015 March *OK Computer* preserved as part of Library of Congress National Recording Registry

Cultural Events

Radiohead
Life and Career

May 21–June 6 *The Panic Office* exhibition, Sydney, Australia—Yorke contributes *Subterranea* soundtrack

August Yorke and Rachel Owen announce separation

September Selway dedicates drum set to Manchester Central Library in memory of Scott Johnson

November *Junun* released

December Yorke performs solo set of new Radiohead songs at United Nations Climate Change Conference in Paris

December 25 "Spectre" released on audio-streaming site SoundCloud

2016
June "Brexit" vote
November election of Donald Trump

2016
May 8 *A Moon Shaped Pool* released as download
December death of Rachel Owen

2017
February *Radiohead Complete*—400-page songbook of lyrics/guitar parts

June nominated for Rock and Roll Hall of Fame induction; *OK Computer—OKNOTOK 1997 2017* released

July 19 controversial Tel Aviv performance

September *Let Me Go* released

November "Water" released on vinyl (with Australian Chamber

Cultural Events	Radiohead Life and Career
	Orchestra); O'Brien/Fender release EOB Sustainer Stratocaster
	December *Phantom Thread* released; *Tomorrow's Modern Boxes* reissued on CD, vinyl, and streaming services
2018 July 250,000 protestors demonstrate in London against Trump's first UK visit	2018 March *You Were Never Really Here* released
	July composition for solo piano "88 (No. 1)" released as sheet music

INTRODUCTION

My first encounter with Radiohead occurred when a guitar student brought in "Creep" as the next song he wanted to learn. The name of the band didn't register with me at the time, only the song. Already having taught this individual for a considerable duration of time, I'd begun to get the impression he was less genuinely interested in learning how to play guitar than in the prospect of gaining the kind of popularity that sometimes attaches to those who play the instrument—especially and, ironically, the kind of popularity that appeals to potential romantic interests. It wasn't the first time I'd heard the song, but it had certainly not made an initial positive impression, and it would not be until some years later that I'd begin to get to know the group's work.

In fact, I was not to become properly aware of Radiohead until the release of *OK Computer* in 1997. Later that year, I began to perform alongside another local musician, who soon introduced me to that landmark album, along with its impressive 1995 predecessor *The Bends*. I was immediately impressed with how the band downplayed photographs of themselves on album sleeves and covers, as well as with the evident high sophistication involved in the production of both recordings. Over the course of the next three and a half years that our duo performed together, prior to my partner moving to another part of the country, we incorporated into our repertoire our own versions of many of the songs that comprise these two albums. I've continued to incorporate miscellaneous songs from subsequent Radiohead recordings into my ongoing solo performances.

I am roughly the same age as the members of Radiohead. In fact, while I'm younger than Philip Selway, Ed O'Brien, and Thom Yorke, I'm older than Colin and Jonny Greenwood. All of us belong to "Generation X," a phrase that, even in the 1950s, was associated with alienated youth, as with Billy Idol's punk rock band that took the formulation as its name in 1976. It wasn't until 1991, in any case, when the Canadian author Douglas Coupland released his celebrated book of that title that demographers likewise adopted the name, nearly three decades following the advent of this generational cohort. Prior to this, we'd been labeled "post-boomers," "the MTV generation," or the new "lost generation." The "X," however, was a placeholder for something unknown, of course, a generation that appeared to resist definition.

With this in mind, it is significant that the subtitle of Coupland's book is *Tales for an Accelerated Culture*, since this is a theme that Radiohead's work also addresses, and nowhere more so than with *OK Computer*. This phenomenon that Coupland describes isn't simply limited to our efforts to do things and to get places faster, and the associated technologies that help us to do so. What is also accelerated is the scale and pace of technical innovation, which manifests itself in the general speed-up of cultural change. This element has made contemporary human life qualitatively different to that of our forebearers, given that the dynamic of cultural acceleration is such that it requires our constant personal and social readaptation to new technological environments. Perpetually readjusting to the ever-new conditions of survival that this unprecedented scale of global technological innovation is creating, we collectively constitute explorers whose parts are being played out on almost an entirely new stage.

Many of the questions we face are simply reformulations of earlier ones, but many also present us with new and uncharted territories of concern, whether we're referring to information overload, human cloning, or other forms of biotechnology, mass surveillance, automation, industrial hog farming, global climate change, geoengineering, or the military-industrial complex. One of this book's primary purposes is to trace how Radiohead draws our awareness toward such issues, and I'd suggest that the band's corpus therefore presents an important resource for assisting us in the social and psychic navigation of our new technological age.

Nowhere is this more apparent than in the title *OK Computer*, an album that appeared in the immediate wake of the emerging World Wide Web's rollout in the early 1990s. But as "Fitter Happier," the recording's seventh track, demonstrates with its intoning robotic voice, Radiohead's concern isn't limited to consideration of the newly emerging environment of digital communications. The band's work, in fact, is more broadly engaged with the process of how we shape our tools and techniques overall, and how, in turn, they shape us. As part of this probe, I'll also highlight how the band members have artistically, and commercially, taken charge of their media environment with the aim of harnessing this vast potential toward their own creative ends.

Over the length of their careers, they've also pursued moral and political goals. This is another aspect of the group with which I've always been dramatically impressed, and that I'll foreground in my account of the band and its work. Inherent not only in the messages conveyed by their impressive artifacts of musical multimedia, this orientation was evident too in the band members' prominent roles as political and social activists. Much of their creative work, in fact, provides an emotional backdrop for the haunting significance that attaches to the prospect of our becoming active global citizens, particularly following the chill created in the aftermath of the September 11, 2001, terrorist attacks in New York and Washington.

The paranoid expressions encoded in Radiohead's work that preceded these catastrophic, life-changing, and millennium-launching events, however, were already strongly resonating within the culture. In addition to fear, Radiohead's songs articulate a diverse range of negative emotions, including distress, anger, and disgust. In this regard, James Doheny in *Radiohead: Karma Police* reminds us of Daniel Goleman's suggestion, from Goleman's celebrated 1995 book *Emotional Intelligence*, that "perhaps the most disturbing single piece of data in this book comes from a massive survey of parents and teachers and shows a worldwide trend for the present generation of children to be more troubled emotionally than the last." As Goleman goes on to say, of course speaking now of the Millennials (Generation Y), they're "more lonely and depressed, more angry and unruly, more nervous and prone to worry, more impulsive and aggressive." The relevance of this observation was recently reinforced, with the World Health Organization announcing in 2017 that depression is now the number one debilitating condition for individuals across the globe, and among none more so than Generation Z. Radiohead's songs frequently allow an outlet for the expression of such complexes of emotion, while elucidating, as well, their likely meanings and origins. This makes them a valuable asset for cultural survival.

A further aspect that makes the band's songs an ongoing edifying asset is their general condemnation of violence and all varieties of persecution. This is a theme that runs throughout the group's catalog, and one that possesses renewed relevance of course in the age of Donald Trump and Brexit. That Thom Yorke primarily levels this condemnation at himself, nevertheless, is what makes the band's albums particularly important popular culture texts: they provide hope in the face of our estrangement from the natural environment, from tradition, from each other, and from the structures of power within which we find ourselves so inadequately embedded.

In chapter 1 I trace the early days of the band, which formed in 1985, at Abingdon School in Oxfordshire, England, playing its first gig the following year at the famed Jericho Tavern in Oxford where the group lived. Originally called "On a Friday," even after most of them had left Oxford for universities around the country, the young musicians kept the band together, rehearsing on weekends. In 1991, they began recording demos, performing more frequently, and attracting the attention of Chris Hufford and Bryce Edge, who would become the group's managers, and remain so to this day. After a chance meeting with an A&R representative from EMI, they signed a six-album recording contract and recorded a four-song EP of demos called *Drill* (1992). This was followed by the release of the aforementioned single "Creep," which appeared the next year on their debut album *Pablo Honey* to little immediate acclaim, until the now-famous song was picked up in Israel, and by an alternative radio station in San Francisco. The band began its first American tour just as the song's video went into high rotation on MTV, and this development combined with their nonstop, intercontinental touring over the course of the next two years taught the band what was involved with being part of the star-making machinery, the effects of which would nearly lead to their early demise. Though Radiohead's initial offering admittedly lacks the sophistication of their following work, there are reasons for this that I shall explore here alongside the legacy of "Creep."

In 1994, the band interrupted work on its second album to continue touring, and so chapter 2 will explore how the group, and especially Yorke, soon became disillusioned by the complexion of their newfound fame. Later in the year they released the EP *My Iron Lung*, which included a number of what were to become B sides of the singles off their modestly successful second album *The Bends*. This album sees the band begin to explore themes that would preoccupy them in the coming years. Among them were the electronic communications revolution in "Planet Telex" and a paranoid estrangement found in "The Bends," as well as the artifice associated with technology's commercial voice in "Fake Plastic Trees" and the apocalyptic strains of our civilizational decline in "Street Spirit," with its quasi-religious directive to "immerse your soul in love," fittingly offered as the ultimate antidote to such possibilities. *The Bends* showcases the group's increased musical and technical sophistication as recording artists, and it's with this album that they would also first meet their longtime producer/collaborator Nigel Godrich. Still a collection of generally unrelated songs, Radiohead would wait until its next offering to adopt the concept album form that would appear as a kind of staple of their future output.

Chapter 3 details how further recording and touring in 1996 preceded the 1997 release of *OK Computer*, a recording often compared to Pink Floyd's *Dark Side of the Moon* (1973), both for its artistry and for the effects that each production's massive success had on its respective group's career and creative experience. The album debuted at number one in the UK charts and propelled the group to international stardom and critical acclaim. Expressing a looming, end-of-millennium, and Y2K sense of dread, *OK Computer* appeared, just as the digital age began its shift into high gear. The album's concerns are expressed via futuristic science-fiction imagery, and range from the ill effects of recent technical developments to economic globalization and our increasing propensity for demonization—as conveyed in the title of their yearlong "Against Demons" world tour, concurrent with the album's release. Following them around on the tour, filmmaker Grant Gee documented the band's experience of dealing with the trappings of the music industry and the music press in his film *Meeting People Is Easy* (1998), which illustrated that things were, once again, weighing heavily on the band,

and especially Yorke. During this period, the band released two more EPs, *Airbag/How Am I Driving?*, which further explores technological themes, and *No Surprises/Running from Demons*, comprised of B sides from *OK Computer*. They also released a collection of videos, whose ironic name, *Seven Television Commercials*, betrayed the band members' feelings about this televisual aspect of their business; they soon began the process of reconstructing their shattered selves, primarily by invoking a revolution in their creative methods and approach that included the ongoing experimentation with various technologies old and new. Given the complex nature of *OK Computer*, in chapter 4 I address the album with a close reading of the songs; its richness necessarily permits much longer commentary than any of the band's other work.

In chapter 5, I address how reports began to surface that the band was calling it quits, and it became known that Yorke had fallen into a state of deep depression during this period. This partly had to do with the critical reception of *OK Computer*, especially the close examination of its lyrics and their projection back onto Yorke as their author. Hence, when they returned to begin work on *Kid A* (2000), conditions were very strained over the eighteen-month process, especially as Yorke had also developed writer's paralysis. Notwithstanding, the album was to become highly successful, even a Grammy winner, partly due to its unique online marketing but also as a result of the buzz associated with being leaked on the Napster file-sharing service in advance of its official release. Having turned their creative process upside down, an experience that included adopting numerous different forms of instrumentation and electronic treatments, the band's gradual reconstruction enabled Yorke to continue forging ahead.

Following from *OK Computer* then, *Kid A* and chapter 6 similarly deal with issues related to increasing mass surveillance, propaganda, and the paranoia associated with contemporary political activism, with which the band members were increasingly becoming involved. Returning us to the problem of technology, the album is named for the first human clone, and adorning its cover are images of a coming ice age. We're assured in the first track, nevertheless, that everything's "in its right place." As with *OK Computer*, however, evidence of violence is pictured on the album sleeve's images, illustrating cannibalistic mutant humanoid bears with machine guns. Violence is also evident in lines such as "We got heads on sticks / You got ventriloquists" and "cut the kids in half," which, like the previous album, displays concern for the world we appear to be leaving to our young people, who, along with the rats in the song "Kid A," are left following the piper "out of town."

Because it was the result of the same series of recording sessions, *Kid A*'s follow-up came eight months later with *Amnesiac* (2001), the recording with which chapter 6 is likewise engaged. The album sustains and further explores such themes and others, including issues related to intellectual property, as seen in sketched images on the recording's inner sleeve of a life form, stamped with the copyright symbol. Fore-shadowing September 11, 2001, which was to occur just months after the album's release, there are also images of "twin towers" seen in various places, something that later surprised even the band. On the album's inner sleeve is printed "THE DECLINE AND FALL OF THE ROMAN EMPIRE," once again alluding to the threat of a dark age on the horizon. Of course, civilization is typically linked to the ability to read and write (dark ages are typically linked to the absence of these skills), and this connection is articulated not only in the image of the book that adorns *Amnesiac*'s cover but also through the special collector's "book edition" of the release. It was made plain as well via the references to Ray Bradbury's *Fahrenheit 451* that were featured during the performances that supported the double album release. Technologies of writing oper-ate as forms of transpersonal memory, a theme evident in the title *Amnesiac*, and dark ages tend likewise to be periods of forgetting, when cultures are for the most part unable to either access or remember any kind of recorded past. The focus on technology continues with the song "Dollars and Cents," and violence rears its ugly head again in songs such as "Knives Out" and "Hunting Bears," and in the lines "we are hungry for a lynching," which appear in the album's concluding piece. Sadistic violence was evident as well in an interactive, online image associated with the album, which allowed the user to inflict endless shocks upon a crying minotaur, featured also on the album's front cov-er. This of course foreshadowed immanent reports of the U.S. Central Intelligence Agency's sponsorship of torture, not only in Guantanamo Bay, Cuba, but also around the world.

Having regained their footing by 2002–2003, chapter 7 chronicles the rather more relaxed process that went into the completion of Radio-head's sixth album *Hail to the Thief* (2003). Of course, this was in spite of its being partly a reaction to the devastating 2000 election of George

W. Bush and his imminent launch of the War on Terror. In this regard, the Orwellian reference within the first song's title, "2 + 2 = 5," expresses the creeping totalitarianism that was threatening to emerge. Hope for the fate of the children nonetheless reappears in "Sail to the Moon," written for Yorke's son Noah, but this moment of tenderness is later countered by the narrators of the track "We Want Young Blood." The album bears the subtitle "The Gloaming" (from the Middle English, meaning "twilight"), partly because—as we find out when the singer of "The Lukewarm" berates his listeners—"YOU HAVE NOT BEEN PAYING ATTEN-TION." Another reason for this state of affairs, nonetheless, is clearly identified as information overload, apparent in the album's artwork, which portrays the sense of continuous distraction that characterizes the evolving contemporary information environment. The theme of information glut is evident too in the lines of "Scatterbrain," where "Yesterday's headlines blown by the wind, Yesterday's people end up SCAT-TERBRAIN." Invoking Dante, "The Lukewarm" refers to those who are close to being in hell but are not quite there, indirectly reflecting the Renaissance poet's well-known formulation that "the hottest places in hell are reserved for those who, in times of great moral crisis, maintain their neutrality." The album buttresses an overall foreboding. And intoning that "your alarm bells should be ringing" and how "we are accidents waiting to happen," the album concludes with "The Wolf at the Door"—threatening to steal the activist singer's children, whom he won't see again should he "not pay the ransom."

Following the tour that supported *Hail to the Thief*, the band took a break, in order to spend time with their families and to work on outside projects. And so chapter 8 outlines these efforts, including Jonny Greenwood's soundtracks to the films *Bodysong* (2004) and *There Will Be Blood* (2007), and Thom Yorke's debut solo album *The Eraser* (2006). When Radiohead's contract with EMI ended, they began to forge a new path on which to proceed within a music industry experiencing the ongoing effects of the digital communications revolution. Work for *In Rainbows* (2007) began toward the beginning of 2005, and the recording was released as a pay-what-you-want download on the band's website, a move that provoked worldwide discussion about the future of the music industry. A box-set edition of the album included both vinyl and CD versions of a second disc of songs from the recording sessions, along with a hardcover book of associated artwork. They released the album physically a few months later on independent labels XL Recordings in the UK and TBD Records in North America, and the album charted at number one in both countries, before proceeding to win the 2009 Grammy Award for Best Alternative Music Album. The album's protagonist finds himself again on a journey marred by scenes of persecution, making a brief escape, before arriving at the pearly gates by the end of the album in "Videotape." This return to apocalyptic imagery is preempted in "Reckoner" and "House of Cards," with the latter's suggestions that "infrastructure will collapse" and its refrains of "denial" and "your ears should be burning." In 2008, Radiohead launched W.A.S.T.E. Central, which serves as a social networking service for Radiohead fans, while EMI released its greatest hits album *Radiohead: The Best Of*, without approval or involvement from the band. During the last half of the year and into early 2009, the group promoted the album, with tours in Europe, North America, South America, and Japan.

Chapter 9 recounts how Radiohead and Nigel Godrich began new recording sessions later that year and released a tribute song to the last British veteran of World War I, titled "Harry Patch (In Memory Of)," donating the proceeds to the British Legion. Immediately following, another new song called "These Are My Twisted Words" was uploaded (possibly by the band itself) to BitTorrent; one week later the band released the song for free download on their website. Yorke was also beginning to put together a new group called Atoms for Peace that included Godrich and the Red Hot Chili Peppers' bassist Flea; Atoms for Peace performed a small number of North American shows in 2010, the year that also saw the release of drummer Phil Selway's first solo album *Familial*. Radiohead launched its eighth album *The King of Limbs* at the beginning of 2011, first as a self-release through the band's website, followed a month later by retail vinyl and CD releases. The beginning of 2012 saw them undertake their first extended North American tour in four years. For this they recruited Portishead drummer Clive Deamer to participate in the band's performances of the new repertoire. *The King of Limbs* is less overtly apocalyptic than its predecessors, though it employs similar imagery to that found on *Hail to the Thief* and *In Rainbows*, including fairy-tale-like references, such as "Mr. Magpie," and the visuals of forests and ghoulish specters featured on its cover. Hints of savagery abide, and Yorke sustains his use of space and water imagery from its similar employment on *In Rainbows* and elsewhere. The overriding strain, and one that has been present throughout their work, is a spiritual one. And death makes itself known once again toward the end of the album, in the lines "I think I have had my fill / I think I should give up the ghost." Similarly, the promotional newspaper that featured alongside the album's release points out that its newsprint is written on a type of paper that will yellow quickly, "mirroring the inexorable decay of all things." The penultimate page of the newspaper, however, reads "Love?" and the album closes with the song "Separator" in which the singer intones, "If you think this is over then you're wrong."

Following the tour in support of *King of Limbs*, Radiohead took another break, and as detailed in chapter 10, early 2013 saw the release of an Atoms for Peace album called *Amok*. Early in 2014, Radiohead released their *Polyfauna* app for iOS and Android phones, which used imagery and musical elements from *The King of Limbs* and saw the band collaborating with British digital arts studio Universal Everything. Toward the end of the year, Yorke released a second solo album called *Tomorrow's Modern Boxes*, and Selway did likewise with *Weatherhouse*. Jonny Greenwood, meanwhile, composed another soundtrack, this time for the film *Inherent Vice*, which was released around the same time. Radiohead had also begun work on a new album, and according to Greenwood, the band had changed its methods, once again imposing limits and using both "very old and very new technology." In 2015, an installation of Radiohead artist Stanley Donwood's artwork called *The Panic Office* took place in Sydney, Australia, for which Yorke contributed a soundtrack called *Subterranea*, and that year the band sued Parlophone/EMI for the troubling "packaging" deductions that had long been made from downloads of their back catalog. Illustrating his ongoing commitment to fighting climate change, Yorke performed a solo set of new Radiohead songs at December's United Nations Climate Change Conference in Paris, and on Christmas Day the band released on the audio-streaming site SoundCloud a new song called "Spectre," a captivating piece that was intended for the most recent James Bond film but was in the end rejected for that purpose. The song was likewise made available as one of two bonus tracks with the 2016 boxed set version of Radiohead's ninth album *A Moon Shaped Pool*. Once again employing a number of fairy-tale-like references, the album emphasizes themes of love, attachment, and loss, and it seems to modulate back and forth between a "ragdoll mankind" that "we can create" and one that is "helpless to resist" and entering into "our darkest hour." Prior to the album's release, some of the band's fans received a mysterious postcard reading "we know where you live." This "low flying panic attack" reflected a return to themes of paranoia, polarization, and scapegoating evident in the song's opening track "Burn the Witch."

Finally, chapter 11 details a band looking backward, to some extent, as they approach midlife, with aging children, a partner lost to cancer, and the release of the remastered version of *OK Computer—OKNOTOK 1997 2017*, among numerous other projects.

The band is still also very much in the present, however, concluding its 2018 tour dates and courting controversy along the way. Though I never thought I'd have occasion to say it, the Presidency of Donald J. Trump has made George W. Bush seem like a statesman. Given our present circumstances, should we wish to survive him, we'd best hold on to our seats, *pay attention*, and actively resist. Nothing's inevitable should we be willing to do so and, in the words of Henry David Thoreau, should we have the ability to maintain the courage for letting our lives be "counter-frictions" to the "machine."

1

BECOMING RADIOHEAD

Pablo Honey and the Legacy of "Creep" (1985–1993)

Jonathan Hale recounts how, in the early days of Radiohead's career, Thom Yorke pointed out that all the band's songs "come from a state of conflict, and if you listen to them in the right way, you're bound to feel that conflict as well." Colin and Jonny Greenwood, in this regard, lost their father when the former was seven years old and the latter five, and it's well known how artistic creativity often helps to provide a type of symbolic repair for the victims of such circumstances. Yorke, fortunately, didn't suffer such a tragic personal loss, but his childhood was characterized by endless ridicule, as a result of his notable deformity. Born with his left eye paralyzed and fixed shut, he endured five operations before his sixth birthday, only to be left with a drooping eye. Though born in England, he spent his childhood in Scotland, and his family moved a number of times, as a result of his father's work. This required him to be always reencountering victimization from fresh groups of children, leading to his frequent involvement in fights, a tendency that was to follow him, at least briefly, into his university years. First inspired by Queen's *A Night at the Opera* (1975), his first song, written at the age of eleven, was called "Mushroom Cloud." This Cold War image, of course, gave constant definition to the cultural context of Generation X, though Yorke's song was apparently not concerned so much with atomic warfare's potential massive destruction as with the image as technological and visual marvel. Notwithstanding, Yorke was later to say, as Hale again records, "A lot of our songs—the good ones, anyway—come from crisis points in my life. Songwriting, for me, is therapy."

Even when he entered the school outside what is now his home base of Oxford at which he was first to meet his future bandmates, the posh and private Abingdon School for boys, he was soon endowed with the nasty nickname "Salamander." In his typically understated manner, as Tim Footman notes in *Radiohead: A Visual Documentary*, Yorke was to tell the now-defunct magazine *Melody Maker* of the school, "It was purgatory. It nurtured all the worst aspects of the British middle class: snobbery, lack of tolerance and right-wing stupidity." Yorke was especially unenamored with the school's headmaster, whom he made the subject of a 1996 B side called "Bishop's Robes," and whom he referred to as "a fascist idiot," when introducing the song the previous year, prior to a performance in Stockholm. Among the song's lines are "Children taught to kill, to tear themselves to bits on playing fields," apparently reflecting the school's promotion of competitive individualism. In contrast, Radiohead, on an early version of the band's website, included a quote, popularized by Ernest Hemingway, but apparently an old Hindu maxim: "There is nothing noble in being superior to your fellow men. True nobility is being superior to your former self." In this relation, according to Jonny Greenwood, while at the school, the band members attended church services every morning, reflecting another aspect of the school's mission—to "forever sing praises to the Lord" and to "give boys an understanding of the Christian heritage," an interesting element of the band's experience to which we shall return.

At Abingdon, Yorke first met up with bassist Colin Greenwood and guitarist Ed O'Brien, and they soon invited drummer Phil Selway to join them. Along with three female saxophonists, only later was the younger Jonny Greenwood invited to join, the irony being that he was ultimately to become Yorke's closest collaborator within the group. Among the band's most prominent early influences were Magazine, the Smiths, Joy Division, the Fall, Joe Jackson, Talking Heads, U2, Japan, the Pixies, Elvis Costello, and R.E.M. Concerning the influence of Costello on his writing, and particularly of his song "I'll Wear It Proudly," Yorke was to remark, as Hale includes, "It's really upsetting, but I feel better afterwards, which is my ideal ingredient for a song."

Well into honing their craft together at Abingdon, the band members, like most Gen Xers who'd been sold the idea that education would guarantee them meaningful and reliable employment, took a hiatus in order to attend university but returned home on holidays and weekends to reconvene for rehearsals. As the eldest, Selway was the first to graduate. After taking a year off in order to work, he went to Liverpool Polytechnic to study English and history. O'Brien, meanwhile, entered Manchester University for politics and economics, while the elder Greenwood attended Cambridge to major in English, particularly post–World War II American literature. Yorke, on the other hand, also deciding to take a year off, took advantage of staying in Oxford, to develop his working relationship with the younger Greenwood, who had yet to complete his studies at Abingdon. The following year, however, Yorke pursued his education in art and English literature at Exeter University, where he purportedly found himself within a comfortable and creative environment. During this time, he developed an affinity for electronic dance music and DJing, as well as for the technique of scanning and overlaying digital images with the art school's new Macintosh computers, a skill that was put to use in producing future Radiohead album cover art. While there, he met Dan Rickwood, better known as Stanley Donwood, who, along with Tchock (Yorke's pseudonym), became the group's resident album cover artist following *Pablo Honey*. As Donwood was to say, notes Trevor Baker, "I think that my obsession with nuclear apocalypse, Ebola pandemics, global cataclysm and Radiohead's particular brand of unsettling melody have gone together quite well."

In his third year at Exeter, Yorke became increasingly politicized, helping to found an anarchist collective and becoming part of an antifascist club. He participated in protests involving approximately 200,000 demonstrators in the wake of UK prime minister Margaret Thatcher's 1989–1990 short-lived introduction of a Community Charge (or poll tax), and years later, the video to the track "Harrowdown Hill" from his first solo album *The Eraser* (2006) was to include footage of this massive demonstration. Meanwhile, Selway, having completed his degree in Liverpool, returned to Oxford, began working, and became involved with the Samaritans, an organization that counsels troubled and suicidal teens and for which he was to become a kind of spokesman in future years.

It was not until 1991, when everyone except Jonny Greenwood had finished his degree, that the band began to think about pursuing a recording contract. Since their Abingdon days, the group had been known as "On a Friday," in reference to the day they'd typically been able to rehearse. They soon invested in a three-song demo, recorded in a sixteen-track studio on the outskirts of Oxford, and for better and for worse began living communally. Around this time they attracted the attention of Chris Hufford. Hufford attended a performance at the Jericho Tavern in Oxford and then, with his partner Bryce Edge, offered cheaply at their Courtyard Studio to produce a new five-song cassette demo that became known as *Manic Hedgehog*, after the name of the Oxford indie record store where it was made available for purchase. Upon conclusion of the sessions, Hufford and Edge were so impressed with the results that they offered to become the group's managers, a proposition that the band accepted. Working in a local record shop following the completion of his Cambridge studies, Colin Greenwood, during a fortuitous encounter in the summer of 1991, gave a copy of the recording to Keith Wozencroft, a former EMI sales representative, who was just beginning work as an A&R representative for the company's subsidiary Parlophone. Wozencroft followed up, seeing the band on a couple of occasions, the last of which featured around two dozen other A&R people from various companies in attendance. On December 21, therefore, at the end of a year in which it remarkably performed less than ten club shows, the group signed a six-album deal with Wozencroft and EMI. And so, Jonny Greenwood, after only a few weeks of attendance, left the Oxford Polytechnic, where he had been enrolled to study music and psychology.

In February 1992, *Melody Maker* gave the band its first national media coverage, but this came under the name "On a Friday." The record company and band mutually understood that a new name needed to be immediately forthcoming. So, drawing on a Talking Heads song from *True Stories* (1986), the band determined upon "Radiohead." Of the image conjured by the name, Yorke was to say, noted again in Hale, that it's "about the way you take information in. The way you respond to the environment you're put in" and, ordinarily, one's typical "passive acceptance" of that environment. Yorke's reference to information environments and taking information in is relevant, particularly if we acknowledge that *any* environment functions as a complex message system that instructs us how to think, feel, and behave, as well as when to speak and what kinds of things we can say. Though we might think of courtrooms, classrooms, or places of worship, this of course goes as well for more explicitly "technological environments" as we shall touch on herein.

In the spring of 1992, Radiohead released an EP called *Drill*. Two of its songs—"You" and "Thinking About You"—had appeared on the *Manic Hedgehog* tape,[1] while the others were the new tracks "Prove Yourself" and "Stupid Car." The first three were to be rerecorded and to appear on their debut album *Pablo Honey*, which they didn't begin working on until they'd completed their first UK tour in support of Catherine Wheel. Chris Hufford had produced *Drill*, but it was decided that the band's recording would continue instead with American producers Paul Kolderie and Sean Slade, known especially for their work with Buffalo Tom and the Pixies. By the fall, they had released a second EP introducing "Creep," which was backed by the songs "Lurgee," "Inside My Head," and "Million Dollar Question," only the first two being later included on *Pablo Honey*. Although the UK release was not commercially successful, *New Musical Express* named "Creep" among the top ten singles of 1992. As the end of the year approached, the song, an early version of which Yorke had written while back at Exeter, was getting picked up in Israel and in San Francisco, where it soon spread along the California coast, inducing EMI's "sister company," Capitol, to also release the song as a U.S. single, notwithstanding the relative lack of interest the UK release had generated. In early 1993, the band released its third offering, the anthemic "Anyone Can Play Guitar," backed by the songs "Faithless, the Wonder Boy" and "Coke Babies," the latter two, again, not appearing on *Pablo Honey*, which was released just a couple of weeks later at the end of February.

The debut album's name derives from an underground tape of New York's Jerky Boy phone pranksters, who made an art out of executing and recording the prank call. In this particular case, a Jerky Boy called up someone pretending to be their mother, beginning the call with a falsetto voice saying, "Pablo, Honey." Touring prior to and immediately following work on the album, the recording sessions took place within a schedule of three weeks, a punishingly tight duration for a group of relative novices, upon whom the album's final mix was, more or less, imposed. "The situation required somebody to take the situation in hand or the record wouldn't have been made," the band's longtime producer Nigel Godrich was to say, as Baker records, in relation to the role played by producers Paul Kolderie and Sean Slade. "As a result, they felt, quite justifiably, that they hadn't had as much of an input as they'd liked. They hadn't made a record they felt was completely theirs—even the artwork was done by somebody else." While *Melody Maker* aptly and famously appraised the album as "promisingly imperfect," many Radiohead commentators have been comparatively relentless in their somewhat simplistic dismissal of its quality. With no reverb on the album, as was the style of Nirvana and Suede, Ed O'Brien was to refer to *Pablo Honey* in terms of "a collection of our greatest hits as an unsigned . . . naïve, young, impressionable band,"[2] while Jonny Greenwood was to add, also recorded in Martin Clarke's *Hysterical and Useless*, "*Pablo Honey* was our first time in the studio, so what can you expect? The Beatles' first album was almost all covers." Yorke, meanwhile, told *Mojo*'s Nick Kent in 2001, as Mark Paytress recounts, "I just don't recognise myself at all," and has likewise said of the work, included in Hale, "I like the first album, but we were naïve. We didn't really know how to use the studio."

What the album thus lacks is exactly the technical richness that, with later recordings, came to characterize Radiohead's use of the recording studio. Nevertheless, representing a not insignificant level of maturity, its various subtle guitar arrangements and production techniques are impressive, being best heard with headphones. Though it also lacks the cohesive conceptual richness of their later work, much of the imagery and themes that Radiohead was subsequently to employ we get a glimpse of here. For instance, though it's never clear whom the song addresses, the opening track "You," with its interesting and irregular meter, introduces the apocalyptic theme into the band's work. Speaking as it does of self-doubt and the imminent end of the world, it features "you, me, and everything" being "caught in the fire" and "drowning." Clearly, this sentiment segues nicely into that associated with the second track "Creep," but given the song's reappearance as an alternate version at the end of the recording, and its overall significance to the band, I'll return to address it at the end of this chapter.

The album's punkish next song "How Do You?" is typically dismissed, even by the band itself, and features aggressive playing, alongside the barely audible sample of the Jerky Boys' "Pablo, honey" sketch, from which the album takes its name. The song is sung in an exaggerated manner, critically describing "a bigot" that "cheats," "steals," and "bullies," but the chorus ironically prompts listeners to question themselves, asking "how do you?" This is followed by "Stop Whispering," the oldest song on *Pablo Honey* and largely a two-chord progression in the manner and style of U2 that is likewise a call to action and freedom of expression, which prompts the listener to "stop whispering" and "start shouting." With its suggestion of having a "complaint," forgetting what it is, and concluding that "it doesn't matter anyway," this strain of low confidence and self-doubt that the song confronts is sustained throughout "Thinking About You." Both on the album and in relation to previous versions of the song, two alternatively strummed acoustics, with the addition of subtle background harmonium and very sparse, clean electric guitar, replace the former ground of distortion. Adopting the intimacy of the confessional singer-songwriter style, "Thinking About You" intimately expresses the singer's masturbatory estrangement from a lover who now appears unobtainable as a result of the individual's new-found fame.

In this relation, Yorke himself appears to have had a long-held desire for stardom, apparently articulating the ambition "TO BE A POP STAR" in an art show booklet from his final year. This sentiment is satirized in the next track "Anyone Can Play Guitar," whose singer intones that he wants to be Jim Morrison, so that he "won't be a nothing anymore." Having recently seen Oliver Stone's 1991 film *The Doors*, and critiquing its portrayal of Morrison as "some type of Arthurian legend or something," Yorke says, in Baker, that while the song has mostly been taken as sarcastic, it is also a celebration of playing the guitar: "I do want to be in a band when I'm in heaven"; he said, "It's the best thing you can do with your life." True to its title, the song's introductory soundscape features everyone who'd been working at the studio, including all band members, the producers, and even the cook, each with their own track, obtaining different electric guitar sounds. For his track, Jonny Greenwood was to use a paintbrush on the strings.

As throughout *OK Computer*, in "Ripcord" we get images of airplanes and accidents, in this case the addressee dropping from the sky and being unable to open the parachute, a fate identified as "the answer to your prayers." We also get intimations of technology ("soul destroyed with clever toys for little boys"), speed ("1,000 miles an hour"), and political innocence ("politics in power that you don't understand"). The protagonist of the next track, however, powerfully asserts that he's not a "Vegetable," a tag often meaning that an individual has no personality, is stupid, or lives a dull life. Interestingly, the song is an early manifestation of Yorke's later tendency to alternate between contrasting dispositions of a protagonist within the same song. In this regard, "Vegetable" features pronounced dynamic contrasts between its softer verses and bridge (during which we may be more prone to identifying with the singer) and the powerfully distorted, assertive, and aggressive persona that takes over during the choruses and prechoruses, and who boasts, "I spit on the hand that feeds me" and "I will not control myself." This dynamic is apparent throughout the song's bridge. Invoking a shift to the relative minor, its initially soft and sober purifying waters that "spray" and "run all over me" are followed by a crescendoing distortion that expresses the desire for getting even. This is immediately followed by a forceful and powerfully backed guitar solo.

An earlier version of "Prove Yourself" had been the lead track from the *Drill* EP, and the song features a narrator who, despite his aspirations, occupies a hostile environment, in which he "can't afford to breathe" or "sit without a gun." Along with everyone else, looking back up to "the cathode ray" (our now-obsolesced TV and computer screens), he repeatedly resolves that he's "better off dead." The next song, "I Can't," continues with another protagonist's "strange and creeping doubt" and his repeated resolution that, despite trying, he just "can't" succeed.

This sense of malaise gets at least a temporary remedy in the next track "Lurgee," a word meaning illness or ailment. In this context, however, the singer "got better" and "got strong," particularly after the departure of his apparently toxic addressee. Allegedly a companion song to "Creep," it is, according to Yorke, purportedly about "getting rid of someone who'd been hanging round for ages and fucking you up." For all intents and purposes, however, this sense of comfort dissipates at the end of the song, and *Pablo Honey* concludes with the once again troubled narrator of "Blow Out," who finds himself with decayed feelings and in danger of coming apart. "Everything I touch turns to stone," sings the narrator, and the song transitions from its Latin-tinged first section to the heavy, "blow out" dissonance with which the song and album terminate.

As noted above, *Pablo Honey* concludes with the rerecorded reprise of "Creep,"[3] minus the earlier version's prechorus expletive, to help facilitate potential radio play. The song was recorded largely live, and—as part of a zeitgeist of songs that included Nirvana's "Smells Like Teen Spirit" and Beck's "Loser," James Doheny notes—"became adapted as a Generation X anthem of affirmational self-loathing and alienation." The origin of the song's notable highlight, its ominous rifle-cocking guitar effect, had two alternative explanations; the first had Jonny Greenwood simply checking his guitar volume, and the second had him expressing frustration with a song he didn't particularly like. About an allegedly unobtainable girl with whom Yorke was obsessively infatuated, his deadpan delivery betrays that the song is not to be taken entirely seriously, though the entry of an acoustic piano inflates the slow, final chorus with a sense of authenticity. As Mac Randall notes in *Exit Music*, the song *was* taken seriously, however, by a British inmate serving time for murder and who sent a chilling letter to Thom saying, "I'm the creep in that song. I killed this bloke. They made me do it. It wasn't me, it was the words in my head." Along with the collection of pressures that accompanied sudden fame, this served to amplify Yorke's considerable psychic discomfort.

During what Greenwood was to dub "the 'Creep' tour," the band performed 350 shows in support of *Pablo Honey* over the course of nearly two years. "We joined this band to write songs and be musicians," Greenwood said in Clarke's book, "but we spent a year being jukeboxes instead." Having to play the same songs over and over was to prove highly arduous, as the group was now eager to get on with writing, recording, and releasing new work. To add insult to injury, although in the UK audiences would generally stay for their entire shows, those in America would often leave in large segments after the group played "Creep," even if it had been the band's second number. The song, of course, put Radiohead on the charts worldwide, helped sell millions of copies of *Pablo Honey*, and made the group an MTV staple (they even mimed the song at an *MTV Beach Party* and were incorporated into the program *Beavis and Butthead*). Subsequent singles, however, weren't to do as well, their big hit pigeonholing them and proving "a major-league millstone," hailed as it was by the readers of *Melody Maker* and *NME* as "single of the year" and by *Rolling Stone* writers as top choice for the best song of 1993. Although he started to refer to

"Creep" as "Crap," Yorke would likewise joke about "the house that Creep built," that is, the house that he bought for his partner Rachel Owen and him in the Oxford suburb of Headington with the significant royalties that the song had brought him and the band. "We sucked Satan's cock," he was soberly to say, as Clarke records, adding however, "It took a year-and-a-half to get back to the people we were . . . to cope with it emotionally." But as manager Chris Hufford remarked of the singer, "Thom found it particularly hard, because all the attention was on him. That whole dilemma of the commercial success against artistic integrity. It was hard for him to find where he sat in that whole framework. Who he was, what he was." Presumably as part of finding and working through some of these details, the group dropped "Creep" from their set, eventually resurrecting the song years later, during a triumphant 2001 homecoming performance in Oxford's South Park. This formed part of the band's adaptation to how the legacy of "Creep" was to become funneled into further existential issues, as the band began recording and then promoting their next album *The Bends*.

2

TOWARD TECHNOLOGICAL APOCALYPSE

Where Do We Go from Here? (1994–1995)

Generation X was to come of age in a decade characterized by "an existential crisis of sorts."[1] The culture of the 1990s was one of both optimism and despair, and an era of disruptive and startling changes that laid the foundations for a different order to emerge in the pending new millennium. The end of the 1980s saw the fall of the Berlin Wall, followed by the dissolution of the Soviet Union in 1991 and the apparent consequent disappearance of the threat of communist totalitarianism. For some, this appeared to illustrate that Western-style capitalist democracy was the paramount form of government, and our expanding electronic information environment facilitated the shift toward "economic globalization." As part of this shift, finance and investment rapidly began to cross borders, while manufacturing sectors began to be located or relocated in so-called developing countries, wherever the price of workers was cheapest and labor and environmental laws typically most lax. The world's people likewise continued increasingly to cross borders, and with immigration now being much more globally and ethnically diverse than in previous waves, this led to further profound and disorienting alterations in national demographics and identity. Wiping out many independent retailers, the period also saw the appearance of national chains of "big box" retail stores that continued the process of bringing a bland type of sameness to metropolitan commercial areas. In a 1991 speech, meanwhile, president George H. W. Bush described the "new world order" as one that would see the United States lead the world in containing aggression and chaos and enforcing the rule of law. But it would soon be revealed that this type of action would only be applied in areas that threatened to destabilize the emerging system. Thus, we saw American intervention and the changing technological face of battle in Iraq during the wars in the Persian Gulf. We saw it as well in the Balkans (1991–1999), a conflict characterized by campaigns of ethnic cleansing. But there were no such actions taken with regard to the 1994 Rwandan genocide. This all took place alongside a rise in homegrown antigovernment extremist movements, as well as the first attack organized by Islamic militants on U.S. soil in the 1993 World Trade Center bombing.

All this provided much of the backdrop to Radiohead's own crises of experience recounted above. Playing 130 shows in fourteen countries, Jonny Greenwood was to comment on the internal conflict that had begun to plague the band throughout the extensive touring of 1993: "Strife infers arguments and things being thrown, but it was *worse* than that. It was a very silent, cold thing, away from each other. No one was really talking to anyone, and we were just trying to get through the year, which was a mistake." As he was to explain further in Mac Randall's *Exit Music*, "There were never rows or anything, which is worse in a way. Everyone withdrew . . . we could never play for fun anymore. We never got to rehearse. We weren't writing songs."

Things were to subside briefly at the beginning of 1994, however, as the band did not have further performance commitments for the next five months. Their plans to get back into the studio at the beginning of January were delayed until late February, allowing them time to reconvene in their newly acquired rehearsal space, a converted apple shed, located near Didcot, Oxfordshire, and later dubbed "Canned Applause." At this point, they were able to begin working on new songs, though some of these in fact predated *Pablo Honey* by a year. As their recording began at RAK Studios in northern London, pressures began to build as the record company established an initial release date of the new album for October, entailing a production schedule that was ultimately to prove highly unrealistic. In its request also that the group begin concentrating first on its next lead-off single, EMI created considerable additional pressure for them. No one could agree what the lead-off single should be, so it was narrowed down to four songs, and the band set off trying successively to record four hit singles. The effort of trying to match the success of "Creep" also posed its own problems for the band members' relationships with each other. According to Ed O'Brien in Martin Clarke's *Hysterical and Useless*, however, "We were questioning everything too much, questioning the fundamentals of what we were doing," adding amusingly, "that's the problem with a university education. You just end up thinking too much."

Given the background of their situation, Radiohead was fortunate to be able to work with producer John Leckie on the tracks that were to become *The Bends*. Leckie began life as an EMI engineer and over time had worked with Phil Spector, George Harrison, John Lennon and Yoko Ono's Plastic Ono Band, Pink Floyd, XTC, the Fall, the Verve, and the Stone Roses. But it was Leckie's work on Magazine's 1978 debut *Real Life* that had primarily won him Radiohead's endorsement. That he was generally very hands off was also to endear him to the band, as did the fact that he came as a package deal with engineer Nigel Godrich, another Generation Xer with whom the band was to form a profound and long-lasting creative relationship in the years to come.

Compounding the ensemble's difficulty in making progress was the fact that someone from the record company or management continued to drop by every three or four days to hear how things were going with the next hit singles. Of the painful self-analysis that the band and Thom Yorke were undergoing at this time, included in the mix were the strained relations that the singer was having with manager Chris Hufford, and Yorke was later to refer to the whole situation as two months of "total fucking meltdown." Relations at the end of this period were likewise strained between Yorke and the rest of the group, partially due to the ego ramifications of the singer's increasing stardom and partly because, while the band wanted to take a break, Yorke wished to carry on working. Given the situation, Leckie suggested that he carry on working with Yorke and that the band take a few days off. He then asked the singer to play the songs that he had ready, just with acoustic guitar accompaniment, and "Fake Plastic Trees" was the first song they completed in this manner. "It all comes from Thom really," Leckie was to report in Clarke's *Hysterical and Useless*, "and they all sort of gather round and support him. It's a good chemistry." Leckie's technique allowed them to make a breakthrough of sorts, and O'Brien was to posit that the band became cognizant of something they really hadn't been aware of in relation to *Pablo Honey*: that was, as Randall's *Exit Music* records, "if it sounds really great with Thom playing acoustic with Phil and . . . [Colin], what was the point in trying to add something more? Everything that was added had to make the track better."

Radiohead was unable to finish the album's sessions at RAK, because they had touring commitments starting in May that would take them to Europe, then back for a few UK shows, before making their first trips to Japan, Hong Kong, Australia, and New Zealand. In reference to another reason for their not keeping to the established production schedule, Leckie was to note of the members of Radiohead in Randall's *Exit Music* "that they're very democratic." As he then explained, "Usually when I go into the studio with a band, someone in the band becomes the central figure and steps into a production role with me. But what happens with Radiohead is that everyone's comment is valid." Consequently, he continued, "when everyone has an opinion, the process gets lengthened."

Radiohead was to continue recording back in England in mid-June, but the sessions were now resumed at Richard Branson's rural Oxfordshire studio complex known as the Manor. Things proceeded well, and almost all the material for *The Bends* was completed there, while what little else remained unfinished was to be accomplished at London's famous Abbey Road Studios. Following their late August debut at the Reading Festival, the band took a brief break from performing and recording in order to allow drummer Phil Selway and his longtime girlfriend to celebrate their marriage and honeymoon. But a month later, EMI released the first product of the Leckie sessions with the *My Iron Lung* single, its four different UK versions all released with different B sides, an industry ploy at the time used—until regulators curtailed it—in order to try to inflate a single's success on the charts, in the expectation that some fans would buy multiple versions or formats. The single entered the UK charts at number twenty-four, at which position it also disappointingly peaked, but it topped the U.S. college radio charts, and this began to enhance Radiohead's appeal to the American nonmainstream music press.

In support of *My Iron Lung*, the group performed another short, ten-show British tour that included Yorke's alma mater Exeter University. This was followed by two nights in Bangkok and an eight-day stint in Mexico, where the band was once again to come to a head, the difficulties they had faced in the studio and on the previous tour having been left to brew unresolved. "We were all completely knackered on this Mexican tour bus," O'Brien recounts in Randall's book, "12 of us, with six bunks and they were about five foot six inches long, so you're getting no sleep. It was just ridiculous. It was something we'd been spending eight or nine years working towards, and it was like, we'd never been totally honest with each other." As Yorke was to add there as well, "Years and years of tension and not saying anything to each other, and basically all the things that had built up since we'd met each other, all came out in one day. . . . We were spitting and fighting and crying." Nevertheless, the venting seemed to prove for the better, overall, and they returned to the UK and Abbey Road, where they were finally to conclude work on the album. In addition to having Leckie finish mixing the project there, a copy of the master tapes was sent to Sean Slade and Paul Kolderie for remixing, in order to hear what the American duo might also make of the tracks. In the end, of the recording's twelve songs, nine of the final mixes were those of Slade and Kolderie.

Radiohead's first official order of business in 1995 was to return to the United States to shoot a couple of videos, the first for "Fake Plastic Trees" and the other for "High and Dry." The latter was released as the band's next UK single in late February, two weeks prior to the worldwide release of *The Bends*, backed by the B sides "Maquiladora," the electric version of "Killer Cars," and two alternative mixes of "Planet Telex." But its performance was lackluster, peaking on *Billboard* at only number seventy-eight in early 1996. "Fake Plastic Trees," released mid-May, was the next single and peaked in June at number twenty. And it featured the B sides "India Rubber" and "How Can You Be Sure" (the only Radiohead track ever to include female background vocals prior to *A Moon Shaped Pool*).

Prior to working with Leckie, Yorke was to say of himself and the band in James Doheny's *Radiohead: Karma Police*, we "never really looked at the studio as an extension of what we were doing, more as an obstacle to get around." But the producer was to teach the group a great deal about making records and how the studio ought to be used. In the words of Jonny Greenwood, as Jonathan Hale records, Leckie "demystified the whole process of recording." Radiohead learned to employ the studio as an instrument, and as Greenwood was also to add in

Doheny, "Using the technology in front of you to actually write something completely opened my head to how we should be doing things." As Doheny was effectively to summarize in this relation, the sounds of *The Bends* are those of a "rock band informed, influenced, and facilitated by the technology and methods of the recording studio."

All this new exposure to recording studio technology and techniques was experienced in the context of massive technological and cultural change taking place in the general shift from an analog to a digital information culture. With the 1989 rise of digital wireless mobile communication and Timothy Berners-Lee's internet-enhancing invention of the World Wide Web, there began a consequent increased public adoption of these technologies by 1993 (I remember first using the internet in 1994). Meanwhile, the fears of Y2K breakdown played out against the impending background of millennial angst. While the electronic information environment was hastening people's abilities to send digital information around the world at the speed of light, transportation technologies had already begun doing the same thing, but shuttling *people* around the world at increasing speeds. Take, for example, Yorke's memory of coming to the United States for Radiohead's first American performance as recorded in *Exit Music*: "We drove overnight from Paris, caught the ferry, drove to Heathrow, then flew to New York. So in 20 hours we covered Paris, New York, and London, and then we drove straight out to Boston." Yorke went on to say, "I woke up on a coach, walked into this hotel in Boston at seven o'clock in the morning, switched on MTV, and there was 'Creep.'"

THE BENDS

It was of course "Creep" and the associated trappings of the band's early success that are referenced in the title *The Bends*, the name of a condition that sometimes characterizes deep-sea divers. Being in deep water increases the level of nitrogen in our bloodstream, and if divers surface too quickly, the rapid change in pressure doesn't permit the nitrogen to dissipate, leaving bubbles in the blood that typically create severe and agonizing discomfort. This provided an analogy for Radiohead's rapid ascendance to stardom, with its grueling tour demands, its record company pressures, its existential crises, and its inevitable critical backlashes. The album cover featured a photograph of Yorke's face, blended with the image of a plastic dummy of the kind with which local medical staff trained people in resuscitation. The image's expression, "somewhere between agony and ecstasy," according to Yorke in *Hysterical and Useless*, made it "just right for the record." The imagery signals the album's emphasis on disease, illness, and injury: "It's a really medical album for me," according to Jonny Greenwood in Randall's *Exit Music*. "Thom went into a hospital to take pictures for the cover artwork, and it struck me the other day how much it's all about illness and doctors. It kind of makes sense, because we've all been on a cycle of illness."

In this regard, Doheny recognizes three overarching themes expressed throughout *The Bends*, all of which are connected to this medical imagery. These themes are alienation (from others, from one's environment, or even one's self), transformation (from one form or setting into another), and technologization (technology's influence largely on the previous two elements). An example of how this came into play was apparent in the tours undertaken to promote *The Bends* throughout the first half of 1995, some of which featured Yorke and Jonny Greenwood performing "unplugged" as an acoustic duo. This led to too much time in and out of airplanes, as the constant processes of pressurizing and depressurizing were causing fluid to build up in Yorke's ears. Fearing that he was going deaf and that it would be difficult to know if he was singing in key, he was advised to wear earplugs for the first part of the tour, and was thus to do so. When the band arrived in New York in May, Yorke had a near breakdown and wanted to leave the tour to return home. At this point the group determined that it was imperative for them to be able to continue working on new material, and so, from this point on, they were to rent rehearsal space for their days off from performing. "It's the only thing that keeps us going," Yorke reported in *Exit Music*, and this adaptive measure carried them through to their final show for this leg of their performance schedule on June 15 in Los Angeles. After a quick trip to Japan, however, the band returned to the United States to do a tour of club dates in more remote and out-of-the-way locations.

Great news came in the form of an invitation, from Radiohead's early idols REM, to open a number of their shows across Europe and then America, setting off at the end of July and carrying them into

September. Yorke was to forge a meaningful relationship with lead singer Michael Stipe, from whom the Radiohead singer learned a lot about coping with the pressures of the job. As Yorke was to say of Stipe a couple of years later in *Exit Music*, "He's helped me to deal with most things I couldn't deal with." In this regard, shortly following their stint with REM, the band began to travel almost entirely separately on the road, to prevent previous types of tension from building up again. The group started another U.S. tour in October in support of Soul Asylum, and the younger Greenwood was suffering from repetitive strain injury, and so began to perform regularly with an arm brace. They also frequently began to suffer illness, especially Yorke, who at a December performance in Munich finally actually collapsed onstage, after only a few songs into their set. In relation to this incident, and reminiscent of a scene from Pink Floyd's *The Wall*, Yorke describes the predicament in *Hysterical and Useless* that bands can find themselves in when sick on the road: "The doctor came round at four o'clock because every time you don't do a show, you have to get a doctor's certificate saying you are too sick to do a show, just like school, so you have a fucking sicknote." As he was to add, "If you don't get the sicknote, you get sued for thousands and thousands and thousands of pounds . . . of course the doctor was paid for by the promoter. He says, 'you're fine, you're fine to do the show,' and I was like, 'I can't fucking speak, let alone sing.'"

But beginning with its opening track "Planet Telex," the only song to be written in RAK studios, *The Bends* also explores a profound sense of *cultural* sickness. Although nixed due to its being a registered trademark, the song was originally called "Planet Xerox," named for the American global company that advanced, among other things, important developments in the evolution of personal computing, including the "mouse," the desktop metaphor, the graphic-user interface, and desktop computing. Appropriately beginning life as a drum loop, the track's opening riff features keyboards, which are more prominent throughout this album than on *Pablo Honey*. With its refrain that "everyone" and "everything" are "broken," the song highlights how electronic communications have made the world into a "global village," changing its forms of human interassociation and patterns of personal and political interdependence. This transformation alters the meaning of our relationships, as well as that of our general experience, with some, as here, intimating that the world has been significantly impoverished in the process. The lyrics suggest that any kind of effort the addressee makes is doomed to failure, even if one breaks "all the rules."

A song that had apparently preceded *Pablo Honey*, the album's title track was recorded in one take at the Manor. Yorke had also sonically captured a scene with a cassette recorder outside his hotel window on one of the band's U.S. tours, and this can be heard at the beginning of the song: "There was this guy training these eight-year-old kids, who were parading up and down with all these different instruments," he recounted. "The guy had this little microphone on his sweater and was going, 'Yeah, keep it up, keep it up!'" This drill sergeant reflects the band's own punishing imperative to "keep it up," and as a kind of prelude to *OK Computer*, the song's protagonist is portrayed "alone on an aeroplane"; when he announces "my blood will thicken," the character betrays that he has the bends. We likewise learn that his girlfriend also has the bends, but his own injured state is indicated further when the character describes himself lying down in a bar with his "drip feed on," wishing he could be happy. "People sometimes ask me if I'm happy and I tell them to fuck off. If I was happy, I'd be in a fucking car advert," Yorke was to say in *Hysterical and Useless*. "A lot of people think they're happy, and then they live these boring lives and do the same things every day. But one day they wake up and realise that they haven't lived yet. I'd much rather celebrate the highs and lows of everyday life than try to deny them." As Ed O'Brien was to add there as well, in this relation, "We like bands that have an element of melancholy in their music. Unfortunately, this element tends to get lost in most pop or rock music." The character portrayed in "The Bends" proceeds to announce that "we don't have any real friends," and as Jonny Greenwood was to remark in Randall's *Exit Music*, "That represents how we felt. . . . There is a sense of isolation being in Radiohead," something that was further explained there by his brother Colin: "You go away for two, two-and-a-half months at a time . . . then come back, then go away again, and meanwhile your friends have gone on with their lives." Nevertheless, the song's narrator intones that he wants to live and breathe, and "be part of the human race," from which he evidently feels a profound detachment. He also sings that he wishes it was the 1960s, in part perhaps a satirical reference to the flourishing Britpop movement, which included bands like Suede, Blur, the Boo Radleys, and Oasis, with whom Radiohead did not feel a particular affinity, especially as a result of the movement's backward-looking aesthetic, which highlighted and celebrated the influence of 1960s British bands like the Beatles, the Rolling Stones, the Kinks, and the Who. When asked if he wished it were the 1960s, Yorke was to say, "Levi's jeans might wish it was . . . I certainly fucking don't." But the protagonist of "The Bends" is also pictured as "waiting for something to happen." In this relation, one way that Yorke *might* have wished the world was more like the 1960s is for the 1990s to be characterized by a similar degree of activism and social protest, something that might have made him feel he was more significantly "part of the human race." Though 1994 did see a major demonstration against economic globalization in Madrid, as the World Bank and International Monetary Fund celebrated their fiftieth anniversaries, Yorke and company would have to wait for the massive civil society backlash that shut down the Organization for Economic Cooperation and Development's (OECD) Multilateral Agreement on Investment (MAI) in 1998, and for international protests that rocked the G8 at the beginning of 1999, and which, at the end of that year, culminated in shutting down the World Trade Organization (WTO) meeting in the so-called Battle of Seattle. Yorke himself participated in 1994 protests against plans to launch a UK "Star Wars" missile defense system and referred to the planet as "a gunboat in a sea of fears"; it is significant that the protagonist of "The Bends" recounts how "they brought in the CIA," along with tanks and the marines, to blow him "sky high," illustrating the sense of paranoia that can accompany the effort to become more politically involved in such actions. Around the same time, Radiohead played a charity gig for Rwanda in Abingdon, and donated the studio version of "Banana Co." to a compilation called *Criminal Justice! Axe the Act*.

"High and Dry," the oldest track on the album, was recorded in 1993 and written while Yorke was still at Exeter; he even performed it with his university band "Headless." Yorke, Selway, and Colin Greenwood laid down their parts for the three-chord song first, while the other two musicians came in later to add their contributions, primarily, according to O'Brien, because they "weren't really into doing the song." The track features a soon-to-be maligned character, whose Evel Knievel–like daredevil feats attempt to mask apparent inner insufficiencies. The injury is internal this time, and all of the protagonist's "insides fall to pieces." While he soon finds out that the best thing he ever had "has gone away," the song's narrator entreats the other not to leave him "high and dry."

"Fake Plastic Trees" documents the overwhelming effects, for some, of the approaching near omnipresence of inauthenticity within our technological culture, with its endless development and consciousness-colonizing commercial values that wear people out. Each verse documents the experience of someone different, the first a woman, the second the "cracked polystyrene man" whom she lives with, and the third the narrator of the song, who sings of his "fake plastic love" that she "tastes like the real thing." In the end, the song's narrator laments his own inauthenticity, bemoaning the fact that he can't always be the person that his addressee wants him to be. In this regard, the song's video pictured Yorke in a grocery cart being pushed around a surrealistic supermarket, playing up the sense that Radiohead is just another commodity for sale, or in Yorke's words from *Hysterical and Useless*, "one more element of the entertainment industry's attempt to distract." The video made it to MTV's *Buzz Bin* and, like "Creep," was featured also on *Beavis and Butthead*, but its success was relatively muted. As with "High and Dry," the authenticity and intimacy of the singer-songwriter confessional is communicated through the prominence given to the acoustic guitar, the subtleties of Jonny Greenwood's Hammond organ, and his and Yorke's tasteful score for violin and viola accompaniment.

Recorded at the Manor on the same day as "The Bends," the next song, "Bones," continues the injury motif, the narrator singing that he doesn't want to be "krippled kracked." Feeling it in his bones, which feel as if they're "ground to dust and ash," he's unable to climb the stairs, instead "crawling on all fours." This sense is conveyed through the dissonance of the distorted guitar effect with which the track opens; that his pain is really psychic, however, is betrayed by his reference to "Prozac painkillers," and his admission that he "used to fly like Peter Pan"—as did the children when he touched their hands. In this regard, the album's liner notes include a sketch accompanied by the words "it's so beautiful up here I don't ever want to land," and this is the first Radiohead song to make reference to "the children," a constituency that becomes a staple for inclusion in much of Radiohead's later work as we shall see.

"(Nice Dream)" returns us to the texture of acoustic guitar with string accompaniment, and its parenthetical title, initial tonal ambiguity, and driving triple meter throughout contribute to the song's dreamlike quality, as do the other-worldly whale sound effects heard at the end. The first verse outlines the narrator's dream of being loved and protected like a brother and having the basics of life that bring happiness. The second verse indicates that the character requires help, and the dream takes an interesting twist when he calls up his friend "the good angel," who, strangely, is out with her Ansaphone. Consequently, though she says she would love to come, if she did, "the sea would electrocute us all." Such thoughts are a nice dream, but as Ed O'Brien sings in the background, only if you think you're both "strong enough" and "belong enough." A dramatic contrast emerges, meanwhile, between the restrained acoustic verses and choruses and the heavy, distorted electric guitar instrumental interlude. As Yorke ushers in this section, his last sung refrain of "nice dream" transforms from a sweet kind of expression into one characterized by rage. "There was a great danger of it being too airy-fairy," as the singer was to say in *Radiohead: The Complete Guide to Their Music.* "We wanted it to sound a bit sinister," in part at least, presumably to represent the harshness of reality.

Though he still wrote the album's lyrics, the songwriting on *The Bends* is not quite as Yorke-centric as that on *Pablo Honey*, and "Just" was largely written by Jonny Greenwood. The opening seems a deliberate allusion to Nirvana's "Smells Like Teen Spirit," perhaps a deliberate effort to align the band with American grunge rather than with Britpop, and the dissonant sustained note heard toward the end of the song prior to the riffing outro was produced with Greenwood's pitch-shifting Digi-Tech Whammy pedal. The narrator addresses a character in the song that has been "suckered" by someone whose "stink" he can't get off, and despite having "changed the locks three times" he can't manage to get rid of this person. As he's "hanging out the fifteenth floor," however, he doesn't get the narrator's sympathy, and we learn in the chorus that this is "just," since the character does it to himself and thus has only himself to blame for his situation. The song's video pictures the character beginning his day and heading out into the world, but he soon lays down on the concrete sidewalk, where an unsuspecting man trips over him. After a crowd gathers and the man is unsuccessful in determining what is wrong with him, the character finally tells the crowd, but unlike the remainder of the narrative, this scene does not include captions. The group has never revealed what the character was to say, a statement that prompts the crowd to all lay down on the sidewalk around him as the band members bewilderedly look down from their performance space.

The album shifts once again from psychic imagery to that of physical affliction with "My Iron Lung." Named for the devices used as respirators during the first half of the twentieth century's polio epidemics, these were giant metal tubes in which people were placed, with only their heads emerging from the top. The contraptions created a vacuum inside that would help people to breathe, facilitating their lungs' expansion and inhalation of oxygen. The song was largely written the day that the band had to pull out of what was originally to have been their Reading Festival debut, as Thom had lost his voice, and the track was recorded essentially live during the band's May 1994 performance at the Astoria in London, with only the vocal redone later and the crowd noise eliminated. As the album's first single, the song was written as a response to "Creep." With its lines "this is our new song, just like the last one, a total waste of time," the song was intended, according to Yorke in *Exit Music*, as "the final nail in the coffin . . . of the previous song that shall remain nameless." Nevertheless, the song is acknowledged not just for the pain of its "eternal itch" and for being a uniquely "twentieth century bitch" but also for its tremendous resuscitating power as a "life support." That the song is to be interpreted more broadly is also apparent in its later section, where Yorke sings, "if you're frightened, you can be frightened . . . it's okay." This juncture is relatively placid, particularly compared to the raucous and heavy sections that bookend it, and that feature the bizarre lyrics that are absent from the printed lyrics of the CD jacket: "The headshrinkers they want everything, my Uncle Bill my Belisha beacon." *The Bends* is dedicated to Bill Hicks, the like-minded American comedian who had recently died of cancer at the young age of thirty-two, and it may be he that is referenced here as "Uncle Bill." As a social critic who was to counter much of the propaganda of "the headshrinkers," it's possible that Hicks provided a "guiding light" of sorts to Yorke, particularly as his influence appears to color some of the band's later lyrics.

"Bulletproof . . . I Wish I Was" is certainly one of the most beautiful Radiohead songs, and its impressive atmospheric guitar parts were created by O'Brien and Greenwood without simultaneously listening to the track. Once again foregrounding the acoustic guitar, and the sense of intimacy that it conjures, we continue to confront inner ills, masked as external ills, as expressed in the song's opening lyrics: "Limb by limb and tooth by tooth, tearing up inside of me." Though it's not clear who the protagonist is addressing, it's evident that they're perceived as responsible for his predicament, in the manner of a voodoo doctor manipulating a doll. Inviting the addressee to "take a shot" and to "leadfill the hole" that the protagonist feels in himself, his vulnerability is conveyed through Yorke's fragilely high and soft singing. The comfort of the idea of being "bulletproof" is conveyed, as the chorus of the song shifts to a major key, but the character recognizes that, were he so fortified, he would no longer be himself. Rather, he would become a "surrogate," who would likely burst the bubbles of many around him through his desensitization, and the song's jarring and dissonant conclusion thus reflects his irresolute situation.

Recorded with Nigel Godrich one day when Leckie was away, "Black Star" retains the interior focus but portrays it as part of an alienated domestic situation, and since the song employs the rare effect of a fade-in, it suggests that the problem has been a longstanding one. By the third verse, the relationship is over, but the character is still affected, suggesting that he's going to suffer a "melt down," and at the end he sings, "This is killing me." In the chorus, initially it looks as if he will again accuse external mediating forces, including the "black star" and "the falling sky," but he proceeds to shift the blame back toward himself and to how he extends himself technologically through "the satellite that beams [him] home." After all, he tells his partner that he hasn't slept with her for "58 hours." Nor presumably has he been at home for that duration.

Though you would never know it from the lyrics, apparently the basis of the rarely performed "Sulk" was written in 1987 in response to what became known as the Hungerford massacre, where a twenty-seven-year-old male shot and killed sixteen people in the small town of Hungerford, due west of London, before turning the gun on himself. Reportedly, the last line of the song was changed from "just shoot your gun" to "this is killing me" so as not to be mistaken as a reference to

Kurt Cobain's recent suicide. The lyrics of the song yield none of this sense by themselves and rather employ the image, pictured in one of the liner note sketches, of a big wall that "bites back" and eats the narrator alive.

"Street Spirit (Fade Out)" is the album's concluding song, a piece that Mark Paytress of *Mojo* appropriately refers to as "apocalypse rock," and in this regard it can be said that Radiohead's oeuvre has tended to become progressively more apocalyptic over time. The song's minor key and hypnotic and meditative droning quality contributes much to this effect, as does the heaviness of the "rows of houses bearing down" on him, the "machine" that "will not communicate" his thoughts and sense of strain, and his probing of the weighty matter of death. The song was allegedly inspired when Yorke, as he was getting off a bus, witnessed some dead baby sparrows lying on the pavement next to their eggshells. In this regard, the last verse's "cracked eggs dead birds," though already dead, "scream as they fight for life."

In the English author and poet Thomas Hardy's novel *Jude the Obscure* (1896)—a book that nearly inspired Radiohead in their earlier days to call themselves "Jude"—the protagonist is illustrated as having had a remarkable sense of identification and empathy with the natural world, a quality that certainly belongs to Yorke too. It is quite possible that the singer had a pronounced sense of affinity with the character, particularly as much of the book is set in Radiohead's home base of Oxford. Hardy's narrator describes the young Jude as follows:

> He had never brought home a nest of young birds without lying awake in misery half the night after, and often reinstating them and the nest in their original place the next morning. He could scarcely bear to see trees cut down or lopped, from a fancy that it hurt them; and late pruning, when the sap was up and the tree bled profusely, had been a positive grief to him in his infancy. This weakness of character as it may be called, suggested that he was the sort of man who was born to ache a good deal before the fall of the curtain upon his unnecessary life should signify that all was well with him again.

Though Jude is meant to be scaring the birds away from a farmer's crops in an earlier scene, he deeply sympathizes with their thwarted desires, for like himself they appeared "to be living in a world which did not want them," a world that was becoming devoid of any cohesive sense of meaning to which young protagonists could attach themselves. Apocalypse means "revelation," and whether we will collectively be able to create such meaning will determine whether we "fade out again," or alternatively whether we acknowledge the imperative to "be a world child, form a circle" and ultimately to "immerse [our souls] in love" as the song concludes.

As Yorke was to say, *The Bends* was a "leap for us as a band" but "not a leap for us commercially," at least in the American market, where the album peaked in June at number 147 in *Billboard*, before reentering the chart a year later and peaking at number 88. In the UK market, however, the album debuted on the charts at number six in 1995 and peaked at number four in 1996. This momentum appears to have been sustained by their ongoing single releases, including "Just" at the beginning of August that peaked at number nineteen and whose accompanying video garnered a lot more attention (including major airplay on MTV). The album's fifth and final single, "Street Spirit (Fade Out)," meanwhile, was released in January 1996, peaked at number five, and featured the B sides "Molasses," the full electric version of "Banana Co.," "Bishop's Robes," and "Talk Show Host"—the band's first foray into trip hop. By April of that year, *The Bends* had been certified gold in the United States (500,000) and platinum in the UK (500,000).

As James Doheny was to write, *The Bends* is an organic product of the band's "feelings, interests, knowledge, and experience at the time," and in this regard, Yorke confirmed of the recording in *Radiohead: The Complete Guide to Their Music* that it was an "incredibly personal album." That it illustrated an impressive longevity and appeared to capture the general mood of the times was reflected in *Q Magazine*'s fifteenth-anniversary 2001 poll, in which *The Bends* was voted the number four album of all time; the number one album, meanwhile, was *OK Computer*, to which we'll now turn our attention.

3

A SGT. PEPPER FOR THE "NET" GENERATION

Probing *OK Computer* (1996–1998)

Radiohead broke for the holidays at the end of 1995 and did not recon-vene at their rehearsal space until February of the new year. By this point they'd also decided to self-produce their next album with Nigel Godrich, whom they enlisted to purchase $150,000 worth of new mo-bile recording gear for them. They wanted to avoid working in studios, as they hadn't found them to be environments conducive to enjoying their work, and although the master recordings for *OK Computer* were once again eventually to be sent to Sean Slade and Paul Kolderie, the American duo's mixes were not in the end used. So with John Leckie also now absent, the Gen Xers—Radiohead, Nigel Godrich, and Stanley Donwood—set out on their own across the high seas of record produc-tion.

They had already done so by the previous September, in fact, when they recorded the first of the suite of songs that make up *OK Computer*. In August, Brian Eno's charity Warchild, an organization set up to pro-vide assistance to the children of war-torn Bosnia, had approached them in regard to contributing a song to a fundraising recording. They agreed and recorded "Lucky" on September 4, and then the charity album was released five days later. Toward the end of the year the song was released as a UK single but was only to reach a disappointing number fifty-one. When Radiohead reconvened in February, their first project involved supporting the "Rock the Vote" campaign. This was an effort organized to encourage British youth to vote, a campaign in which REM had participated in the American context. "One of the reasons it struck a chord with me," said Ed O'Brien, "is that I have to admit that at the last General Election I didn't vote, because I was disenchanted with politics." With regard to the estimates that Rock the Vote sent the band, O'Brien was to report in Jonathan Hale's *Radiohead: From a Great Height* that, in 1992, "43% of those under the age of 25 who were eligible to vote didn't vote. That's 2.5 million people. Those kind of statistics are quite frightening. It means that we could have had a different government in power for the last four years."

When they embarked on yet another U.S. tour from mid-March to April, the band had accumulated many new songs, and in between European festival appearances in May and July, they began two months of recording at Canned Applause, where their new equipment had now been installed. Toward the end of these sessions, however, Godrich recommended that the band members' proximity to their homes was interfering with their progress. Therefore, following thirteen U.S. dates that August, opening in arenas and stadiums for Alanis Morissette, they resumed the sessions at a fifteenth-century mansion just north of Bath called Catherine's Court, owned by the British-American actress Jane Seymour. They had booked the mansion for the month of September but were unable to complete the project within that duration, so, following more rehearsals at Canned Applause throughout October, they returned to Catherine's Court for the month of November, during which time *OK Computer* was practically finished, except for string parts, which were to be recorded at Abbey Road in January 1997. At the same time Donwood had started getting together the band's first website.

Their first single, "Paranoid Android"—backed by the B sides "A Reminder," "Melatonin," "Polythylene," and "Pearly"—debuted in May at number three on the UK charts. It featured an innovative animated video by Magnus Carlsson, the Swedish creator of the animated series *Robin*, and the video portrays an adventure of the character Robin and his friend Benjamin. That month Radiohead also began a four-day marathon session in Barcelona for the official European launch of *OK Computer*, an event that included meetings with international EMI representatives, internet press conferences, two club performances, and an almost nonstop series of interviews with various media. Some scenes from this event appear in Grant Gee's 1998 film *Meeting People Is Easy*, which Radiohead commissioned in order to document this stage of the group's career and which included following the band around during the tours that it undertook in support of the new album. "From the start it was quite clear that they were quiet and articulate people being put through this industrial process of sort of being vacuumed for image and information and quotes and thoughts," Gee was later to say of this event in Andy Greene's "Oral History." "That might have brushed off their backs if they were thick-skinned, but I got the sense they were going to react in a thin-skinned kind of way." As those who have seen it will know, Gee's film well captures this reaction.

OK Computer debuted in June at number twenty-one in *Billboard* but at number one in the UK charts, where it lingered for two weeks and then stayed for months in the top ten. They performed at the Tibetan Freedom Concert in New York and at another event in California, where Thom Yorke was to collaborate with one of his favorite techno artists, DJ Shadow, on a song called "Rabbit in Your Headlights," eventually to appear on a 1998 album accredited to UNKLE called *Psyence Fiction*. He was also later to collaborate with Drugstore on a track called "El Presidente," while he and Jonny Greenwood also worked with Michael Stipe on the soundtrack for *Velvet Goldmine* (1998). They returned to Europe for a number of shows, including their celebrated Glastonbury debut, before heading back to the United States in late July for their first monthlong tour in support of the album. Late August saw the release of their next UK single "Karma Police," which peaked at number eight and featured the B sides "Lull" and "Meeting in the Aisle"; then the band was to embark on an eleven-date UK tour, prior to completing a full European jaunt that took them through the autumn. During this time, the band was to set up a mobile studio on their tour bus, but this didn't seem to address the group's previous tensions and difficulties, which were again beginning to show. In mid-November, they were back in England for some arena dates, and as Yorke was to say in *Exit Music*, regarding their performance in Birmingham, "I came off at the end of that show . . . sat in the dressing room and couldn't speak. People were saying, 'Are you all right?' I knew people were speaking to me. But I couldn't hear them. And I couldn't talk. I'd just *so* had enough."

Since the band still had months of commitments in the coming year, it was good that during their December holidays, their efforts were broadly critically celebrated. Such acknowledgments included being awarded Band of the Year in *Rolling Stone* and *Spin* and Album of the Year in *New Musical Express* and *Q*, as well as being nominated for two Grammy Awards, including Album of the Year and Best Alternative Rock Performance, the latter category being one they were to clinch a couple of months hence. In addition to their embarking on further performance dates in Japan, New Zealand, and Australia, January saw the band release its third UK single, "No Surprises," which reached number four and included the B sides "How I Made My Millions" and "Palo Alto." The song's video, like those for "Paranoid Android" and "Karma Police," continued the trend of the group not appearing in their videos. Only Yorke performed cameo features in the latter two, and all were released a few months later as *Seven Television Commercials*, which also included the band's videos from *The Bends*. Though they were soon to be in the United States for another monthlong tour in March, they declined to attend the Grammy Awards ceremony, since they hadn't been offered a performance slot. At this time, *OK Computer* reclimbed the *Billboard* chart, scaling all the way from 179 to 37. And just as it was declared platinum in the United States (one million copies), the band's North American EP release *Airbag/How Am I Driving?* debuted at number fifty-six, containing the title track, along with all the UK B sides. Before breaking for a summer vacation, Radiohead made what was to be its last 1998 U.S. appearance in June at the third Tibetan concert in Washington, D.C., appropriately bookending this period of the band much as it had begun the year prior in New York.

OK COMPUTER

Aptly denoted by Mark Paytress as "the *Sgt. Pepper* for the net generation," and eventually deemed culturally and aesthetically significant enough to be preserved as part of the Library of Congress National Recording Registry in 2015, *OK Computer* communicates meaning through a rich symbolic interplay. Yorke and Donwood created images for the CD jacket cover, which were then laid out for all to see. "I love the cover," Phil Selway was to comment in Hale's *Radiohead: From a*

Great Height, "because it all came together in the same studio, and seeing it develop alongside the music, it becomes much more personal." Eric Gorfain—a violinist for whom *OK Computer* was sufficient inspiration to later arrange and record his own string quartet version, titled *Strung Out on OK Computer: The String Quartet Tribute to Radiohead* (2001)—was to concur with an interviewer's mention that much debate in the "Radiohead world" was over the album's being a "theme album" along the lines of other "opus records" like Pink Floyd's *The Wall*. "I think it's totally relevant," Gorfain said to *Then It Must Be True*. "I have a hard time listening to those songs one by one; it doesn't make sense. . . . I mean, I think of *OK Computer* as a classical work with electric instruments and distortion. I don't think of it as songs; even *The Bends* is much more song-oriented. With *OK Computer* there was that flow that went through it; whether it was literally songs being connected or whatever, it's more of a concept album."

Compare Gorfain's comments with the following exchange from MTV, where Yorke and Colin Greenwood respond to the following question posed to them on the show by a fan through email: "Could you discuss the term 'concept album' and how it applies to your work?"

Greenwood: Oh God.

Yorke: I'm not doing that.

Greenwood: The only time we think about that is, we spend like a week putting the songs together at the end. We choose things that will sound good after each other, but before that they're all individual things.

Yorke: *OK Computer*. For people to suggest that's a concept album . . . That's frankly terrifying.

Greenwood: Yeah but it is to them, though.

Yorke: Yeah, it could be to them. But to us, the only concept we had, was that it was gonna be called "OK Computer." That was all we had for the record. The title.[1]

To explore this conflict of perspectives, it's helpful to delve into musical heritages. Though he's done much work in the rock music field, Gorfain clearly has at least one foot firmly in the Western "art music" tradition, so it may be unsurprising that he should perceive the album to be in the character of a cohesive and extended "classical work performed with electric instruments and distortion." Radiohead, as we've seen, on the other hand, emerged from the "nonmainstream," postpunk tradition of bands like Magazine, Joy Division, and the Smiths. The group's members appear as well to have adopted the tradition's apparent ideological stance, which was firmly opposed to the artistic pretensions of "corporate" classic rock, and its perceived "musical elitism," particularly in relation to the technical aspirations of instrumental virtuosity in some of the music considered to be "progressive" or "art" rock.[2]

With the term "concept album" being so intertwined with the evolution of these styles, it's not surprising that its attachment to Radiohead's work should make the group uncomfortable. I would suggest, though, that there's a general confusion over what these terms really mean, the use of the word "progressive" in discussions of rock music being perhaps as difficult to pin down as its use in politics. For some, the monikers "art rock" and "progressive rock" conjure, specifically, bands like Genesis, King Crimson, and Emerson, Lake and Palmer, all of whose music featured complicated rhythmic meters, synthesizers, and borrowings from "classical" music styles. An interviewer named Nick Kent from *Mojo* pointed out to Yorke, however, that the "golden age" of progressive rock had as much to do with Can, Soft Machine, and Captain Beefheart as it did with Gentle Giant and Yes. He added, "Being associated with that is not something to be ashamed of, surely?" To this Yorke replied,

> No, I guess not. (Pause) But I don't really see us as "progressing." You walk down one particular path—that's what you choose to do. You're in the woods and you take a path and you just keep taking it. Sometimes you'll get lost and sometimes you won't. . . . But if you really love music, you don't want to repeat yourself. That's all it is. And also, if you hear other people's music, you're influenced by it. The things you love really inspire you and make you go off and do something else. And if that's what "progressive" is—then yeah, that's us. But trying to be clever, trying to be difficult or bloody-minded is not what we're about at all.

In my own view, the terms "art" and "progressive" rock refer to that transition in rock music, during the late 1960s through the 1970s, from a music comprising primarily dance compositions to one that was composed expressly for listening. The music also began to encompass an expanded ideational content in comparison to what had previously characterized the genre. Sophisticated use of the recording studio as a compositional and orchestral tool began to develop with musicians during this period as well, alongside of which developed diverse recording techniques. These trends are most popularly attributed to manifesting first in the work of George Martin and the Beatles on *Sgt. Pepper's Lonely Hearts Club Band* (1967), an effort that was to take seven hundred hours of studio time, in comparison to ten hours for the first Beatles LP in 1963. The new employment of extended musical structures also characterizes this transition and was a development that corresponded to the "album" taking on its appearance as a distinct, compound musical form, following the widespread commercial availability of stereo equipment and experimentations in stereo. Prior to this, it was only in "classical" music and recent jazz that extended playing time had been widely utilized. This expanded structure evolved into a multimedia form, attaching itself to the realm of the image with album covers, and to that of the printed word with the increasing inclusion of song lyrics—first with LPs and then with CDs. For this reason, a discussion of *OK Computer* is much different from a discussion of *Pablo Honey* and *The Bends*, particularly in the sense that it's a much longer and much richer affair.

OK Computer draws on elements of the genre often referred to as "science fiction," defined by Isaac Asimov as that branch of literature that deals with human responses to changes in the level of science and technology. Although the genre arose initially in literature, Mary Shelley's *Frankenstein: A Modern Day Prometheus* (1818) often being cited as its initial exemplar, its diffusion then extended through radio, film, television, and subsequent media formats. Often characterized by the coexistence of "futuristic man" with computers, robots, and the like, or by his interactions with outer space and potential advanced technological beings from other solar systems, science fiction, as Asimov suggests, is generally interested in the ongoing interaction between human beings and their contemporary techno-scientific culture.

In the following exchange with Yorke, excerpted from the same MTV appearance to which I referred earlier, the host alludes to these influences in Radiohead's work:

MTV host: On *Kid A*, *Amnesiac* and even *OK Computer*, there's so much recurring sci-fi imagery . . .

Yorke: Is there? . . . Right.

MTV host: Subterranean Homesick Aliens? Paranoid Androids? Clones called Kid A?

Yorke: Yeah, I know . . . but I wouldn't . . .

MTV host: Ice ages coming and . . .

Yorke: Is that science fiction, then? Maybe . . . yeah. Yeah.

MTV host: Wouldn't you say so?

Yorke: Yeah . . .

MTV host: Well, why all the futuristic imagery?

Yorke: I don't know . . . I really don't know. I don't even necessarily think it's in the lyrics, it's even in the music as well. The whole atmosphere of it . . .

The general tone of *OK Computer*, as Yorke explains, is imbued with this futuristic or science-fiction imagery, including its CD cover art- work, where, for example, the jewel case's back cover features the im- age of what appears to be a spaceship reminiscent of the starship *Enter- prise* from the television series *Star Trek*—that is, until you notice it's actually a modern underground train system in miniature. The science- fiction imagery extends also to the album's first track, "Airbag," as does the metaphor of travel. In part exhibited by its protagonist's traversing the vast expanse of the universe at the speed of light, as expressed in the song's lyrics, it's also realized through this persona's being related to the "Paranoid Android" of the second song, with which "Airbag" is sonically connected. This gesture helps to establish a sense of narrative extension that continues with "Subterranean Homesick Alien" and beyond. Similarly, we can discern in "Airbag" the jackknifed juggernaut of "Lucky," along with the protagonist's intimations of being reborn in "Paranoid Android"—an event that begins during the second song's elegiac "rain down" middle section. Yorke appropriately begins the album and its first song, "Airbag," singing, "In the next world war, in a jackknifed juggernaut—I am born again." That to what he was referring was shortly to become known the world over as the "War on Terrorism," I suspect he had little clue. But then, this was also a time before the world was to know anything about social media, the ubiquity of five-inch screens, or Google.

The album's title derives from Douglas Adams's 1979 book *Hitchhiker's Guide to the Galaxy*. When on tour the group used to listen to the audio book version, hearing its characters constantly addressing their cyborg companions, "OK computer!" In this way, the album's title is one of its most enigmatic characteristics. To be specific, it is its ambiguity of attitude to the beginning of the digital age of technology, which quickly evolved in the late 1970s with applications of the microchip, without which we would not be in possession of the saving power of the "airbag." It seems as though it should be read as a question—Ok, *what*? What about the computer? In this relation, the album emphasizes the boundless supremacy that our society grants to technical progress and how broadly some of the effects of our technologies reverberate across our global culture. It also stresses that technologies cannot be viewed as unequivocal friends that necessarily always improve our lives; rather, their gifts sometimes come with heavy costs attached. Thus, the title *OK Computer* suggests a posture of readiness to surmise the ways in which digital and other new technologies might manifest themselves as both friend and foe.

There's no question about Radiohead's enthusiasm for the tools of digital technologies, however, in many of their commercial, communicational, political, artistic, and musical dimensions. For instance, the band was eventually to use computers to create what it called "blipverts," short animated audio/visual clips, which were used to promote both *Kid A* (2000) and *Amnesiac* (2001) on the internet—a medium that the band also began to use in various ways as a means of communication with their international audience. Their website has continually featured links to other sites that provide updates on the band's activities through electronic mailing lists, while also featuring links to the sites of various other organizations devoted to political causes. The computer is employed in various ways as an instrument throughout OK Computer and has become increasingly used thus in the group's offerings since.

The greater portion of the words, pictures, and sounds that comprise OK Computer, however, do not convey much of this apparent eagerness. Yorke was to reinforce the title's intended ambivalence, explaining that it "refers to embracing the future, it refers to being terrified of the future, of our future, of everybody else's." And it might be obvious why one should seek to embrace the future, but it was not entirely evident to all in 1997 why one ought, perhaps, be "terrified" by it. On the other hand, some were aware of the malaise even prior to the advent of the Orwellian "War on Terrorism," including the editor of Adbusters, a magazine published by the Vancouver-based Media Foundation. The month following the 2000 U.S. election, the cover of the Canadian publication featured a photograph of the newly elected president George W. Bush, accompanied by the sobering caption, "We're Fucked!"[3] Responding to the positing of Mojo's Kent, "You must be thrilled by George W. Bush's recent election?" Thom Yorke replied, "I was chuffed to bits. I think it's actually great, to be honest, because it's going to radicalize people. People who've never been into politics are going to suddenly wake up and realize that they actually have to fuckin' do something about it." As we'll see, this is a sentiment that recurs throughout much of Radiohead's work.

4

BACK TO SAVE THE UNIVERSE, I'M YOUR SUPERHERO!

The Songs of *OK Computer* (1996–1998)

"AIRBAG"

Originally titled "Last Night an Airbag Saved My Life," after Indeep's disco hit "Last Night a DJ Saved My Life," "Airbag's" protagonist is portrayed as a kind of comic-book superhero, and the character actually refers to himself as a superhero by the album's next to last song, "Lucky." The characteristics of spelling and punctuation in the printed text of the song ("in an intastella burst, I am back to save the universe!!") alludes to the style of the comic-book medium and serves to illustrate Yorke's tendency to encode meanings also in the printed song lyrics of the CD. "I am an airhead on this record," he points out, betraying the strong sense of satirical self-subversion that runs largely throughout the album's narrative voices, which generally tend to alternate between the roles of "hero" and "antihero."

The overall content of the album's dynamic opening guitar and cello riff in "Airbag" reflects the polar frame of temperament characterizing Yorke's suggestion that the title *OK Computer* refers to "embracing the future" as well as "being terrified of the future." Not only does the riff continuously alternate between a major and minor mode, but also when it's heard combined with the fast repeated background notes a number of octaves above, an additional alternating sense of consonance and dissonance is established. The protagonist confidently counters the hints of negativity with his vocal entry's heroic ascending melodic leap, repeated twice each time, before descending the pitches of the major scale, comfortably concluding each phrase on the primary note of the key. His confidence is bolstered throughout by the punctuated gestures of the bass guitar, which along with the drums also contribute to the song's overall momentum. The verses maintain a pedal point or drone, which the character transcends with each appearance of the song's refrain during his heroic "intastella burst": Ascending a whole step, it's during these meteoric moments of "affective elevation" that he presents himself as the potential savior of the universe. A sense of the heroic is also established sonically from the beginning of the song with the sound of sleigh bells, which conjure the childhood hero Santa Claus, the mythical entity who functions just as valiantly in his role as the patron saint of merchants throughout Christendom and beyond.

As per Yorke's suggestion that the futurist or science fiction imagery in Radiohead's work is represented musically too, electronic music tends to connote "technology." And the initial and fleeting appearance of synthesized electronic sound effects in "Airbag" is heard during the first of three repetitions of the refrain, occurring in tandem with the protagonist's initial high technology "intastella burst." The bulk of electronic effects in "Airbag," however, are to be found toward the end of the song during the "juggernaut's jackknifing"—an event conveyed by the series of disruptions to the song's general motorial flow.[1] This temporal fallout serves to illustrate that the phenomenon of "dissonance" occurs across various musical parameters, and often among a number of them simultaneously, as in this case.

Whereas Superman is "faster than a speeding bullet," this character, as we've seen, travels instantaneously between distant stars. But who is this hero, we should ask, and how is he going to save the universe? Some may conjecture that he's "the artist," exceptional artists often being portrayed as generally more aware of their surroundings than the rest of us, and it's notable in this regard that in "Airbag," the protagonist sings of being reborn in the "deep deep sleep of the innocent." In fact, Yorke's general conception of the role of the artist seems congruent with such a view. "I'm quite an absorbent person," the singer explained in an interview in 2004 with Brian Draper—recalling Ezra Pound's idea that artists are "the antennae of the race"—"I have quite a low shield, or force-field or whatever, so I can get very affected by things around me. I just absorb things and sometimes it will make me go to a weird space for a week. But that's part of being creative, I think." Yorke explains that this process of "retraining" and "updating" sensibility is one that for him requires an accompanying attempt to "stay sane." Notwithstanding, he also simultaneously recognizes the privilege of his position:

> I was thinking about this last week, that I should count myself most lucky just to be able to stand back and look at what goes on around me—having the time just to zone out and absorb things and think about them. It's an incredible privilege, because most people's lives are full up from the moment they're born to the moment they die, and I don't have that. I spend a lot of my time watching that process without actually participating in it. Which is a kind of shamanic thing to do. That's always been the role of artists in a way, and it's incredibly important that someone's doing it. (I would say that, wouldn't I?) But you know what I mean? It's not as easy as it sounds, either. For me, it's quite difficult. In some ways, you are tempted to fill your life up with other noise instead.

Yorke confirms a characterization of the artist as a type of mystic outsider who at times is capable of divining the future. "The other interesting thing, I think, is that sometimes really powerful music can presage things that then happen," he says. "Like any artform, there's that element of seeing into the future, no matter how dimly and naively. I've had it with artwork as well," he says, explaining that "*Amnesiac* came out in the summer of 2001 and almost every other image on the album is two towers collapsing. That freaked us out a bit." In this respect, Yorke might have also made reference to the numerous images of planes flying and crashing throughout the *OK Computer* sleeve.

"A good piece of music . . . is like knocking a hole in the wall so that you can see out on another place you didn't know existed," Yorke affirms to Draper, mirroring an emphasis on the effects that art has on our awareness. "If your consciousness is not constantly evolving somehow or other and you just keep going round the same room again and again," he recommends, "then you're sort of trapped, and every good piece of music—or art or writing—stops you feeling trapped." Elsewhere, in a December 2001 interview with *New Musical Express*, Yorke posits that "the reason you create music or art or write is in order to put things in a way you can possibly deal with [them]," indicating that Radiohead uses music as a way of "turning bad energy into good energy," or "making something out of inexpressible emotion, which could be useful."

I'm tempted to suggest that this hero could also be the celebrity idol. Interestingly, Yorke has attempted to resist being made into such a social hero and emphasizes his disdain for the creation of such a caste in Martin Clarke's *Hysterical and Useless*:

> The whole idea of being Thom Yorke, "the personality" . . . I don't want to die having been just that. That whole thing that most pop stars are desperately trying to attain [is] immortality through their cult of personality . . . this phenomenon, this Sunday review section, glossy front page. . . . It's like "No!, actually. No!" I don't want to be remembered for this, I want to be remembered for doing pieces of work that people like, and other than that I don't really want to know. I'm not into this for immortality's sake. Sixty years from now, I'm going to be dead, and that will be that.

In *Meeting People Is Easy*, he adds, "It's an absolute fascination to us that celebrities in America just live on a higher plane. They're absolutely untouchable," adding that "English people are not impressed." Certainly, however, there is something of the celebrity's superheroic attributes that are satirized in the song's protagonist. And when asked to describe what "fame madness" had felt like, Yorke replied in Jonathan Hale's *Radiohead: From a Great Height*, "There was lots of bullshit involved that ends up feeling eventually like it's real and then you have to go away and tell the difference. You actually start believing your own bullshit," he adds. "Like John Cleese said . . . 'I can only do about three weeks promo because after a while I start to feel less like I'm really human, just a little bit . . . false.'" He refers to the idea of feeling "two-dimensional," of being "a moving target," and he told another interviewer in the December 2001 *New Musical Express*, "I think now it's all about trying to get your head round what you do and not actually subscribing to the personality crap that goes with it, and the way that people project it back onto you personally, which can be quite a debilitating thing if you actually take any of it seriously."

Celebrities and the entertainment industry are of course both manifestations or characteristics of the wider phenomenon described by some as "commercial culture." In fact, one might say that these "glitterati" function as the heroes in its mythological starscape. In comparison to the formerly less influential role of commerce, "commercial culture" differs in the degree to which market principles have permeated almost all facets of private and public life. In this relation, I've noted the protagonist's sung reference to "the deep sleep of the innocent" and that the absence of wakeful awareness is one of the most pervasive themes, not only of *OK Computer* but of subsequent Radiohead work as well. We should be careful to observe, however, that I've misquoted him and that his expression is actually encoded with the detail "inno$ent," demonstrating again—along with the tendency for meaning within the album to be specially embedded in the medium of printed type—the relation of this phenomenon to the world of commerce. The evolution of commercial or business power under globalization can be described as both dangerous and scary, but this remains a much marginalized perspective that seems largely invisible to "the inno$ent," for the majority of whom the possibility of being "completely terrified" is in large part a remote one, as illustrated by the two words being crossed out on the *OK Computer* CD sleeve. This overall sense is likewise evident in the album's tenth song, "No Surprises."

Regarding the automotive metaphor of "Airbag," it should be noted that in Britain, the word "juggernaut" is also used to refer to a large heavy motor vehicle, especially an articulated lorry (or "tractor trailer" as we say in North America). In this relation, it's interesting to consider how, at the highest levels, contemporary societies tend to be envisaged primarily as *economies* that are "driven" as though they were vehicles. A former governor of Canada's central bank announced, for instance, that he was raising interest rates in order to cool "the engine" of the country's economy. In response to some critics' suggestions that by doing so he was perhaps "putting his foot on the brakes," the central banker replied that he was merely "taking his foot off the gas pedal," illustrating the variety of automotive metaphors that have entered the commentary of official economic and monetary policy. In these terms, it's difficult not to construe the jackknifed juggernaut as the global economy in the coming 2008 financial meltdown, which Yorke can be seen forecasting toward the conclusion of Grant Gee's film *Meeting People Is Easy.*

A major facet of commercial culture, advertising serves not so much to advertise products as to promote consumption as a way of life, and as the necessity of limitless economic development replaces economic necessity, the appeasement of basic and generally recognized human needs gives way to the ongoing fabrication of artificial needs. In other words, advertising exists to manufacture desire, to stimulate the consumption necessary to drive the machinery of the economy to ever-increasing growth and development, and we should note that the procurement of technical knowledge or services and the purchase of a tangible good or commodity tend to be at the heart of commercial activity, alongside technological innovation and exploitation. That the futility of searching for happiness through the endless gratification of desire, particularly via the acquisition and consumption of material things, is a mode of life deplored by the ancient Hindu texts, the Qur'an, the Jewish Prophets, Buddha, and by Christianity ought to lie in uneasy contradiction with the materialism of the evolving global commercial culture.

But the character is "born again" within the electronic cultural context, complete with the characteristic religiosity of its ubiquitous "neon sign scrolling up and down," the scrolling imagery being highly appropriate to the new computer age. "There is nothing to prevent me from profiting by the light that may come out of the West," wrote the Indian spiritual and political leader Mohandas Gandhi. "Only I must take care that I am not overpowered by the glamor of the West. I must not mistake the glamor for true light." In connection to this sentiment, it's worth observing that the underlying ideology of commercial culture can be identified as *technological theology*, with advertising representing the most prominent and paradigmatic form of its religious literature. Technological theology presents technology as our collective savior, and it's therefore interesting that the protagonist seems to attach great metaphysical import to the idea that he was "saved" by an airbag. Those of us on the other hand who do not recognize technology as our savior are meanwhile often looked at with suspicion and widely viewed as either infidels or exemplars of *technological* innocence.

"PARANOID ANDROID"

In *The Hitchhiker's Guide to the Galaxy*, Marvin the paranoid android is a melancholic misanthrope who displays an "utter contempt and horror of all things human." Of the "Genuine People Personalities" line, he's a robotic "personality prototype" from among the latest products of the Sirius Cybernetics Corporation. On the floor of its brand-new spaceship, Marvin finds the company's latest sales brochure, the tone of which he describes as a lot of "the Universe can be yours" type stuff: *"Be the envy of other major governments,"* says the brochure, describing how the ship passes through every point in the universe at the moment when its drive reaches "Infinite Improbability." Marvin, mimicking the style of the sales brochure, says mockingly, *"All the doors in this spaceship have a cheerful and sunny disposition. It is their pleasure to open for you, and their satisfaction to close again with the knowledge of a job well done."*

A similar euphoria is apparent in the Sirius Cybernetics Corporation marketing division's definition of the word "robot" as *"Your Plastic Pal Who's Fun to Be With."* This definition is in stark contrast to that provided by what author Douglas Adams calls the "Encyclopaedia Galactica," which characterizes a robot as a mechanical apparatus designed to do the work of a man. "The Hitchhiker's Guide to the Galaxy," a publication that sports the words "DON'T PANIC" inscribed in large friendly letters on its cover, has come to supplant the "Encyclopaedia Galactica" as the depository of all knowledge and wisdom within the world constructed by Adams. The guide's title conjures the automotive imagery of the pedestrian "hitchhiker" transposed into the world of interstellar space travel, and defines the marketing division of the Sirius Cybernetics Corporation as *"a bunch of mindless jerks who'll be the first against the wall when the revolution comes."* A footnote observes that the editors welcome applications from any nonparanoiacs interested in taking over the post of robotics correspondent.[2]

Apparently inspired by the multiple sections of the Beatles' song "Happiness Is a Warm Gun," it's musically evident from the outset of "Paranoid Android" that the protagonist is in a disturbed state of being, a condition that, as I've suggested, was latent in the underlying dissonances of "Airbag." Because the song foregrounds the solo acoustic guitar at this point, it initially lends the piece an aspect of the confessional intimacy typical of the singer-songwriter genre; thus the character's apparent internal conflict initially evokes pity, as he expresses his distress when he plaintively pleads, "Please could you stop the noise im tryin a get some rest?" Unlike the inno$ent in their deep and peaceful sleep, we comprehend that this character is much of the time "completely terrified," not unlike the readership of "The Hitchhiker's Guide to the Galaxy." Our sympathy is aroused through the blended elements that comprise the song's first section, including its minor key, its chromaticism, and the predication of its unsettling bass figure and harmonic content on the tritone—the most jarring and unstable interval in tonal music (interpreted by the European Middle Ages as "the Devil's interval"). Attesting to the irrationality typical of our "postmodern" experience, the protagonist's initial remark is testament to the fact, articulated by General Alfred M. Gray of the U.S. Marine Corps, that communications without intelligence is "noise."

The protagonist also seeks respite from the interior "noise" created by what he calls "all the unborn chikken voices" in his head. The image conjures that of the "cracked eggs dead birds" in the song "Street Spirit"[3] from *The Bends* that, though already dead, "scream as they fight for life." The effects of the character's alienation from his humanity are signaled in the adoption of the "paranoid android" of Douglas Adams. "Huh what's that?" he sings, followed immediately by the apparently subconscious synthesized voice of the Macintosh Simple Text Reader, heard in the background of the soundscape. "I may be paranoid but not an android," it intones, perhaps what a Freudian perspective would designate his "superego." Attempting apparently to proclaim his "humanity," he betrays at the same time that he's—in a sense—*posthuman*. Of course the computer voice is that of "Fitter Happier," a piece that, as Yorke explains, pertains to "mental background noise": "Some days, you're in a disturbed state and it moves to the front," he says in Mac Randall's *Exit Music*, referring to the increasingly disturbing stimulation created by the musical processes and sonic effects that emerge from behind the computer voice within that scene. With regard to *OK Computer* in general, Yorke remarks, "It was just the noise that was going on in my head for most of a year and a half of travelling and computers and television and just absorbing it all."

One of the most problematic things that we face at present of course is the phenomenon of information overload, and in the face of the communications inundation of our time, it's been suggested that the surest way for avoiding complete schizophrenic breakdown is through desensitization, which can spare us from having to remain alert to the bombardments of our information environment. But whatever has significance for the sensorium, of course, has relevance as well for the sensibilities, and the singer of "Paranoid Android" would appear to demonstrate that it's a matter of desensitization that pertains here. As our superhero transforms into a supervillain, we recoil, bearing witness to the oncoming intolerance, hatred, and fury he directs toward his addressee, the opinion of whom "is of no consequence at all."

Intolerant people typically emphasize group differences, while de-emphasizing the differences between individuals within a loathed group. And it's thought that they devalue individuals because their own identities are too insecure to permit what Carl Jung called "individuation." In this regard, Yorke told an interviewer at the end of 1995, as Martin Clarke records in *Hysterical and Useless*, "I'm obsessed with the idea that I'm completely losing touch with who I am, and I've come to the conclusion that there isn't anything to Thom Yorke other than the guy that makes those painful songs." Meanwhile, Clarke reports that "Paranoid Android" was inspired by a bad experience Yorke had one night in a Los Angeles bar, where, apparently unbeknownst to him, practically everyone present was on cocaine. Clarke's account describes Yorke as finding himself surrounded by "parasitic groupie types and pretentious California posers," and the singer is quoted as saying, "The people I saw that night were just like demons from another planet. . . . Everyone was trying to get something out of me. I felt like my own self was collapsing in the presence of it, but I also felt completely, utterly part of it, like it was all going to come crashing down any minute. . . . Basically [the song is] just about chaos." Apparently, Yorke was particularly horrified by one "especially vicious lady who had a drink spilt over her dress and whose face contorted in venom at the culprit." Although we're never informed of Yorke's reaction to this situation, it's this woman who purportedly provides the model for the "kicking, squealing Gucci little piggy." It's well known how affect or emotion has the constant potential for contagion and escalation, and Yorke's comments suggest that he may himself have become caught up in a situation of vicious imitation.[4] Regardless, at this point he's not the oppressed pig we see at the conclusion to "Fitter Happier." Rather, he's an oppressor of "the Gucci little piggy," the target of his own venom.

Intolerant people aren't able to see themselves as contributors to making and maintaining their individuality, and hence cannot see others as contributors to the construction of their identities either. Instead, they abstract and depersonalize the other, transforming individuals into ciphers or carriers of hated group characteristics, a situation that creates a primal opposition of "them" and "us." In this connection, the Esperanto word "malamikigi"—found on the bottom of the same page in the *OK Computer* CD booklet as the lyrics for "The Tourist"—means to "antagonize," "alienate," "estrange," or "make enemies" with notable animosity. The word "demonize" also effectively conveys this idea—noting of course that the character is "against demons," as the sketched symbol of a circled star carrying that phrase located underneath the *OK Computer* CD jewel case demonstrates. Indeed, Radiohead's tour in support of the album was likewise appropriately dubbed the "Against Demons" tour.

Freud maintained that intolerance is connected to narcissism—a condition where individuals are "preoccupied" with the self, or isolated and withdrawn to the extent that their libidinal attachments appear to be predominantly to themselves. The roots of intolerance thus appear to be found in the tendency to overvalue ourselves, and so, only if we're able to disassemble the fantastic elements in our own self-perception are we likely to be able to break down abstract and stereotypical images of others. As I've suggested, this is a significant component of the characterization of the song's protagonist as a type of satirical comic book superhero. But our "ambitious" revolutionary-celebrity antihero proclaims, "When I am king you will be first against the wall," alluding to the earlier quoted passage from *The Hitchhiker's Guide to the Galaxy*. In contrast, however, to the song's first verse, where through his employment of the high range of Thom Yorke's vocal melody the character exposes frailty, his singing of the second verse occurs within a much more confident and comfortable tonal range.

Perhaps fueling the comparisons that commentators were making between Radiohead and Pink Floyd, the band are reported to have said—following early performances of "Paranoid Android" prior to the song's being recorded or even finished—"Ignore that. That was just a Pink Floyd cover." Interestingly enough, however, "Pink Floyd," the protagonist of *The Wall*, a role that Bob Geldof portrays in the work's film version, is an excessively narcissistic rock star, whose own grandiose fantasies amount to being a powerful and adulated fascist leader who isolates individuals from various recognizable "groups" of his audience. Ordering them "up against the wall," he then goes on to say, "If I had my way I'd have all of you shot." The work explores the process that leads to this character's creation, portraying it largely as the gradual "decay" of the feelings necessary for the expression of love and empathy, and their subsequent replacement by hate and anger. The "human" aspect of the character symbolically dies, giving way to the inhuman, a process paralleled here by the looming electronic computer voice, which reminds us again that the song's protagonist "may be paranoid but no android." The digital voice is now, however, more appropriately conceived of as Freud's "id" rather than superego, insofar as it serves to represent a nonhuman entity devoid of emotional and moral intelligence.

The character's enlarged sense of self-importance and self-assurance finds ominous expression with the change of scene in the second section of the song (with its shift in modal center). This event is accompanied by a change in texture, characterized predominantly by the acoustic guitar's low bass riff and later doubled by a prominent and abrasive electric guitar with phase effect. The range and melodic outline of this riff—the same melody sung to "ambition makes you look pretty ugly"— also comprises a tritone, and its accented notes form a chromatic descent, both of which help to convey his disturbance. His disjointedness is expressed through the modulation back and forth between this figure and another in a mixed major mode, which features the interjection of an odd 7/8 rhythmic meter, in addition to Yorke's articulation of some bizarre hysterical vocalizing. An electronic sound effect, heard just before the lyrical entry, signals the beginning of his flip into persecutory mode.

The protagonist's authoritarian strains seem to reflect his overvaluation of self in direct proportion to his devaluation of ambitious "Gucci little piggies" and "yuppies" excitedly "networking" (not to mention those in the corporate marketing division of the intergalactic Sirius Cybernetics Corporation). Formerly considered among the inno$ent, these are now perceived as impure—polluted by consumer values[5] and the world as organic economic machine. Adding further insult and ire to the mix, the "Gucci little piggy" doesn't even remember the comic book celebrity king's name, and this fury finds expression in the startling violent entry of drums and distorted electric guitar, followed shortly thereafter with the ensuing order of "off with his head man." In the midst of the chaos that ensues, the character learns that the anthropomorphized "piggy" does remember his name after all. But far from expressing regret for his action, one hears what can only be imagined as the ongoing "crackle of pig skin."

Hitler, invoked later on the album in "Karma Police," redefined the assimilation of Jews as a form of pollution requiring "purification" and "cleansing," and this represents the most elemental language of narcissism. Cleanliness, in this regard, is what distinguishes humans from nonhumans and the valued from the despised. That the character obtains an archaic sense of transcendence from violently exerting power over those whom he despises is apparent in his triumphant octave-vocal leap, which occurs on the last sung word of the heavy section ("does"). This sense is reinforced by the guitar solo—so rare in a Radiohead song that the listener immediately understands it's meant to provide a dose of whimsical and satirical content.

This musical violence comes to a crashing close and gives way to the sound of a receding, dreamlike trance, an effect created by a keyboard tremolo, which provides not only a return to the song's original key, where the present interlude began, but also a reversion of scene that returns us to the original inner space associated with it. We are clearly now in the realm of the Freudian superego, that component of consciousness representing the accumulated learning and behavioral codes of a culture, at the heart of which lies the social order established with the institutionalized rituals of religion and their quest for moral and spiritual purification and transcendence.

If, as Kenneth Burke, suggests in *Counter-Statement*, beauty is the term we apply to the poet's success in evoking our emotions, then the scene that's often referred to as "the otherworldly section" of "Paranoid Android" represents the utmost of such aspect. The transition from tonic major key to tonic minor, combined with the return of the acoustic guitar and the music's sudden reduction in overall texture, volume, and rate of activity, serves to establish a sense of sobriety, as does the low-sounding synthesized bass choral voices, especially as set off against Yorke's lone plaintive voice. The descending chromatic bass pattern has been considered to represent lament from at least the seventeenth century forward, and in this context, lament is tied to the character's apparent remorse. It's not so much an affiliation with his victim for which he seems to long, however. Rather, it's for the saving power of the sacred, a force with which he yearns to reestablish a transcendental connection, with his entreaty for its cleansing power to rain down upon him, "from a great height."

Speaking of the deep underground sources of our experience, purification by water is central to imagery associated with the rite of baptism, a religious practice common to many cultures. Within Christian theology it's of course central to cleansing the individual from the stains of "original sin." Insofar as the "otherworldly section" of "Paranoid Android" musically alludes to Christianity in its tonal harmony, counterpoint, and simulated choral background voices, it's interesting to note the extent to which, in their early years, the members of Radiohead seem to have been immersed in a Christian religious environment. As previously mentioned, according to Jonny Greenwood, who composed the "otherworldly" section of "Paranoid Android," the band had a religious education that entailed attending church every morning at Abingdon Independent School for Boys, where the band members originally met. Prior to starting there in the early 1980s, Yorke attended Standlake Church of England Primary School in Witney, where his mother also taught.

But when Brian Draper asked Yorke in a 2004 interview if he'd ever look to the Bible for spiritual enlightenment or inspiration he replied, "No, not really, no. To me, it has too much baggage." And according to Jonny Greenwood two years earlier in the Draper interview, distinguishing Roman Catholicism from earlier remarks he makes in regard to what he describes as the "wishy-washiness" of the band's Church of England education,

> I'm all confused. I don't know. Lots of the music that I love is very religious . . . things like Messiaen, who was fervently Catholic. But then Elgar was Catholic as well and he's the most English composer you can think of which is quite strange. And lots of my favourite writers, like Evelyn Waugh, were Catholic. . . . So I'm curious from that standpoint because I know nothing about it. And yet lots of the people that I admire . . . kind of had very strong Catholic faith.

The apparent ambivalence in the remarks from Yorke and Greenwood is not an uncommon position within our contemporary cultural conditions, where what Neil Postman identifies as "the technological world-view" has come to eclipse what can be designated "the traditional world-view." This dynamic, of course, is apparent in the present song's android imagery and in the album's use of the computer voice in general. Tools and technologies in American civilization have not been integrated into the culture, as is typical of traditional societies, but have continuously attacked and bid to become the culture, thereby threatening and demoting foundational aspects of tradition, including social mores, myth, politics, ritual, and religion. People such as Copernicus, Kepler, Galileo, Descartes, Newton, and Francis Bacon were immersed in the theology of their age and could not have imagined the world without God, or of not caring when the Last Judgment would come.

In this regard, the modern West has its roots in the medieval European world, from which three profound inventions emerged, each significant in creating a new relationship between tools and culture. The first, the mechanical clock, provided a new conception of time. The second, the printing press with movable type, attacked all knowledge associated with the oral tradition. And the third, the telescope, attacked the fundamental propositions of Judeo-Christian theology and metaphysics. With this attack came a collapse of the moral center of gravity in the West, which had permitted people to believe that human beings were of special interest to God, and that the Earth was the stable center of the universe.

This, it would seem, is something like the picture portrayed on the third page of the *OK Computer* inner sleeve: a young, late 1960s family with what appear to be firmly reinforced religious or spiritual convictions. By the time we advance to the images found on subsequent pictorial pages, however, there exists the newly open question of the meaning of existence and the Judeo-Christian worldview in decline. Jesus's hands, in increasingly background televisual image, are all that is subsequently seen, the Earth now wandering lonely through an obscure galaxy somewhere in a hidden corner of the universe. This altered perspective left us in the Western world to wonder whether God had any interest in us at all, and moreover, it served to vanish the kind of cultural satisfaction wherein moral and intellectual values were integrated.

Under information overload, the connection between human purpose and information is confused, and in huge volumes at frenetic speeds we encounter indiscriminate information, not directed at anyone in particular and detached from theory, meaning, and purpose. It's important to acknowledge, however, that our two-thousand-year-old traditions are, in essence, antagonistic toward the technocratic way of life, providing as they do a thought-world that largely admonishes it. This idea imbues the presence of the Esperanto word "malamikigi" on the *OK Computer* sleeve with another layer of meaning, this time on the cultural, not the individual, level.

This dynamic of the technological worldview eclipsing the traditional worldview is enacted again toward the end of the sacramental "rain down" section of "Paranoid Android." The voice of the enlightened first persona is gradually overpowered by the reappearance of the shameless, persecutory android antihero that the second voice portrays, and by the violent "crackle of pig skin" he unleashes. This event reflects a suggestion that we may culturally be moving further toward conditions conducive to an increased cultivation of negative rivalry, an hypothesis affirmed by the frequent return of the album's antiheroic persona throughout the recording, and by the recurring theme of violence in much of Radiohead's subsequent work. With the reappearance of the persecutory android antihero, we see the reemergence of his disgust, and one can hear the sneer of contempt in Yorke's voice, as he sings of "the yuppies networking." Serving to monopolize his psyche, while submerging all feelings of shame and guilt, the scene becomes increasingly more toxic as it concludes in the character's quest for transcendence through violence. The character demonstrates his state of aesthetic alert when singing to the "Gucci little piggy" that "ambition makes you look pretty ugly," and now he signals his fear and disgust, as he imagines future scenes of "panic" and "vomit"—animated visions of "the yuppies networking." Appropriately, Yorke was to say in *Thom Yorke: Radiohead and Trading Solo* by Trevor Baker, "I think people feel sick when they listen to *OK Computer*. . . . Nausea was part of what we were trying to create."

One better understands this powerful mixture of emotion when one undertakes some investigation into the word "yuppie," a concept that, as Douglas Coupland's *Generation X* articulates as well, was particularly strident in Gen Xer's lives. Coined in the early 1980s, "yuppie" is an acronym for middle-class "young urban professionals," and it competed at first with "yumpie," which translated as "upwardly mobile professional/person/people." Certainly the latter meaning remains contained within the image of the "yuppies networking," and in their "ambition" for self-advancement. The word first gained currency in 1982 when it was used in a syndicated newspaper article entitled "From Yippie to Yuppie," a piece about the business networking group that Jerry Rubin had recently put together. Formerly a high-profile radical activist, and leader of the countercultural "Youth International Party," in the wake of the Vietnam War, Rubin had turned entrepreneur businessman. Given digital computing's introduction of the "networking" metaphor, it's also worth noting that he was among the first investors in the Apple computer company. Rubin's past notwithstanding, "yuppie" values are considered synonymous with "Reaganite" values: those of putting competition at the center of life and winning at all costs in every domain of social existence, including one's career, dating, and sports. But in this regard we should recall Radiohead's inclusion on an early version of the band's website of the old Hindu maxim: "There is nothing noble in being superior to your fellow men. True nobility is being superior to your former self."

"SUBTERRANEAN HOMESICK ALIEN"

Much of *OK Computer*'s edifying force derives from its employment of science-fiction imagery. In *Hysterical and Useless* Yorke said, "When I was a kid at school," recounting the apparent germination of the album's third song, "Subterranean Homesick Alien," "one of the very first essays I had to do was this essay that asked, 'If you were an alien landing from another planet, how would you describe what you saw?' I just thought, that's a really mind-blowing question." Of course, what this query particularly requires of its answerer is adoption of what might be called the outsider stance, a necessary component of what might otherwise be labeled the anthropological perspective, a point-of-view that permits individuals to be part of their own culture and, simultaneously, to look at it from the outside. "Subterranean Homesick Alien" promotes this effect not just through its reference to aliens and spaceships but also through its employment of the image associated with the title of the album's final track "The Tourist," evident in the alien space tourists "making home movies for the folks back home." But whereas the figure that appears in "Paranoid Android" does so predominantly in the guise of the antihero, "Subterranean Homesick Alien" illustrates him once again in his heroic aspect.

What I'm calling the anthropological perspective received profound technological amplification in December 1968 when homesick Apollo 8 astronauts took photographs of the Earth during their mission to the Moon. As Stewart Brand observed, allowing humankind truly to see itself from the outside for the first time gave an enormous boost to the ecology movement, the first Earth Day occurring shortly thereafter in April 1970. In the wake of the industrial revolution, nature had been "upgraded" into an artistic vessel of spiritual and aesthetic values, and the persona of "Subterranean Homesick Alien" reflects this in his declaration of constantly forgetting "the breath of the morning" and "the smell of the warm summer air." The alien imagery effectively reflects not just his general sense of alienation but also his estrangement from nature, living, as he does, in a town "where you can't smell a thing." "Subterranean Homesick Alien" was inspired by the silent darkness that followed Yorke's running over a pheasant while driving one night down a country lane, the same location from which the song's persona wishes himself abducted by aliens. Yorke's immediate destructive action upon the natural world—as a result of the "juggernaut" force that his car unleashes—reflects the broader and unintended destructive effects of our technologies upon our selves, our habitats, and our fellow species.

The character's estrangement from the natural world—and from himself as a part of it—is reflected also in the general alienation that the alien outsiders witness in "all these weird creatures," locking up their spirits and drilling holes in themselves to live "for their secrets." Alienation, Erich Fromm suggested in *The Sane Society*, is a mode of being where one experiences oneself as an alien. Estranged from yourself, you're no longer experienced as the creator of your own acts or as the center of your world. As out of touch with any other person as with yourself, this is something you indicate clearly, going about town as "you watch your feet for cracks in the pavement." The word "alienation" has also been used to refer to where human beings do not rule their own actions.

This use of the word "alienation" is identical to that which the prophets of the Old Testament identify as *idolatry*, where individuals project into another entity the richness of their being and experience this richness as something that is no longer theirs but something alien and deposited elsewhere. The same situation pertains when people are subject to irrational passions, or caught up in addictions—the image presented here of people "drilling holes in themselves," or "clinging on to bottles," as in *OK Computer*'s fifth track "Let Down." No longer experiencing the limitless richness of themselves as human beings, one partial striving that they project as an external aim comes to enslave them. For instance, people who exclusively give themselves to the pursuit of their passion for money become possessed by their striving for it. Money becomes the idol they worship, the projection of one isolated power in themselves, caught up within the feedback loop of their desire for it.

It's worth quoting at length Fromm's estimate of the breadth of our estrangement as he saw it in the late twentieth century:

> Alienation as we find it in modern society is almost total; it pervades the relationship of man to his work, to the things he consumes, to the state, to his fellow man, and to himself. Man has created a world of man-made things as it never existed before. He has constructed a complicated social machine to administer the technical machine he built. Yet this whole creation of his stands over and above him. He does not feel himself as a creator and center, but as the servant of a Golem, which his hands have built. The more powerful and gigantic the forces are which he unleashes, the more powerless he feels himself as human being. He confronts himself with his own forces embodied in things he has created, alienated from himself. He is owned by his own creation, and has lost ownership of himself. He has built a golden calf, and says "these are your gods who have brought you out of Egypt."

It's apparent that "Subterranean Homesick Alien" expresses much of its alienation musically, and turning to sonic considerations, the Western film music tradition tends to encode futurist or alien themes with the use of electronic sounds and dissonance. With the exception of drums, the song's performing forces are all electronic, and the spacy tremolo of the Fender Rhodes electric piano is particularly exotic (inspired by Miles Davis's celebrated 1970 recording *Bitches Brew*). The electric guitar effects, for their timbres and use of echo throughout, are equally so. In combination with the abundant use of reverb in the song's three-chord intro/outro and during its verses, these effects serve to create the illusion of a vast sense of space that isolates the listener. During the second half of the track, the protagonist sings about wishing to be abducted by aliens so they might show him "the world as he'd love to see it." Recounting how he'd tell all his friends of everything he's seen, he suggests that they'd never believe him. Rather, they'd think he'd "finally lost it completely."

This isolated and utter estrangement is indicated in the title's use of the word "subterranean," and we should not fail to note the song's allusion to "Subterranean Homesick Blues," the opening track from Bob Dylan's 1965 album *Bringing It All Back Home*. Not only has Dylan had a massive influence on most people who've worked with American-inspired popular music forms, but also he was a reluctant figurehead of American unrest at the time of the album's release during the American civil rights movement, for which songs like "The Times They Are a-Changin'" and "Blowin' in the Wind" had become anthems. Dylan's estrangement from his peers in the folk song community also began with this recording, the first half of which, including "Subterranean Homesick Blues," features an electric rock-and-roll backing band. But on the acoustic second half of the album, Dylan also distances himself from the protest songs with which he'd become identified, his lyrics continuing their inclination toward more personal and abstract expression.

In the first verse of "Subterranean Homesick Blues," Dylan nonetheless sings that he's "thinking 'bout the government," and a general sense of unease or paranoia pervades the song's lyrics, something similarly portrayed in the album jacket photo, featuring an earnest-looking Bob with two uniformed policemen behind him. This is also played out in the album's liner notes, where Dylan writes about an individual running for district attorney who points him out as "the one that's been causing all them riots over in vietnam," and who then turns to a group of people and says that "if elected, he'll have me electrocuted publicly on the next fourth of july." We could similarly note how a couple of years later the aforementioned yippie Jerry Rubin was twice hauled before the House of Un-American Activities, or how the FBI investigated Bob Feldman, after his discovery and publication of Columbia University's obscure institutional affiliation with a weapons research think tank, connected to the U.S. Department of Defense, led to major student demonstrations in 1968.

Leaving aside the paranoia that might accrue to initiating such activities, it's interesting to consider the report of an external fact-finding commission that Columbia set up to examine the events that had led to the situation, and which thus concluded, as Joshua Meyrowitz notes in *No Sense of Place*,

> The present generation of young people in our universities is the best informed, the most intelligent, and the most idealistic this country has ever known. . . . As one student observed during our investigation, today's students take seriously the ideals taught in schools and churches, and often at home, and then they see a system that denies its ideals in actual life. Racial injustice and the war in Vietnam stand out as prime illustrations of our society's deviation from its professed ideals.

The process of recognizing the schism between these professed ideals and our cultural realities can be a painful one, causing significant suffering for many people, since it involves a continuous attempt to negotiate the many contradictions between these two different orders of reality. But the undertaking is made easier with the more people that surround you who're identifying and drawing the attention of others toward similar things. Given that 1968 was a year during which massive student demonstrations were occurring not only in the United States but also around the world, it's in this sense that Yorke, as suggested in the previous chapter, in relation to the title song from *The Bends*, may in part sing about "wishing it was the sixties." Certainly his reaction to the gathering malaise in that song—singing about the authorities bringing in the CIA, tanks, and marines to blow him away—isn't unlike that which Dylan exhibits.

Perhaps providing further insight into the paranoia of the "Paranoid Android," Yorke was likewise to express concern about his own perceived political activity, as he indicated when Chuck Klosterman, an interviewer for the popular *Spin* magazine, asked him in 2003 how becoming a father had changed his political beliefs and affected his songwriting on *Hail to the Thief*. In the interview, during which he muses whether our children will even have a future, Yorke responds, "The trouble with your question—and we both know this—is that if I discuss the details of what I'm referring to in *Spin* magazine, I will get death threats. And I'm frankly not willing to get death threats," he says. "And that sort of sucks, I realize, but I know what is going on out there."

With wonderful poetic economy, Emily Dickinson (1924, I/vi) expresses the social alienation that must always precede what she here calls the process of being "handled with a chain":

> MUCH madness is divinest sense
> To a discerning eye;
> Much sense the starkest madness.
> 'T is the majority
> In this, as all, prevails. Assent, and you are sane;
> Demur,—you're straightway dangerous, And handled with a chain.

Prior to the nineteenth century, "alienation" denoted a psychotic person, the word "alienist" still being used in English for a doctor who cares for the insane—the absolutely alienated individuals who have entirely lost themselves as the center of their own experience, or lost the sense of self. Though this sounds like our comic book superhero in another context, here he explains that though his friends would shut him away, he'd be all right, since, like all the other alienated people, he's "just uptight." In this regard, notwithstanding all the mournful elements that connote the inevitable distress of the character's alienated condition, that he's not overwrought is evident in the employment of a major mode in "Subterranean Homesick Alien," and in its concluding three-chord figure's optimistic movement from the tonic minor to tonic major. Considerably signifying positive movement, the psychological affluence that accrues from his imaginative thought-experiment demonstrates his potential for a heroic hopefulness, a posture that he'll struggle to attain and retain in "Let Down" but that first dissipates, again, in the next track "Exit Music (for a film)."

"EXIT MUSIC (FOR A FILM)"

It's significant that the fourth song on *OK Computer* is directly connected to tragedy, particularly in its association with Baz Luhrmann's 1996 film *William Shakespeare's Romeo and Juliet*, for which the song was commissioned, and in which the B side "Talk Show Host" also appears. Yorke originally tried to incorporate lines from the play into the song, an aspiration he eventually abandoned. In part inspired by the film's closing scene, where Juliet holds a Colt 45 pistol to her head and proceeds to use it, Yorke was also apparently affected by the 1968 film version as well: "I saw the Zeffirelli version when I was 13 and I cried my eyes out," says Yorke in *Radiohead: From a Great Height*, "because I couldn't understand why, the morning after they shagged, they didn't just run away. The song is written for two people who should run away before all the bad stuff starts," adding that "Exit Music (for a film)" is also "[a] personal song." Jonny Greenwood is also recorded by Hale as saying of the song, "I think we knew as soon as we finished that it had to go on our record, and not the soundtrack. . . . It was about more than the film, which is a bit arrogant to say, 'It's bigger than Shakespeare.'"

What one *can* say about the song, however, is that Shakespeare's work, to be sure, forms what Greenwood once called a "sub-text" to the song, and to *OK Computer* as a whole. It's been observed that *Romeo and Juliet* (1597) is developed in terms of remarkable symmetry around three scenes of tumultuous action devoted to the feud, which has long existed between the young lovers' families. Feuds were a common social convention of the time between families of nobility, as was the necessity of taking personal revenge for an insult to one's honor.

One of the first things we see in the Luhrmann film is the enormous statue of Jesus overlooking the city of Verona. From the perspective of one particularly effective shot, it stands between two tall buildings, respectively marked by the corporate logos "Montague" and "Capulet," the families of Romeo and Juliet. References to Christian nonviolence[6] are apparent within the work, as when Benvolio, the nephew of Montague and friend to Romeo, in the first of these scenes alludes to the words of Jesus, when he says to servants of the two families involved in fighting, "you know not what you do" (1.1.62). Juliet, too, alludes to Jesus's words when, after meeting Romeo and learning his identity from her nurse, she muses, "Prodigious birth of love it is to me / That I must love a loathéd enemy" (1.5.140–41).

A remarkable characteristic of *Romeo and Juliet* is that everyone involved in the feud seems to carry a sword, or in the case of the Luhrmann film, a gun. After the first outbreak of violence, the Prince rebukes his subjects, speaking of their "pernicious rage" and admonishing them for being "enemies to peace" (1.1.79). We learn from him that the Montagues and Capulets have already been responsible for three prior civil brawls and that any further outbreaks of violence will now be punished by pain of death. Enlisting the help of the Friar, Romeo arranges for Juliet and him to be secretly married: "For this alliance may so happy prove," the Friar hopingly remarks in favor of the matrimony, "to turn your households' rancor to pure love" (2.3.91–92).

Until the second explosion of the feud, the action of the play has been in the cause of love's harmonious force—from Capulet's speaking of Romeo's virtues at the feast while rebuking his nephew Tybalt to the young Montague's own attempts to transcend the feud's inescapable snares. Following Tybalt's attempts to provoke Romeo, his friend Mercutio expresses his disgust at the latter's "calm, dishonourable, vile submission" (3.1.72). But Romeo reminds them both that Mercutio's own relative, the Prince, has forbidden such bandying in Verona's streets. The hopeful possibility that his match with Juliet can bring reconciliation to their families shatters, however, after Mercutio dies from a wound inflicted during the ensuing melee. Now imitating Mercutio, Romeo speaks of Tybalt's slander in terms of a staining of his reputation, remarking to himself, "O sweet Juliet / Thy beauty hath made me effeminate / And in my temper soft'ned valour's steel" (3.1.111–13). Moments later he resounds, "Away to heaven respective lenity / And fire-eyed fury be my conduct now!" (120–21). Proceeding to engage and kill Tybalt, Romeo, eventually succumbs to the revenge code's deadly logic, as does Lady Capulet shortly afterward when she demands of the sovereign, "Prince, as thou art true / For blood of ours shed blood of Montague" (146–47). To her mother, even Juliet feigns a desire to avenge her cousin Tybalt's death (3.5.86–87).

The feud begins to take the lives of some who aren't even blood relatives of the families, but ultimately, impelled by love, a Montague and a Capulet both do violence upon themselves and, as the chorus of the play tells us in the prologue, "Doth with their death bury their parents' strife" (8). The last scene of violence is not an outbreak of the feud itself but a consequence of the secrecy and plotting that it has enforced, and at the end of the play it's the survivors of a society forsaken of its youth that occupy the stage. When the Capulets and the Montagues are assembled in the last scene, the Prince says to them, "See what a scourge is laid upon your hate" (5.3.292), and Capulet concedes, suggesting that their children are ultimately "poor sacrifices of our enmity!" (304).

On one level, the singer of "Exit Music (for a film)" would seem to be Romeo, singing to Juliet the morning after they "shagged"—and about to play out Yorke's preferred treatment of the scene through an escape from the violence of the feud. The arrangement of the lyric in the *OK Computer* CD jacket is an element of the work that I've saved to address until now. The disjointedness of their layout is typical to all of the songs where the antiheroic aspect of the album's character is predominant. Interestingly, the track for which the lyric is most ordered and free of typos (typos being another common feature of the antihero's printed lyrics) is that of the apparently well-adjusted and robotic persona in "Fitter Happier."

"When I write, I suppose I have a thing about having 8 or 9 different people within me," Yorke told *Melody Maker* in 1994, less than two years before working on *OK Computer*. "Everybody has different characters following them around. I think that everyone with the first album was presuming that there was this one character who was writing this stuff. I don't agree." Given that the reverb on the recording sounds more like the acoustic environment of a tomb than that of a bedroom chamber, one might construe the song's singer to be more likely the Friar—in particular, as portrayed during the play's final scene, just after discovering the corpses of Romeo and Paris at the Capulet tomb. In the second part of the song, the entry of male choral voices (the band's first use of their newly acquired mellotron) lends itself to this interpretation, helping to conjure the image of the Friar as religious teacher. Urging Juliet not to lose her nerve but to keep breathing and choose life, this moment parallels that in the play when the Friar says to Juliet, following her awakening from the potion-induced sleep that he himself had procured,

> Lady, come from that nest
> Of death, contagion, and unnatural sleep
> A greater power than we can contradict
> Hath thwarted our intents. (5.3.151–54)

Referring to Satan—the "greater power" of which he speaks—the Friar, hearing a noise and fearing they will be discovered, beckons for Juliet to come along so he can help her escape the feud by disposing of her "among a sisterhood of holy nuns" (157). But Juliet replies, "Go, get thee hence, for I will not away" (160), following which he hastily departs.

With the conclusion of the mellotron segment, however, and the return to the original harmonic section of the song, Juliet complains of a chill and requests of the Friar that he sing them a song of consolation, in order to keep them all warm. Replacing the mellotron for the duration of this verse is an enigmatic background loop, wherein one can discern the sound of children's voices, and which thus suggests, as does the play, that Juliet and the others are really symbolic of youth in general. Concern for the youth, as I've previously suggested, represents one of the most persistent and prominent themes throughout Radiohead's repertoire.

Ultimately, of course, it's in the character's imagination that the interactions between these personae are taking place, and up to this point, each voice has expressed distress, in combination with a faint sense of fear. But the understanding that the situation can be remedied or escaped has been apparent. We should note therefore that the motif of escape is one that is present throughout the album, as, for instance, in "Airbag," where our superhero claims he is "amazed" at having escaped unscathed a potentially fatal traffic accident.[7] Certainly he's endowed with a sense of feeling extremely "Lucky" to have done so, as we find out later in the album's second to last song, after he survives another manifestation of "a jackknifed juggernaut"—this time in the form of a crashed airplane (presumably one fitted with the aviation equivalent to airbags). A further illustration of OK Computer's symbolic interplay, this event forms part of the visual montage on its front cover, where the passengers of a downed airplane, marked by an emergency cross above, appear hastily to be disembarking from an escape chute, guided by an individual at the bottom. The album's façade includes signs reading "Lost Child," its eerily white background ominously scarred by a shadowy running figure, superimposed on a juncture of motorways or freeways with cars speeding along. No doubt both are images depicting the album's haunted protagonist.

The plane scenario is further developed on the next page of the album's cover booklet, where the caricature of a man is alerted to the alarming news that one of the wings of the plane is on fire. When one notices that the diagram superimposed over the statue of Jesus on the booklet's third page illustrates the plane "cleared for takeoff" and that its last page shows a passenger's aerial view looking down on a vast pillow of clouds, accompanied by the printed word "Lucky," and a sketched diagram of the escape hatch on the plane's surface—one can surely see that some kind of symbolic journey or meta-narrative is being documented here. Evidence of this plane journey also appears in the booklet in the form of what appear to be images of cockpits, airport terminals, and signs advising not to drink lavatory water.

The aforementioned image of Jesus resembles a baptism scene. Two smartly dressed parents circa the late 1960s are seen holding an infant, and on a subsequent page of the insert, the child, at about five years of age, is pictured pleasantly holding the hands of his parents under the guiding image of a digitally enhanced electronic Jesus, while a specter of horror invades the image in the guise of a dark hand in the top right corner, reaching up through broken thin ice. The narrative continues on the next page, where a shadow of the plane is seen flying beneath the digital image (this time of Jesus's other hand) continuing the connection of this "life journey" to the plane journey.

In 1996, Yorke procured a mini-disc recorder with which he recorded many of the looped sound effects that are heard on the album, and with the conclusion of "Exit Music (for a film)," we hear a return to the loop of children's voices and what Mac Randall suggests sounds like traffic noises. But I'd suggest that what we are actually hearing is the sound of water, the lake from which the protagonist—illustrating that he really "can't do this alone"—requires being pulled, following the air crash in "Lucky." The image of children playing by a lake on the page opposite the pig diagram found toward the end of the *OK Computer* CD booklet suggests just such an interpretation.

Of all the characters in Shakespeare's play, the protagonist's disposition at the conclusion of the song seems closest to that of Mercutio, whose dying words to Tybalt and Romeo are "a plague a both your houses!" (3.1.104), representing a complete and utter giving over to violent hatred. With the increased density of texture that accompanies the entry of drums, synthesized bass, and electric guitar, the scene changes to one of increasing toxicity, moving from disgust through contempt, to anger and hatred. The contempt that the character expresses is that which the youths feel "for the adults who have ruined their lives." What had been the Friar's entreaty for Juliet to "keep breathing" becomes the young people's hope that their adult authorities will find their breath choked by their rules and wisdom. The protagonist's unconsoling song of hate illustrates his own entrapment in violent imitation, and finally escaping the feud into what she imagines to be an everlasting peace with her Romeo, it helps drive Juliet to suicide.

In this regard, seven years following *OK Computer*'s release, the World Health Organization (WHO) sounded the alarm about the profundity of the social problem that suicide has become all over the world. Reporting that in most European countries suicide kills more people each year than road traffic accidents and that, globally, it takes more lives than murder and war combined, it also estimated that between ten and twenty million individuals survive failed suicide attempts every year. Most distressing, however, was its report of an alarming worldwide increase in suicidal behaviors among young people aged fifteen to twenty-five.

"LET DOWN"

On another point we must concur with Randall in *Exit Music*, who recommends of "Let Down" that it's "a tremendous achievement and one of Radiohead's most intoxicating creations." But one of the most significant aspects of its impact derives from the fact that the song emerges from the deranged sounding depths of hatred and violence that the protagonist exhibits in his wretched song to the youth at the conclusion of "Exit Music (for a film)." Whereas in *Romeo and Juliet* the Friar reflects a similar idealism to that of the young lovers, the protagonist's moral decrepitude threatens to lead the youth toward a similar fate to that of the tragic couple. In his lambasting of authorities and other unheroic behaviors witnessed elsewhere, the album's protagonist appears to demonstrate the symptoms of what we might call "radical egalitarian let down." Dreams of how things might be don't always simply provide a buoying vision that can lead us all to work on behalf of making things better; they sometimes also afford a rationale for profusely hating the world as it actually is. Evaluating existing institutions against extravagant hopes of what is possible can just as easily produce alienation and violent fantasies as constructive reform—and this, of course, is the direction of the antiheroic trend that we've so far seen.

During the opening lines of "Let Down," the character identifies the estrangement associated with the mechanical repetition of modern urban and suburban life that the images of various transportation systems convey. According to Jonny Greenwood in Mark Paytress's *Radiohead: The Complete Guide*, the song "is about what speed and movement do to someone's mind . . . when you're staring out of a window in a moving train for an hour. All those people, cars and houses passing by." In reference to the nature of contemporary travel, Yorke describes in Martin Clarke's *Radiohead: Hysterical and Useless* the emptiness of what he calls "the transit-zone feeling": "You're in a space, you are collecting all these impressions, but it all seems so vacant. You don't have control. . . . You feel very distant from all these thousands of people that are also walking there." A similar type of estrangement to that which Yorke describes is apparent, too, in the disappointed people, whom the song's protagonist observes "clinging onto bottles." Like him they feel "crushed like a bug in the ground," their smashed shells reflecting their diminished ability to absorb negative affect.

In spite of his apparent distress, the character sings "don't get sentimental . . . it always ends up drivel"—but it's worth noting that industrial society is by nature deeply nostalgic. A characteristic side effect of its rapid rate of change, obsolescence, in the world of business turnover, is a ubiquitous phenomenon, the basic dynamics of technocratic capitalism's forceful powers of "creative destruction." Electronic communications of all types are very much involved in the general creation of melodrama: "Sentimentality is being emotional for the sake of it," suggests Yorke in *Exit Music*. "We're bombarded with sentiment, people emoting. That's the letdown. Feeling every emotion is fake. Or rather every emotion is on the same plane, whether it's a car advert or a pop song."

Though his legs appear to be all right, the persona's broken wings merely twitch, and, in this regard, it's worth pointing out again that one of contemporary culture's most debilitating consequences is its erosion of traditional narratives and the consequent obliteration of possibilities that they once provided for the acquisition of a sense of transcendent meaning and purpose. Powerful world systems that both nourished and distorted the Western intellectual tradition—theologies and ideologies—are now seen as having collapsed in legitimacy. This situation creates skepticism, an agnosticism in terms of judgment, and often a nihilistic sense of world-weariness, where people begin to question distinctions of value and the value of distinctions. For all of his paralyzation, the character in the second verse yet foresees that he's one day "going to grow wings" and acquire a sense of transcendence by way of some type of chemical reaction. But when the soaring heights fail to materialize, it's so disappointing as to leave him "hysterical and useless," and both he and we do well to remember Jiddu Krishnamurti's suggestion that it's not a sign of good health to be well adjusted to a sick society.

Recalling the protagonist's antiheroic attempts to attain a sense of transcendence through violence, I've referred to his suggestion in the second verse of "Let Down" that one day he's "going to grow wings" and instead find a true and legitimate means for the acquisition of transcendence. It's following the second iteration of the chorus in this regard that he begins to script the scene away from one of distress, and toward one of considerably greater psychological affluence. At this juncture, the song's motorial flow collapses, with all performing forces dropping out except for a solo guitar, which plays a short and heroic four-note motif comprising the latter half of an ascending major scale. Heard entirely on offbeats, the motif is uncertain, yet determined and hopeful, and it's heard in combination with an insistent pedal tone that the bass guitar reinforces when the band reenters. Providing solid tonic stability, this sense of satisfaction is further buttressed when Yorke returns, singing the words "Let Down," emphasizing the tonic third through its neighboring suspensions and, therewith, the brightness of the song's major tonality. This middle section continues to build until the appearance of the jubilant-sounding computerized sounds that the band created using Sinclair ZX Spectrum computers—among the initial mainstream home computers released in the UK (comparable to the Commodore 64 in North America) and apparently owned by each member of the group shortly after they were released in the early 1980s. The excitement of this event is enhanced with drummer Phil Selway's long-awaited return to playing toms, while his accentuated fill, heard just prior to the vocal reentry, powerfully prepares the way for the song's final verse.

Sung at a higher range than either of the first two verses, for the first time in the song, Yorke's voice is single-tracked and isolated in the right speaker channel. "You know where you are with," he sings, which suggests a lifting of the tremendous burden of estrangement and alienation associated with the spiritual transit zone feeling. Though the "floor collapses," he finds himself "bouncing back," and it becomes evident at this point that he's addressing his former self, who reenters in the other speaker, singing about "growing wings" and of feeling "hysterical and useless." Speaking not just to himself but to all the other disappointed people as well, the character affirms three times that "you'll know where you are," melodically outlining the aforementioned ascending four-note motif while doing so. The climbing voice triumphantly reaches the upper tonic with Yorke's heroically long-held high note, hopeful in its sense of possessing the ability to construct unalienated experience. Concluding with quiet acoustic guitar and the return of the synthesized ZX Spectrum sounds, Randall appropriately observes of the latter that it "bears an odd quality of triumph."

"KARMA POLICE"

"Karma is important," says Yorke in *Exit Music*. "The idea that something like karma exists makes me happy. It makes me smile. I get more sympathetical." Central to the Eastern religious traditions of Hinduism, Buddhism, and Jainism, the concept of karma refers to the idea that the sum of a people's actions in previous states of existence bears on their fate in future existences. Recalling how in "Airbag" the album's protagonist is born again, the idea of karma implies that we are continually experiencing rebirth in a system of cause and effect that may span a number of lifetimes, a process from which Hinduism holds we can escape only by entering into immortality—an aspiration that one can achieve solely through the consistent performance of unselfish actions without any expectation of reward or punishment. Generally speaking, in the case of Buddhism it's only traditional Buddhists that maintain belief in karma and rebirth, and for them salvation is solely garnered through the attainment of nirvana—that ineffable state of disinterested wisdom and compassion. Karma is also described as the energy associated with one's past moral conduct as manifested in both thought and action, and English-speaking Buddhists, in this relation, describe good or bad karma in terms of creating merit or demerit. Needless to say, the goal of the practitioner is always to work toward the purification of one's inner nature. That is, of course, unless you are the antiheroic protagonist of *OK Computer*, in which case you instead police the karma of others, reinvoking your sense of disgust in order to purify your perceived pestilences—something that, in this context, he puts into effect through the process of having his victims immediately placed under arrest.

In the second verse of the song, the character signals that this is another scene monopolized by disgust. Of the girl with the Hitler hairdo he says she's making him "feel ill," recalling "the vomit" associated with the Gucci little piggy in "Paranoid Android." Yorke's comments from *Exit Music* in fact suggest it's she that he's again referring to here: "I get stressed pretty easily, and having people looking at you in that certain 'malicious' way, I can't handle it anymore. . . . That's what 'Karma Police' was about." Once more, what Yorke seems unable to handle is the temptations of contagious emotion, that is, responding to this type of emotional outburst in kind.

This is what the persecutory antihero's return suggests at least. Now a tyrant king issuing commands of arrest, the conjuring of Hitler makes him seem even more menacing, an effect that the electronically distorted background vocals of his cronies (heard during the second and third verses of the song) serve to enhance. The musical sneer heard in Yorke's voice and the song's minor key further amplify this effect, as does the character's exertions of coercive force and his retributive "this is what you get when you mess with us," as he sings in the song's chorus. As Randall points out, however, the song possesses "a fine blend of the sinister and comic," and elements of the latter are communicated through its rhetorically ironic use of predominantly acoustic or "non-electric" instrumentation. As I have suggested, normally associated with greater authenticity and intimacy, the acoustic instruments serve to create what seems like a deceptive sense of benevolence. This effect is manifoldly reinforced by the Beatlesque quality of the background vocals,[8] particularly during the chorus, as the harmonic framework of the piece changes from a minor to a major modality, and as the performing forces become much reduced with the rhythm section sitting out.

With the character's initial victim in the first verse, we get the idea of "noise" transferred directly to an individual, who "buzzes like a fridge" and who's "like a detuned radio." With regard to this image, Yorke was to say in Andy Greene's "Oral History," "It was partly the way of just expressing how some people just talk and they're not really saying anything." Like a computer, the man also "talks in maths," and it's interesting to note how Arabic numerals were banned in some places when they first came to Europe in the tenth century. It was René Descartes who, ignited by a passion for exactitude and universal agreement, first urged that mathematical laws should be allowed to become "the procedure and norm of truth," and we're now indebted to this procedure, both for our present mastery of the physical world and for our equal helplessness in the management of our social and political affairs.

In this relation, we can address a number of related technological developments that would not ordinarily come to mind when addressing examples of "technology" and briefly consider some of the powerful effects such innovations create. We could refer, for instance, to how the presumed Hindu invention of the zero—unknown to the Classical Greeks and Romans—represents an example of how symbols can create new mindsets and new conceptions of reality. They do this particularly by way of the things they make possible—as with the Arabic numbering system itself, which facilitated the development of a sophisticated mathematics. This, in turn, enabled the elaboration of statistics, which was already being employed toward the late sixteenth century. Statistics are no doubt one of the most powerful technologies currently in use, and one that draws our attention to large-scale patterns by making possible new perceptions and realities. Among some of the areas in which their application has been problematic, however, are domains such as opinion polling and the so-called measurement of intelligence. Of course, what the use of statistics accomplishes, moreover, is to make a significant contribution to the further generation of extraordinary amounts of useless information, complicating the task of determining and locating that which may prove useful. In this respect, statistics become lethal when combined with the computer, as together they generate reams of refuse within our public discourse. We could also mention the electronic spreadsheet, a development that the protagonist's victim of the song's third verse for some might conjure: "'Karma Police' is dedicated to everyone who works for a big firm. It's a song against bosses," Yorke explains in *Hysterical and Useless*, apparently reflecting the singer's anarchist perspective. Although he claims to have given all he can, his victim remains "on the payroll" and presumably "cashing in."

With regard to the phrase "Karma Police," Jonny Greenwood says in Hale's *Radiohead: From a Great Height*, "It was a band catchphrase for a while on tour—whenever someone was behaving in a particularly shitty way, we'd say, 'the karma police will catch up with him sooner or later,'" adding, "It's not a revenge thing, just about being happy about your own behaviour." There's a sense that the song's persona is himself happy about his own behavior when the scene switches from a toxic one dominated by disgust to an affluent one characterized by a relieved sense of excitement and then joy in the final section of the song, its affective elevation articulated through a change in key. As in the refrain of "Airbag," the key ascends by a tone. At this point our antihero spontaneously transforms into the comic book superhero, his identity affirmed by his use of the expletive "phew." With these changes, and in his pronouncement, "for a minute there I lost myself," the character acknowledges his reclamation of self-control—apparently now able to understand and absorb the negative affect he encounters and capable also of transcending negative action or karma.

It's worth considering the fluid and unstable nature of the character's identity, and in this relation, we should draw our attention toward what are referred to as technologies of "social saturation." This ensemble of technologies includes rail, postal services, the automobile, telephone, radio, motion pictures, the airplane, television, the personal computer, and commercial publishing—perhaps even the book. Each of these technologies has fostered a range of relationships that could not have occurred before their emergence, bringing people into increasingly close proximity and exposing them to an expanding range of others. Social saturation is, thus, now the predominant experience of the global villager, and we're coming to reflect the social surroundings with which we've become increasingly entangled through a kind of internalization of other people. In this way, committed identity becomes progressively more difficult an achievement in the electric age, as social saturation gradually adds to the population of the self.

We should note that such complexity and insecurity of identity also results from our continuous interiorization of new technologies. This always requires some degree of personal accommodation, particularly in an environment characterized by continuous change. Since our identities undergo alteration with every new technology that we adopt, every change in our media environment requires personal readaptation, and sometimes significantly so. With the acceleration of contemporary culture, there's an intense and unprecedented pressure to acquire the robotic condition of the well adjusted, heard in the droning computer voice of OK Computer's seventh track "Fitter Happier." This, of course, is also the context for the "fast-track career," a formulation that appears in newsprint-like text at the back of the *OK Computer* booklet, illustrating that, following the fall of communism, the times appear to be gone when having nonprecarious employment meant possessing a singular and recognizable working identity for the bulk of one's working life.

"FITTER HAPPIER"

"Fitter Happier," the seventh track of *OK Computer*, is perhaps the computer's primary cameo on the album. It provides an appropriate entry point in the pursuit of a considered understanding of the recording, a fact that may have had a role in Radiohead's decision to take the stage to the sound of the piece throughout most of their performances, in support of the album. "It came out like a shopping list," Yorke told Mac Randall of the now-defunct *Musician* magazine. "I wouldn't normally use it, but I responded to the way the computer voice pronounced it. That voice seemed a logical extension of this list mentality." Using a Macintosh SimpleText reader, the band created a piece that's rich in meaning, some of whose potency lies, as above, in the idea that the individual who's completely adjusted to the constant change of the contemporary technological environment is like a robot. Likewise, we could refer to the advertising enterprise, and its attempt to extend the principles of automation—in the form of technological theology—to every aspect of society.

Each of these is evident in "Fitter Happier," which commences with a sense of general consonance, particularly in the wake of the dissonant sound effect at the ending of "Karma Police" from which it emerges. The protagonist would seem to be feeling good—"fitter," "happier," and "more productive," and generally treating himself better. Now "a patient better driver," he also has "a safer car" than the fast German model he was driving in "Airbag" and is now responsible too for "baby smiling in back seat." Moving "at a better pace," "slower and more calculated," he's now in possession of "tyres that grip in the wet," a slogan-worthy phrase that appears alongside a "shot of baby strapped in back seat," suggesting that portions of this scene may have been the content of a television commercial parable. According to Yorke in Randall's *Exit Music*, "The reason we used a computer voice is that it appeared to be emotionally neutral." But what at first seems an impartial scene, with the character "no longer empty and frantic" and feeling "no paranoia," gradually becomes immersed in the toxicity of fear and terror, an effect in large part achieved by the haunting melodic and harmonic dissonances of the minor key piano part, and the harsh electronic sound effects heard throughout. He maintains that though he "will not cry in public," he "still kisses with saliva" and "still cries at a good film." But his apparent paranoia is in large part the result of an increasing sense of not only depersonalization but also dehumanization.

The character, we learn, is getting on better with his "associate employee contemporaries," a technocratic formulation pertinent and fundamental to what might be considered the beginnings of technological theology—namely, "scientific management." Otherwise known as "Taylorism," after being thrust onto the U.S. national scene during hearings of the Interstate Commerce Commission (in relation to an application from Northeastern Railroads), the principles of Frederick Taylor's system were applied in the legal profession, the armed forces, education, the church, and even the home. Among its techniques were his famous "time-motion studies," and Taylor's perspective on what comprises culture represents the first formal and clear outline of the assumptions of our contemporary technological society. These involve a number of beliefs, including that the most important goal of human work and thought is efficiency; that technical calculation is always superior to human judgment, which cannot be trusted, as it's characterized by ambiguities and needless complexities; that subjectivity impedes lucid thinking; that what we can't measure is either of negligible value or doesn't really exist; and that it's technical "experts" who can best guide and conduct the affairs of citizens. Under the new system, laws, rules, and principles regarding the "science" of workers' jobs replaced their own individual judgment, along with any traditional rules of thumb with which they may have had acquaintance. Moreover, "scientific management" legitimized the idea that technique can do our thinking for us. Taylor's work represents the first expression of the view that society and human beings are best served when placed at the disposal of their technology and techniques. Since Taylorism remains the essential scaffolding of the contemporary world, and given that there now appears to be "no chance of escape," the fact that the character is "now self-employed" seems of little consolation.

The protagonist's angst derives also from an overwhelming sense of political paralysis. The character is "concerned (but powerless)" and at the next moment, paradoxically, "an empowered and informed member of society (pragmatism not idealism)"—but clearly only if he discards distant ideals and approaches the matter of exercising whatever power he pragmatically has at his disposal. This was of course the case for the emerging global "pro-democracy movement" of the time, which was typically characterized within public discourse as the "antiglobalization movement," its most radical elements usually dismissed as "anarchists." This movement might ultimately be better understood as "anti-totalitarian," though we should also remember that Yorke, while at Exeter University, was involved in founding an "anarchist collective." He had apparently also become part of an antifascist club while there, possessed "strong felt political views . . . and used to get involved on the frontline if it was something he believed in," according to an old classmate quoted in Hale's *Radiohead: From a Great Height.*

It's interesting in this connection to note the inclusion of a quote on Radiohead's 1998 EP *Air Bag/How Am I Driving?*, the immediate follow-up to *OK Computer.* The EP and its cover appropriately proclaims, "This album is aimed at the United States"—and the outlines of an American flag in the hazy ground of the thirteenth page of the *OK Computer* CD booklet illustrate the nation's significance here as well. The quote is from the self-proclaimed anarchist, American social commentator, and world-renowned linguist Noam Chomsky and is apparently excerpted from *The Chomsky Reader* (1987):

> It is an important feature of the ideological system to impose on people the feeling that they really are incompetent to deal with complex and important issues: they'd better leave it to the captain. One device is to develop a star system, an array of figures who are often media creations or creations of the academic propaganda establishment, whose deep insights we are supposed to admire and to whom we must happily and confidently assign the right to control our lives and to control international affairs.

It's worth observing that, in the post–*OK Computer* context, Radiohead inquires not into how the captain is steering but into how the character himself is driving. "It's interesting that it has really taken off in America," Yorke was to say of political activism in *Juice Magazine,* speaking less than a year following the 1999 trend-setting major demonstrations against the World Trade Organization (WTO) in Seattle, Washington, though prior to the events that were to spawn the War on Terror, which no doubt explains his apparent buoyancy. "There's a bit of a tradition of it, but there hasn't really been anything coherent since Vietnam. . . . I think it's because of people like Chomsky. There's a lot of people who've read Chomsky now and people of his ilk and his e-magazine in America and in Europe." Observing that "it's nothing to do with left and right now," he adds, "It's to do with stuff that's come out since the cold war, certain things dawning on people over a long time."

Among the things that have become clearer is the reality, during the Cold War, of the U.S.-backed "Operation Condor," where numerous right-wing South American military dictatorships—including those of Brazil, Argentina, Uruguay, Paraguay, Bolivia, and Chile—participated in a joint campaign across one another's borders to track and kill their left-wing opponents, a campaign that was to last until 1983. Though the official operation was not launched until 1975, it began in 1973—notably on September 11—with General Augusto Pinochet's CIA-backed overthrow of the democratically elected Chilean president Salvador Allende. The official release in 2008 of the telephone transcripts of Henry Kissinger revealed that this plot was taking place at the highest levels of the U.S. government.

The relevance that this has for us is that shortly after "Fitter Happier" begins, the sound of a television enters and we hear a loop that is repeated for the duration of the piece: "This is the Panic Office, section nine-seventeen may have been hit. Activate the following procedure." Although the CD liner notes say the sample comes from "The Flight of the Condor," it actually derives from the 1975 Robert Redford film *Three Days of the Condor* (based on James Grady's 1974 book *Six Days of the Condor*). In Yorke's words, recorded in *Exit Music*, "It's the sequence where all the people have been killed and he's calling the office to tell them," and by "the office," Yorke means that of the character's CIA superiors. Both the book and the film explore the moral ambiguities of the United States in the wake of the scandals that were the Vietnam War and Watergate. And for the contemporary activist, when combined with the knowledge that the United States in the recent past facilitated undertakings such as "Operation Condor," this provides a considerable source of paranoia—if not utter deterrence.

At the conclusion of "Fitter Happier," with "no chance of escape," the protagonist refers to himself as "a pig—in a cage—on antibiotics," a line taken from Jonathan Coe's 1994 satirical novel *Carve Up!* The line is a reference to the contemporary factory farming methods, first developed in the hog industry during the mid-1970s and modeled on techniques previously applied in poultry production. This "scientific" approach to hog production is also conjured by the pig diagram that appears toward the end of the *OK Computer* booklet. According to Nathaniel Johnson at *Harper's Magazine*, the industry found itself considerably "more productive" after adopting its new system of vertical integration: U.S. pork production increased by six billion pounds between 1979 and 2004, while the number of American hog farms declined from over 650,000 to fewer than 70,000. The industry, however, has found that much of its product is being compromised, as a result of a combination of overbreeding and the stress generated by the living conditions of the pigs, which lead monotonous lives in extremely cramped quarters—sows not even being able to turn around in their gestation crates. Under such conditions they frequently develop what some animal behaviorists identify as signals of chronic frustration or neurosis, repeated movements, such as swinging their heads from side to side or biting at the air around them. Just as the protagonist "will frequently check credit at (moral) bank (hole in wall),"[9] fortunately others have similarly checked their moral credit and outlawed such practices in their jurisdictions, including the United Kingdom, Sweden, and numerous American states, including Florida since 2004, Arizona since 2006, and California since 2008.

In the "confinement hog industry," it's common to give antibiotics to an entire herd, in order to increase its growth and to ward off disease, the risks of which are significantly amplified by maintaining such great numbers of animals in so close quarters. This practice, however, in conjunction with human antibiotic overuse, has proven ideal for creating drug-resistant organisms, otherwise known as "superbugs." A good example of unintended consequences of applying techniques and technologies, it's one that demonstrates how although technologies "giveth and taketh away," sometimes—as in their undoing of the efficacy of our present medicines—they provideth more than we ever expected.

ELECTIONEERING

"What can you say about the IMF, or politicians? Or people selling arms to African countries, employing slave labour or whatever. What can you say?" Yorke asked in early 1998, as recorded in *Exit Music*. "You just write down 'Cattle prods and the IMF' and people who know, know. I can't express it any clearer than that, I don't know how to yet, I'm stuck." Yorke's statement acquires particular significance when, toward the end of Grant Gee's film *Meeting People Is Easy*, one sees him exasperatedly attempting to explicate some of the more arcane elements of corporate globalization. And one can get a further sense of what he means from his response to Nick Kent's suggestion in 2001 that he looked uncomfortable in June 1999 campaigning next to Bob Geldof and U2's Bono on behalf of an organization called "Jubilee 2000" at the G8 meetings in Cologne—among the first of the international so-called antiglobalization demonstrations with protests simultaneously organized in dozens of cities around the world:

> I don't think anybody was comfortable. I was sprawling on a pin, I'll tell you (laughs). Half the stuff that was going on, I was going, "I'm not so sure about this." It took a lot of effort just to understand what the issue was. Having to do interviews—the amount of information I'd have to swallow and then spit out was just nightmarish. A lot of what gets called politics now is just fuckin' cowboys and indians and doesn't amount to anything. The really important issues in politics are the Third World debt and the relationship between the First World and the Third World, and trade laws, and NAFTA and GATT and none of this stuff is ever discussed as a political issue. It's all in the realm of the economists and that is fucked up.

Noting the technocratic nature of international politics, Yorke inadvertently refers to the scary and dangerous evolution of corporate commercial power and its colonization of the world's nation states. In Caitlin Moran's "Everything Was Just Fear," he was to add, "It seems rather odd to be choosing between one unworkable, outdated system and another. We need to go beyond that. . . . And the whole myth around economics I find fascinating, it's this century's biggest myth." In addition to the work of Noam Chomsky, among the sources noted to be informing his background knowledge were Will Hutton's 1995 book

The State We're In and Eric Hobsbawn's 1994 book *The Age of Extremes: The Short Twentieth Century, 1914–1991*. According to Yorke in James Doheny's *Radiohead: Karma Police*, "I was totally fucking ignorant until I read those books."

With its heavy and abrasive guitars and drums, *OK Computer*'s eighth song is musically foreign to everything else on the album. Representative of the caustic character of the contemporary neoliberal politician[10] —whom the character portrays here with great satirical ridicule, singing with a sneer, "It's just business" and "I trust I can rely on your vote"— "Electioneering" was inspired by memories of the fury from the 1990 Poll Tax riots in the UK. At the basis of this intense anger lies distress, of course, and through the song's exposure of contemporary foolishness, like all satire, it ultimately seeks to effect reform. But anger overwhelms this distress, much as the London protests degenerated into rioting and looting that was not to abate until sixteen hours after the demonstrations first began.

Otherwise known as the "Community Charge," as previously noted, it was the government of Margaret Thatcher's Conservative Party that brought in the regressive "Poll Tax" that took no account of people's ability to pay, and many observers believe it was the riots that ultimately led to Thatcher's political downfall, resigning as she did eight months later. Much of Thatcher's duration in office corresponded to that of the presidency of her ideological bedfellow Ronald Reagan, in relation to whom the epithet "voodoo economics" first came into being, following George H. W. Bush's use of it in the Republican presidential primaries that Reagan went on to win. "Reaganomics," otherwise known as "supply side economics," consisted largely of cutting taxes for the wealthiest, purportedly in the belief that such a course of action would provide incentive for entrepreneurship and risk-taking, thus stimulating economic growth from which everyone would then benefit. In practice, however, "voodoo economics" led to an increased widening of economic inequality throughout the Reagan era, and recalling our protagonist's disgust at the "yuppies networking," it's in this sense, again, that "yuppie" values are synonymous with "Reaganite" values.

The extent to which such trends of income disparity have continued since the 1980s is apparent. For instance, in 2003 the Internal Revenue Service reported that the four hundred wealthiest taxpayers in the United States had doubled their share of the nation's income between 1992 and 2000 (accounting for 1 percent of the total), while their tax burden significantly declined over the same period. By 2008, as the proportions of the "jackknifed juggernaut" of the global financial crisis were becoming clearer, Washington's Congressional Budget Office projected that twenty-eight million Americans the following year would be using government food stamps for buying essential groceries, the highest number of people since the program for food assistance was introduced in the 1960s. Toward the end of 2014, the Organization for Economic Cooperation and Development (OECD) announced that levels of global inequality were at their worst since the 1820s, and they've only continued since, with the most recent news suggesting that five men presently own nearly as much wealth as one half of the world's population.

The general situation isn't unrelated to the increasing pay packages of corporate executives, a trend that was to begin in the United States, and among whose harshest critics in the late 1990s was the respected management consultant Peter Drucker. In 2002, the *Washington Post* reported that the CEOs of the largest American companies were paid, on average, five hundred times what their hourly wage earners made, an amount that in 1980 had been only forty times as much. The same article notes also that while the average head of a top company in 1960 made twice as much as President Eisenhower, by the days of George W. Bush this ratio had escalated to sixty times the U.S. president's salary. At the beginning of 2006, Justin Blum of the *Post* also reported the Exxon oil company's revenue the previous year had been higher than the gross domestic product of Belgium. Many note how excessive executive compensation tends to accrue, whether or not the companies themselves are operating successfully, as was evidenced in late 2008 when the Wall Street financial firm Goldman Sachs was to set aside £7 billion for the salaries and year-end bonuses of its executives, after receiving a £6.1 billion injection as part of the U.S. government's bailout of the financial industry.

In 2005, research from the Canadian Tax Foundation that detailed how the burden of federal taxes shared between individuals and corporations, although it was about evenly split following the Second World War, was now distributed such that 75 percent of revenues come from individuals, with the business sector furnishing only 25 percent. Numerous factors contribute to this phenomenon, including the race to lower corporate taxes worldwide, unpaid loans from government to businesses, and the growing influence of off-shore tax havens, as was found following the scandalous collapse of Enron, a company that had managed to avoid paying taxes for three of the five years prior to its filing for bankruptcy.

But when the persona of "Electioneering" sings in the chorus "I go forwards, you go backwards and somewhere we will meet," he's also making reference to our increasing disparity in political equality. This is a phenomenon of which not only the international "antiglobalization" or "pro-democracy" protests but also, in more recent years, Occupy Wall Street, the Arab Spring, and other associated movements had been a symptom. The protagonist's invocation of the image of "riot shields" conjures the mass demonstrations that began to take place on an increasingly frequent basis during the 1990s and that, on May 16, 1998, led to what is considered to be the first "global" day of action, coinciding with the second ministerial meeting of the World Trade Organization (WTO) in Geneva. While Yorke was in Cologne at the G8 meeting with "Jubilee 2000" in June 1999, UK activists were busy closing down the country's financial heart in central London, and later that year, a similar mass shutdown was achieved in Seattle at the WTO's third ministerial meeting. Activists continued to launch similar demonstrations in tandem with satellite international solidarity protests, sustaining their targeting of the symbols of economic globalization and attempting to illuminate their lack of democratic legitimacy.

When the protagonist sings, "I go forward, and you go backward, and somewhere we will meet," he's also referring to the increasing disparities between so-called developed and undeveloped countries or, as Yorke put it previously, the relationship between the First World and the Third World. In relation to this issue, Radiohead was to lead a mass lobby of the British Parliament in 2002 on behalf of the Trade Justice Movement—founded in 2000, and a formidable and growing coalition made up of prominent organizations, from the Church of England to Greenpeace, World Vision UK, and Friends of the Earth. It's worth noting that the International Monetary Fund (IMF) and the World Bank were created in June 1944 with the Bretton Woods Agreement, in order to provide the fundamental basis of the postwar system of global finance. Expanding this basic framework in 1947 to take in the General Agreement on Tariffs and Trade (GATT), which in 1995 was to become the WTO, these institutions sought, under the sponsorship of the United States, to reconcile high rates of economic growth, adjustable exchange rates, and increasingly free trade. But we can elucidate the incongruity between the policy that the United States was to follow for the majority of its first two hundred years, and the prescriptions it has recommended for the developing economies of today, largely through the aforementioned international financial institutions, which are in large part perceived as American proxies. As with the early United States, most emergent nations followed a developmental path that used state power to coordinate technical learning and economic development with a considerable measure of sovereignty. But the U.S. government and international private investors have attempted to steer developing economies in a much different direction. This direction has included shying away from public investment, public subsidy, public ownership, and public regulation, while promoting entry for foreign private capital and a ban on any kind of discrimination in favor of domestic producers—policies that the United States and other Western countries have resisted applying in the case of agriculture, given that they heavily subsidize their own producers.

Drawing on Joseph Schumpeter's observations regarding technical efficiency, Robert Kuttner in *Everything for Sale* observes that American history demonstrates much more forcefully the power of *innovative* rather than the market's much lauded *allocative* efficiency:

> One cannot experimentally rerun history. However, it is very hard to believe that the United States in the year 2000 would be a more prosperous nation if the nineteenth-century federal and state governments had never promoted the development of railroads and canals, if we had never set up state universities, agricultural and mechanical colleges, and agricultural extension, if there had been no government program to accelerate development of radio, civil aviation, semiconductors, pharmaceuticals, and basic research in the sciences, and had the immense technical stimulus of World War II and the Cold War never happened. It is even more improbable to believe that Japan or South Korea would be more prosperous today had they just waited for private-market forces to follow the dictates of allocative efficiency and failed to take heroic steps to industrialize.

The emphasis that neoclassical economics places on allocative efficiency is very much related to its assault on the institutions of the postwar mixed economy, and in this relation, the IMF has not been shy about bestowing its advice on developed countries as well. But in return for loans, the IMF has demanded of developing countries such measures as the privatization of their water systems and—despite their various levels of impoverishment—the charging of user fees in the school system and for health-care services. By March 2003, however, the IMF had admitted that there was no clear evidence that so-called globalization was helping the world's poor, and the institution was to admit the following year, moreover, that its policies had crippled Argentina, which had defaulted on its loans two years earlier.

"CLIMBING UP THE WALLS"

Of the recording's chilling ninth track Thom Yorke explains, "This is about the unspeakable." With its bleakly reverberating drum, the dissonant buzzing timbre of its low-pitched Novation Bass Station synthesizer, and the strange echoes of its cold and frightening sound effects, we enter what is doubtless *OK Computer*'s most toxic scene. Also evident from the song's minor tonality and the bizarre effects it employs on Yorke's doubled and troubled voice, it's as though we are left alone with the persona at the conclusion of "Exit Music (for a film)." The imagery evoked in the lines "a pick in the ice" and "15 blows to the back of the head" helps to recount the tale of a violent murderer, whose "toys" have slipped from the "basement" to the attic—identifying himself as he does with the technological extension that is his weapon. "I was fascinated in a kind of twisted way about what is it that makes someone who can go through life and just snap one day and do something that you can't possibly imagine," Yorke was later to say in Greene's "Oral History," suggesting also that British people at the time were not getting the care they required. "Depression for example at the time was something that everybody just went, 'Oh, well, you're just depressed.' But now it can lead into other things like if someone gets ill, they can be a danger to themselves and to other people." Lending substance to the idea of a "dangerous neighbourhood" (another formulation expressed in Esperanto in the *OK Computer* CD booklet), Yorke recounts how he was working as an orderly in a mental hospital during the time that the UK government was returning mentally unstable patients to the streets, suggesting that "it's one of the scariest things to happen in this country, because a lot of them weren't just harmless."

The apparent inhumanity of this heartless killer reminds us of that associated with the unfeeling and misanthropic android; the sound effects heard following the first chorus also serve to conjure the android, particularly as they seem to emulate a squealing little piggy. As he begins the last verse of the song, with its reference to "the kids," we are again reminded of "Exit Music (for a film)," where, in the spirit of Mercutio, we experienced a deranged-sounding protagonist's complete and utter giving over to violence. In that tragic context driving Juliet to suicide, his madness here, again, conjures visions of bringing the kids down, along with himself in the coming plane crash. In this relation, of all the album's songs, the printed lyrics for "Climbing Up the Walls" are the most debauched in presentation, and Yorke's substitution of the word "lock" on the recording for the printed word "tuck" adds to the general chill. The scene is not merely fear laden but also includes a significant component of disgust, whose odor is evident both musically and lyrically. That this particular stench is "of a local man with the loneliest feeling" carries considerable irony and reflects Marshall McLuhan's observation that, in the modern world, we're much like the occupants of an elevator—that is, we tend to experience "proximity without community."

In 1997, MTV Online reported the following interchange with Yorke:

> "The thing is, everyone's capable of murder," Yorke says, then reaches into a knapsack. For a second, it seems like he might pull out a revolver to illustrate his point. But fortunately, his arm withdraws holding a black journal. He leafs through the pages, then finds the desired entry. "This is from a 'New York Times' article dated 19 October, 1991," he says, then quotes the piece: "Was it any accident that of the ten largest mass-murders in America, eight have occurred since 1980, typically acts of middle aged white men in their 30s and 40s after long periods of being lonely, frustrated and full of rage, and often precipitated by a catastrophe in their lives, such as losing their jobs or divorce?"

The same article notes not only the rapid increase in the frequency of mass murders but also the number of victims killed in individual attacks. Highlighting that the homicide rate in the United States has long been the world's highest, it also observes how mass murder, for the most part, has tended to be a peculiarly American phenomenon, in large part the result of the proliferation of firearms and concomitant increases in available firepower, something not lost on the American students who held mass demonstrations following a fatal shooting at a Florida school early in 2018. The article notes as well this trend's connection to "the disintegration of traditional American society," and—emphasizing that we all possess the capacity to commit such atrocity—Yorke remarked, "Some people can't sleep with the curtains open in case they see the eyes they imagine in their heads every night burning through the glass. . . . This song is about the cupboard monster."[11] This monster we encounter with the protagonist's terrifying scream at the conclusion of the song, and his hellish affective experience of disgust, terror, and madness, becomes ours as well—in no small part through the incredible dissonances of Jonny Greenwood's string arrangement, the last chord of which features sixteen violins playing quarter tones apart, displaying the influence of Polish composer Krzysztof Penderecki. "Climbing Up the Walls" thus represents the protagonist's transformation into the ultimate antihero and the nadir of his descent into monstrous villainy.

"NO SURPRISES"

"The Berlin Wall fell more than 10 years ago, and yeah, I think resistance is quite a good way of putting it," said Yorke in Lorin Zoric's article in *Juice Magazine*, in regard to the global movement's massive demonstrations against the corporatization of society. "If nothing happened at all, if so called anarchists just sat home and smoked dope and did fuck all, then we would all just bow down to a global economy and willingly watch millions of people die for no fucking good reason." Yorke is referring to perhaps one of the higher-profile examples of such resistance, but there are other fronts, as well, on which individuals are active in countering some of the ill effects of the contemporary world. The means or tactics are probably innumerable by which they've sought to address the public mind in their attempt to influence change or, in other words, to maximize their information's "action value." And the strategies employed range broadly across a spectrum from consonant to dissonant in character, meaning that each entails distinct attitudes inherent in the tactics themselves, and in the various technologies and techniques they employ. From the writing of books by individuals to the blocking of ocean vessels by organizations such as Greenpeace, the medium of any utterance of dissent is an enormous part of the message. The means employed range broadly from low to high tech—from the distribution of printed matter to the emerging participatory electronic public fora typical of the online world and to the distributed denial of service attacks practiced by a hacktivist group like Anonymous. Attempts to capture the public's increasingly colonized attention within the flooded contemporary information environment are an endeavor to reclaim the sense of public space essential to the concept of democracy.

In some cases, attempts to address the public occur through the reclamation of physical space, as in the international "Critical Mass" bike rides, events where a mass of cyclists gather at a designated intersection and begin riding en masse, forcing cars to yield to them. A group in the city of Montreal humorously refers to itself as the "bikeshevics," and we can say that cyclists and even motorcyclists understand, at least as well as our protagonist, McLuhan's additional observation that the car has become the carapace, "the protective and aggressive shell, of urban and suburban man." Not unrelated to *OK Computer*'s "Airbag," the car for these individuals, as Naomi Klein suggests, in her 2000 book *No Logo: Taking Aim at the Brand Bullies*, symbolizes "the most tangible manifestation of the loss of communal space, walkable streets and sites of free expression." Such events have sometimes been enacted in combination with another form of public address, the "Reclaim the Streets" movement, and Klein reports that such an event drew 20,000 people to Trafalgar Square in London in April 1997. The sites of these giant "street parties" are often cleared of traffic by sweeping Critical Mass rides through the area, just moments before blockades are put up and people arrive. She quotes one participant as saying that the movement "has always tried to take the single issue of transportation and the car into a wider critique of society . . . to dream of reclaiming space for collective use, as commons." Klein's book is particularly notable not only for its distinction of having been read and heartily endorsed by three of the members of Radiohead but purportedly also for the band passing copies of it from the stage. "*No Logo* gave one real hope," Ed O'Brien was to suggest at the time, as recorded in Marvin Lin's *33 1/3 Kid A*. "It certainly made me feel less alone. I must admit I'm deeply pessimistic about humanity, and she was writing everything that I was trying to make sense of in my head. It was very uplifting."

Other examples of efforts to communicate with the public include an activity that Klein refers to as "adbusting," known in the UK apparently as "subvertising." The techniques range from defacing billboards with black magic markers to the less disharmonious digital desktop publishing edits that leave billboards looking not unlike the originals, though altering their messages. Such instances demonstrate that the newly accessible technologies permit "jammers" to use commercial aesthetics against itself. In this regard, "adbusting" is an example of what Klein and others more broadly term "culture jamming," that is, any form of expression mixing art, media, parody, and "the outsider stance"—not an unfitting description of *OK Computer* itself perhaps. "Culture jammers," Klein says, are united primarily by their belief that "free speech is meaningless if the commercial cacophony has risen to the point that no one can hear you." They reject marketing's buying its way into public spaces, advocating instead "freedom *from* expression," which it can be said the people of São Paulo achieved in 2007 with that city's near total ban on outdoor advertising and billboards. As might be expected, along the way there have been examples of counterappropriation of these sentiments by corporate commerce, "the outsider stance" in particular. Examples Klein provides include Nike requesting the longtime consumer advocate and 2000 presidential candidate for the American Green Party Ralph Nader to take a dig at the company in a television commercial. Also, a 1997 ad campaign for Sprite features a young black man who says he has been bombarded with media lies all his life, telling him that soft drinks will make him a better athlete or more attractive. Now he realizes, however, that "image is nothing." Providing another instance is Nike's campaign the same year using the slogan "I am not / A target market / I am an athlete." Radiohead, in turn, jammed this message on the cover of its video *Meeting People Is Easy*, the cover of which reads in bold lettering the slogan "You Are a Target Market."

One can plainly discern how distressing and frightening the outlines of the modern world actually are. As I suggested previously, however, this does not seem to be the case for the inno$ent, who are not "completely terrified" but who rather "look so tired and happy" in their "deep deep sleep," admitting of "no alarms and no surprises." Nowhere is this contrast communicated with more force than in the transition from the alarming conclusion of "Climbing Up the Walls"—with the protagonist's disturbingly dissonant encounter with the cupboard monster to the tonal concordances of the next track "No Surprises," an effect the reassuring sound of the music box–like glockenspiel appropriately reinforces, as does the song's major key. This dynamic is also in play on the second page of the CD cover jacket, where juxtaposed with the image of a man observing the disquieting fact that the airplane is on fire is the following snippet of text: "Jump out of bed as soon as you hear the alarm clock!! You may also find it useful spending five minutes each morning saying to yourself: 'Every day in every way I am getting better and better.' Perhaps it is a good idea to start a new day with the right frame of mind." Responding to a journalist's observation that "Fitter Happier" resembles the pages of a self-help manual, Yorke recounted the following to David Sinclair in *Rolling Stone*:

> I bought a whole load of those how-to-improve-your-life books, and we'd been trying to use them in various different ways. One said something like, "You will never make friends unless you like everyone, genuinely." Oh, well, I'm fucked then, aren't I? And the legacy of these books goes on. You still meet people who really believe that the way to succeed is to adopt that smile and that smile will sell: "Unless you believe in the product, you will not sell the product."

This sort of relentless optimism, which many American self-help gurus, business managers, and religious leaders propound, has been referred to as "the tyranny of the positive attitude." Concerned that there is insufficient space within contemporary American society for people to feel badly, if someone is having a rough time, the pressure to be cheerful, or even just neutral—like the well-adjusted and robotic "OK" computer voice of the album's central track, can make things even more difficult, on account of the resulting stress. This is the experience, of course, that we hear portrayed through the background sounds of "Fitter Happier."

That this phenomenon is not limited to the United States is demonstrated in the film *Meeting People Is Easy*. During an excerpt from the UK's Sky News TV channel, in which the video for "No Surprises" is being shown, one of the three chatty commentators condescendingly refers to it as "music to cut your wrist to" and "the most miserable sounding tune I've ever heard." In this regard, Yorke was to say of the song:

> [It's a] fucked-up nursery rhyme. A desperate bid to try and get back to normalcy and failing miserably. It stems from my unhealthy obsession of what to do with plastic boxes and plastic bottles. You can't throw them all away. Then I got into landfills and general household things. I find landfills really curious. All this stuff is getting buried, the debris of our lives. It doesn't rot, it just stays there. That's how we deal, that's how I deal with stuff, I bury it.

By "normalcy," of course, Yorke presumably means a state of relative psychological affluence, while "failing miserably" would amount to being drawn in the direction of toxicity, as in the image of "a heart that's full up like a landfill." But the "bruises that won't heal" appear, in large part, to belong mostly to the protagonist himself, the inno$ent, as a result of their peaceful slumber, only gradually crumbling under a "job that slowly kills" them.

In this regard, particularly given Yorke's apparent penchant for Buddhism, it's interesting to contrast the "tyranny of the positive attitude" with the outlook of the Buddhist cultures of the Far East. As Andrew Powell explains in *Living Buddhism*,

> The first Noble Truth is that the basic condition of human existence is dukkha, a word usually translated as "suffering." Although not denying that life contains the potential for happiness, the Buddha insisted that it was fundamentally unsatisfactory because of its inherent inability to fulfil humanity's spiritual longing. Rather than being a deeply pessimistic analysis leading logically to despair, the Buddha's teaching is that progress and achievement are possible, but only through looking life squarely in the face, and taking the first step on the road to wisdom, which is the recognition of the ubiquity of dukkha. Persisting in delusion will get us absolutely nowhere and, furthermore, make us far more unhappy than if we adopt a more sensible course.

Clearly one need not live in an out-of-control technological society in order to suffer life's slings and arrows, and, according to "the Buddha"—the "enlightened" or "awakened one"—we'd expect that the inno$ent will, in time, should they choose to look life "squarely in the face," come to recognize their underlying discontentedness and alienation. But looking life squarely in the face involves looking, likewise, at the world itself, since "knowing where you are," as our character sings in "Let Down," depends on being able to situate yourself within your environment. And being awakened to your life environment in the time of the Buddha, although nonetheless certainly a complex affair, is a decidedly different prospect from the demands that the present reality exerts on human consciousness.

I've drawn attention to some of the musical elements that give "No Surprises" its semblance of the inno$ent's presently comfortable state of being, but I should also point out those elements, beyond the song's words, that imbue it with the protagonist's sense of distress. In addition to inhering in its slow tempo and consistent employment of a minor chord on the fourth-scale degree (what would typically be major), this effect is overwhelmingly encoded in the song's melody, which bears an obvious and inseparable connection to the soft, plaintive voice of its singing persona. And just as large, upward melodic leaps indicate a sense of striving, large downward ones tend to convey falling spirits and disappointment, an effect apparent in the song's first two verses, which feature a series of just such descending melodic leaps.

The first take of the first song recorded on the first day of sessions at "Canned Applause," "No Surprises" can nearly be classified as "music to cut your wrists to," as the Sky News commentator suggests. Apparently opting for "a handshake of carbon monoxide," sustaining the automotive imagery, the protagonist—as intimated at the end of "Exit Music (for a film)," unheroically appears to be leading the children in the direction of suicide, longing for "the quiet life" in order that he, too, might encounter "no alarms and no surprises." During the fourth and fifth verses, he expresses this giving over of himself by abandoning the aforementioned distressing melodic motif and seems finally to surrender to a downgraded version of the "quiet life," the archetypal "pretty house" and "pretty garden." Ultimately, however, he manages to maintain his heroic status, rejecting the quiet life entirely—just as "Let Down" makes use of a vocal overdub to signify the protagonist's heroic strain, "No Surprises" employs this technique in the chorus's final repetition, where we hear a background voice singing "let me out of here."

"LUCKY"

Given the dreary conditions of the contemporary cultural milieu, especially in the wake of Donald Trump's 2016 election win, it's worth reexamining the heroic aspect of our protagonist. With the "jackknifed juggernaut" of the crashing airplane, it's during OK Computer's second to last track that the forecasted catastrophic accident occurs. And it's here also that the character explicitly alerts us to the fact that he's our superhero, implicitly having done so at the beginning of the song sequence with "Airbag," where we first learn he's "back to save the universe." In this regard, ultimately what we may be seeing is the heroism of the global "citizen," whose mental melting pot the electronic communications revolution helped to forge. It would seem appropriate, then, to conceive of the hero as the concerned, active, and genuine seeker of opportunities for real participation in public deliberations regarding the governance of human affairs. Describing the citizen-centric nature of a democratic social order, former U.S. Supreme Court justice Robert H. Jackson noted in *The Demon-Haunted World* by Carl Sagan that "it is not the function of our government to keep the citizen from falling into error; it is the function of the citizen to keep the government from falling into error." Likewise, Aristotle distinguished "citizens" from all others because they participate in judgment and authority.

I have detailed, in part, how the members of Radiohead had promoted civic participation during this period of time. But I might also mention again the ensemble's support of the organization "Rock the Vote," a campaign for which bands help motivate young voters to cast their ballots during elections. In an era that has seen a universal decline in the rates of voter participation, not to mention more significant types of civic involvement, it's important to resuscitate the celebrated sense of cultural individualism associated with the famous funeral oration of the Greek statesman Pericles, and manifested in the citizenry's direct democratic government of the Athenian city-state:

An Athenian citizen does not neglect the state because he takes care of his own household; and even those of us who are engaged in business have a very fair idea of politics. We alone regard a man who takes no interest in public affairs, not as a harmless, but as a useless character; and if few of us are originators, we are all sound judges of a policy. We Athenians, in our own persons, make our decisions on policy or submit them to proper discussions; for we do not think that there is an incompatibility between words and deeds; the worst thing is to rush into action before the consequences have been properly debated.

Most interesting about these comments, aside from highlighting the incompatibility of the accelerated conditions of contemporary life with democratic governance, may be their emphasis on reasoned popular discourse in service of the public goal of responsible collective action. This has pertinence to any political entity purporting to be democratic, and to any society that professes to be ethical.

Of course, one of the primary areas of concern for "activists" is the attempt to raise people's awareness, and in this relation, it's interesting to note the diagram superimposed over the pig on the fourth to last page of the *OK Computer* CD booklet. There we find the EEG brain-wave representations from "ACTIVE SLEEP" (or REM) to "QUIET SLEEP" (or non-REM), to the relaxed wakefulness of "Alpha" rhythm, and to the activist's ultimate goal "AROUSE." Of course, the sense of political space has become considerably abstracted from the citizen since the days of antiquity, while the concept of public discourse has similarly taken on new meaning. In this respect, a sense of diminishing social and political potency has accompanied the electronic phenomenon of decontextualized information glut.

"I couldn't really say it directly so much," Thom Yorke explains, in regard to political impotence, "but it's there—the feeling of being a spectator and not being able to take part." His comment was made to Simon Reynolds in relation to *OK Computer*'s immediate successors *Kid A* and *Amnesiac*, and to his experiences at the Cologne G8 summit in 1999, but this "outsider" sentiment permeates *OK Computer* as well. "It's pretty difficult to put into songs," says Yorke. "In a way you have to wait until it's a personal issue or experience."

The extent to which the band has been successful in modeling civic engagement, however, is demonstrated in Naomi Klein's comments to the Belgian magazine *HUMO* from late October 2001:

> When Radiohead started talking about "No Logo" in interviews, I got a massive number of letters from 16 year olds from all over the world. They swallowed every word Thom Yorke said, like it was the happy message. And on his recommendations they all went and read my book. Their letters were very sweet. For most of them "No Logo" was the first political book they read. Many were shocked and wanted to know what it is they can do about it, they wanted to know where they could go, what stuff they may or may not buy. They were very young and naïve, but I took them absolutely serious. I felt an incredible, crushing responsibility to offer them something.

Also suggesting that there are typically three people with Radiohead shirts in the front row of every lecture she gives, Klein illustrates her own heroic aspect and touches upon the underlying way that democracy makes everyone accountable: "Because it is not easy," in the words of John Dewey in *Freedom and Culture*, "the democratic road is the hard one to take. It is the road which places the greatest burden of responsibility upon the greatest number of human beings."

Moving from the harmonious sounds that conclude "No Surprises" to the eerie one that Ed O'Brien achieves on his guitar during the intro of "Lucky," we hear an effect that Yorke apparently imitated for an interviewer in a squeaky, mouselike voice as "ninganinganinga," explaining it was "like nothing we'd ever heard before." Sounding as though it could just as easily be the "Paranoid Android" as the "Subterranean Homesick Alien" who emerges from the air crash, the song's lyrics themselves suggest the latter, while their arrangement in the CD booklet, in combination with the song's minor key and a number of other musical processes, reflect the former. It's clear that though there's a significant amount of distress represented in the song, the character evidently attempts to script the scene toward one more characterized by positive affect, explaining, "I'm on a roll," "I feel my luck could change," and "its gonna be a glorious day." His dazed condition is apparent, and the song's general apocalyptic character is evidenced in the persona's repeated suggestion throughout that "we are standing on the edge"—certainly the album's fundamental message.

In this relation, apparent in the use of simulated choral voices behind the protagonist in "Lucky," this religious imagery helps to convey the album's continuation of Radiohead's apocalyptic message. Just as "Street Spirit" concludes with the imperative to "immerse your soul in love," in the second verse of "Lucky," our superhero protagonist instructs an unknown person named Sarah to "kill me again with love." In this relation, Eric Fromm notes in *The Sane Society* how the sanity of human beings depends on uniting with and being related to other living beings, and how such relationships, again, can take the idolatrous guise of submission to a person, group, institution, or God—or, one can unite oneself with the world by exerting power over it, and thereby transcending the limits of individual existence by making others a part of oneself through domination. But ultimately, as Fromm suggests,

> There is only one passion which satisfies man's need to unite himself with the world, and to acquire at the same time a sense of integrity and individuality, and this is *love. Love is union* with somebody, or something, outside oneself, *under the condition of retaining the separateness and integrity of one's own self.* It is an experience of sharing, of communion, which permits the full unfolding of one's own inner activity. The experience of love does away with the necessity of illusions. There is no need to inflate the image of the other person, or of myself, since the reality of active sharing and loving permits me to transcend my individualized existence, and at the same time to experience myself as the bearer of the active powers which constitute the act of loving.

"THE TOURIST"

Following the release of *OK Computer*, a friend drew Yorke's attention toward a 1984 essay he had discovered online called "Is It O.K. to Be a Luddite?" The essay was written by the celebrated American novelist Thomas Pynchon[12] and was originally published in the *New York Times Book Review*. "Luddites were that lot in the last century that went around and smashed up all the weaving looms or whatever it was," Yorke recounts in *Exit Music*. "And that was a reaction against the dehumanization of production, and the fact that people were only becoming their hands or their feet . . . and not whole people anymore. My friend gave me this thing he found and said, 'There you are; that's what I think of this record.'" Pynchon cites Sir Charles Snow's famous Rede lecture "The Two Cultures and the Scientific Revolution" and refers to Snow's polemical use of the word "Luddite," which he uses in Pynchon's words "to imply an irrational fear and hatred of science and technology," as well as a means by which to designate those with whom he disagrees "both politically reactionary and anti-capitalist at the same time." Typically the term has now come to signify a kind of childish and naïve opposition to technology. Yet the historical Luddites were anything but—rather, they were people who desperately tried to preserve whatever laws and customs or rights and privileges had provided them justice under the traditional worldview.

In our culture, where the technological worldview now has a near monopoly on our thinking (as evidenced by the decline of the humanities within our universities), we encounter a thought-world that's indifferent to the unraveling of tradition in the boundless license it confers upon technological progress. Neil Postman uses the word "Technopoly" to refer to this cultural situation, and in relation to the collapse of theologies and ideologies he observes,

> Into this void comes the Technopoly story, with its emphasis on progress without limits, rights without responsibilities, and technology without cost. The Technopoly story is without a moral center. It puts in its place efficiency, interest, and economic advance. It promises heaven on earth through the conveniences of technological progress. It casts aside all traditional narratives and symbols that suggest stability and orderliness, and tells, instead, of a life of skills, technical expertise, and the ecstasy of consumption. Its purpose is to produce functionaries for an ongoing Technopoly. It answers [Allan] Bloom by saying that the story of Western civilization is irrelevant; it answers the political left by saying there is indeed a common culture whose name is Technopoly and whose key symbol is now the computer, toward which there must be neither irreverence nor blasphemy.

During the late 1970s and 1980s there was a pervasive myth that computer power was going to create more leisure for people, eventually doing most of the work formerly done by human beings. Though this first and rather extravagant projection has surely occurred in some instances, the second continues to do so much more commonly—as in the example of the automobile, for instance, where gasoline attendants and cashiers are in large part now obsolesced and where my mechanic is incapable of repairing the antibrake lock system of my car because its computer dashboard light refuses to stay on.

"The Tourist" is the closing track of the album and was the last song recorded. And that the protagonist's final appearance is a scene of affluence and enjoyment is expressed in the track's sauntering pace, in the confident and long-held notes of Yorke's consonant melody, and in the song's B major tonality, anticipated at the beginning of the album in the triumphant affective elevation evident in the chorus of "Airbag," where our protagonist announces that he is "back to save the universe." Clearly once again in his heroic mode as the "Subterranean Homesick Alien" space tourist, the song is a critique of the "quick to anger," antiheroic persona of the "Paranoid Android," who sometimes gets "overcharged" when he moves "at 1000 feet per second." Of "The Tourist" Yorke explains in *Exit Music*, "That song was written to me from me, saying, 'Idiot, slow down.' Because at that point, I *needed* to. . . . So that was the only resolution there could be: to slow down." Intimating, however, that the "hey man" of the song's chorus is also intended to refer to "mankind," Yorke added, "If you can slow down to an almost stop, you can see everything moving too fast around you and that's the point."

I've referred to the generally accelerated rate of cultural change that human beings now experience. I've noted also that though technical change for our predecessors often had enormous consequences, the intervals between which major innovations tended to occur, and the scale upon which they unleashed their operations, were typically much more negligible, allowing the requisite time and space for personal and social adjustment to new situations. But contemporary human life, in contrast, possesses a continuous source of underlying tension—the result of being relentlessly required to readapt to the ever new, "environmental" conditions to which our technics give rise.

It's often unclear in the initial stages of a technology's development who will mostly gain by it and who will mostly lose. Many people, for instance, have benefited enormously from the computer in many ways beyond its usefulness as a word processor. Among such benefits we could include the ability to collect, organize, and store vast quantities of easily accessible data; the ability to establish and maintain relationships and contacts with people in your city and around the world; and the ability to access online encyclopedias, dictionaries, academic journals, and library catalogs, in relation to which we can recall or renew our materials or consult them at any time of the day or night, whether they're down the street or across the world. Illustrating that technology is always a double-edged sword, however, many will doubtless develop injuries related to their eyesight, or conditions such as the increasingly common carpel-tunnel syndrome. Moreover, all are likely to suffer from the effects of information overwhelm, as a result of the computer's bias in favor of generating vast quantities of information. "The slow movement of the eye along lines of type, the slow procession of items organized by the mind to fit into these endless horizontal columns," as McLuhan wrote in the early 1950s in the article "Culture without Literacy," with regard to the printed word, "these procedures can't stand up to the pressures of instantaneous coverage of the earth," adding that "it is the almost total coverage of the globe in time and space that has rendered the book an increasingly obsolete form of communication." As McLuhan was otherwise to put it, "The future of the book is the blurb." But if this was his take in the mid-1950s, there's little doubt what he would have thought with regard to the information deluge that the World Wide Web now makes possible.

Overall, perhaps we can retrospectively conclude that for Radiohead the benefits of computer technology seem generally to have outweighed its drawbacks, but certainly the band is not unaware of other deleterious social effects that accompany the technology's increasing use. For instance, as Yorke explained to Coke Babie around the time of OK Computer's release, inadvertently referring to "big data,"

> The thing that worries me about the computer age is the fact that people know so much about you. It's an incredible invasion of privacy. And no matter where you are in the world people can monitor you if you're using your credit card. I heard this weird rumor on the internet about how the military are funding this great big research project, and basically they believe that in the future, the balance of power won't be determined by who has the most nuclear weapons, but by who has all the information. I'm not afraid of being taken over by computers though, because the thing is, computers cannot resist. You can always smash 'em up, and they're totally defenseless. All we need are more people with hammers.

Yorke's concerns over the computer's assault on privacy were to become ever more validated over time, especially after the revelations of Edward Snowden, and computer technology has also served to reinforce people's belief that human progress equates to technological innovation. As reflected by the intoning computer voice of *OK Computer*'s seventh track, "Fitter Happier," the computer is the defining technology of our age, because it suggests a new relationship to work, to power, to information, and even to nature itself. In this regard, it's been suggested that computers have redefined human beings as information processors and nature as information to be processed. Their basic message is that we're thinking machines, and this is the reason they're the quintessential technology for the present. Broadly apparent in the language of those involved in artificial intelligence, as well as being evident in the widespread machine-as-human metaphor, computers help relieve human beings of responsibility, and we should expect bureaucrats to embrace a technology that serves to create the semblance that decisions are not under their control, which it does through its kind of magical tendency to direct attention toward itself as the true source of authority, and away from those in charge of bureaucratic functions.

Observing how our confidence in human subjectivity and judgment has been shaken and how faith in the power of technical calculation has replaced and devalued respect for the unique human capacity to perceive things integrally in all their psychic, emotional, and moral complexity, the computer advances the view that our most pressing problems, at both the personal and public levels, require solutions of a technical nature by way of instantly accessible information that would be unavailable in its absence. Even more fundamentally, computer technology has yet to touch the printing press in its ability to generate significant and radical religious, social, and political thought.

In the personal experience of many, the overall situation I've been outlining herein gives rise, in addition to a lot of bad affect, to profound states of dislocation, dispossession, disillusionment, and paralysis. Though *OK Computer* certainly contains its revelatory and reveling aspects, the aforementioned emotional strains form an undercurrent typical of much of the album. Ultimately, it is by transcending these feeling states and by persevering in the effort to translate ideas into action that the heroic character of our protagonist ultimately reemerges, as it does in "The Tourist." At the end of the day, as Gandhi witnessed, "you may never know what results come from your action, but if you do nothing, there will be no results." And as the egalitarians among us would similarly do well to remember, Benjamin Barber suggests that "our ideals and aspirations must be cut close enough to the pattern of the actual to give hope the aspect of the possible."

By the end of *OK Computer*, it's obvious that there are four key things that we must all strive to possess in order to be able to overcome the potential for falling into despair and the temptation to exhibit the antiheroic tendencies associated with such emotional states throughout the album. These things are especially necessary in order to be reconciled with the belief in one's power to create a better world, and in addition to hope, they include the virtues of faith, patience, and love. In this relation, it's interesting to note that the character reiterates throughout "Airbag" that he's "born again," one of the central symbolic ideas of religion, as I've pointed out. Ed O'Brien remarked in Clarke's *Hysterical and Useless* that "Airbag" encapsulates "the wonderful, positive emotion you feel when you've just failed to have an accident; when you just miss someone and realize how close it was and stop the car and just feel this incredible elation. There's something joyous about it—life seems more precious." As Yorke was to add in *Exit Music* concerning "Airbag," whose lyrics were in part inspired by the *Tibetan Book of the Dead*, the song is also about "the way I've been brought up and most of us are brought up, we are never given time to think about our own death." And as the singer pointed out to James Sullivan, he was also "absolutely obsessed with death all the way through *Kid A/Amnesiac*," presumably wrestling with the Epicurean conundrum that "experience is no guide to the cessation of experience." As Leon Wieseltier otherwise puts it in "On Love and Death," when it comes to the matter of our dying, we're all pragmatists.

The detail that our superhero travels in a *fast* German car, as we've seen, is a significant one, as is the fact that he traverses space in interstellar bursts. It's as a result of his traveling so fast, however, that he was nearly to become a fatality, and herein would appear to lie *OK Computer*'s locus of significance for us: we've been reborn in a further speeded up world, one that allows us to do things faster, to get places ever faster, and to accomplish many things in shorter amounts of time than ever before possible. But it was in the nineteenth century that time first became an enemy that technology could conquer, a proposition whose fallout we've been dealing with ever since. To be a mortal human being, as Wieseltier observes, is to be a temporal creature: "I think speed is the single most salient and dangerous characteristic of contemporary life," he suggests, "[and that] historians of medicine will eventually record that it became a medical problem as well." Like others, Wieseltier recommends how "generally—spiritually, culturally—we have been enemies of time. We've been trying to live outside of time, and we've lost patience with time."

Radiohead, like Wieseltier, appears to have determined that the only revolutionary act yet to be performed is to slow something down. Yorke apparently agonized for a couple of weeks about *OK Computer*'s track order, and it was important for him that the album should reach some resolution as noted in Trevor Baker's *Thom Yorke: Radiohead and Trading Solo*. "When we chose to put 'Tourist' at the end . . . we did find that it was the only resolution for us—because a lot of the album was about background noise and everything moving too fast and not being able to keep up." Certainly the band found the appropriate resolution for the album, and quite likely for society as well. But this sense of resolution was not to linger, particularly in light of the media fallout of *OK Computer*, to which we now turn.

5

THE MEDIA FALLOUT OF *OK COMPUTER*

Meeting People Is Easy? (1998–1999)

As noted previously, essential for psychic and social survival in the contemporary age is our successful navigation of the continuously accelerating bully-blow of technological change characteristic of advanced technocratic capitalism's extraordinary powers of "creative-destruction." Given the constant flux in how our experience of the world is mediated, we require the ability to map and give shape to the environments that our technologies create. This is so we're best able to optimize our interactions with them at both the individual and the collective levels. It's informative, therefore, to attend to Radiohead's process of adaptation to the media fallout surrounding the immense success of *OK Computer*. This process entailed the numerous means by which the band created an upheaval in their array of creative methods. And this disruption included a number of different measures: the exclusion of printed lyrics from not only CD liner notes but also Radiohead's collective creative process; the employment of Dadaist technique in the composition of the lyrics; the avoidance of melody and the use of extensive vocal processing; the adoption of new musical instruments; and the establishment of a variety of new performance and publicity techniques. Taken together these constituted a thorough reconfiguration of Radiohead's technological "extensions" and their presentation of self.[1]

As Grant Gee's film *Meeting People Is Easy* records, Thom Yorke was seriously troubled in the wake of *OK Computer* and its lengthy accompanying tour—an experience he summed up in conversation with fellow band members during an uncomfortable scene toward the end of the film as "a complete head-fuck." "We were in a situation where people were trying to persuade us to carry on touring for another six months," according to Yorke, who added, "we should have said no but we didn't and I went bonkers." The film project documented the media exposure associated with the immense critical attention and acclaim that the band was receiving, including reports in the United States of high-profile celebrities attending their concerts. *Meeting People Is Easy* also chronicled the promotional procedures favored by the enormous multinational entertainment media oligopoly and their contribution to wearing down the band.[2] These factors caused a sense of disintegration, and murmurs briefly emerged that the group's members had thoughts again of calling it quits. For Yorke, the sum of the effects that this experience generated were no less than losing all confidence in himself and losing faith in what he was doing and in the direction the band was going, and these factors led him to believe he could not continue with it. Having always used music as "a way of moving on and dealing with things," Yorke felt the thing that had helped him do so had been "sold to the highest bidder" and that he was simply "doing its bidding."

Yorke's remark indicates that the crisis was in no small part one relating to authenticity, and in this, it's interesting to ponder the ubiquitous comparisons that have been made between Radiohead and Pink Floyd, particularly because the experiences of the two bands possess a number of interesting parallels. These comparisons began to circulate even prior to the release of *OK Computer*, the recording that in a way can be seen as Radiohead's *Dark Side of the Moon* (1973).[3] Both works, conceptual in scope, pinnacled the creative careers of each band with their release, while catapulting their creators into the dominant mainstream, with its accompanying mythologies and pathologies of superstardom. Both bands were thus "mired in the crisis of following up works that many of their contemporaries had already hailed as perfection." Pink Floyd's 1975 album *Wish You Were Here* was largely a response to the conditions that its more famous predecessor had created, and like Roger Waters, Yorke told *New Musical Express* in 2000 about having been "very ambitious" but that his head had become "done in" after he realized these ambitions. "I thought when I got to where I wanted to be," he said, "everything would be different. I'd be somewhere else. I thought it'd be all white fluffy clouds. And then I got there. And I'm still here."[4]

Both groups, the respective group leaders in particular,[5] found this realm highly destructive and depersonalizing, and both suffered a major bout of creative and existential paralysis as a result. Both records led to larger-scale performance situations and an accompanying alienation from certain elements of the situation and its new mass audience.[6] Both acts were comprised mainly of unschooled instrumentalists who hailed from the oldest of England's university towns (Cambridge and Oxford), and each had to negotiate the frustrating paradox of trying to create serious artistic projects in the context of a multi-billion-dollar commercial entertainment industry. Both stand out also, of course, for their effective employment of electronic instruments, advanced musical technologies, the self-production abilities demonstrated through using the studio as a compositional tool, and for the rich semiotic tapestries that both bands have stylistically weaved.

As with *Dark Side of the Moon* and Pink Floyd, every Radiohead album since *OK Computer* appears to be a conceptually complete unit with interrelated lyrics, music, and artwork, though, as we shall see, the character of the band's work in the wake of *OK Computer* has undergone significant transformation. When asked by Nick Kent in 2001 whether the group was planning for future internet distribution of their music (noting that Radiohead's initial terms with record company EMI were almost fulfilled), Yorke remarked in the negative, saying, "We still want an excuse to print all the packaging. . . . For me, it's an integral part of what's going on with the record itself. I know this sounds wanky but it's true: if the music's not inspiring the pictures, then I'm not comfortable."

Radiohead endured a great deal of distress in association with the crisis that accompanied the "fame-madness" spawned by the *OK Computer* experience, an ordeal that at one point led Yorke to fear for his mental health. The subsequent creative struggle for a renewed sense of authenticity that constituted the making of *Kid A* and *Amnesiac* (albums that were to be released a mere eight months apart) also proved to belong very much to this trying time. In Kent's "Happy Now," Yorke explains in reference to the sessions that "there were lots of depressingly frank exchanges of opinion into the night," adding that "the sad thing about it is that very few of our arguments were to do with music: it was just 'fall-out.' Really sad. Personally speaking, during that time I was just a total fuckin' mess. No one could say anything to me without me turning round and launching a vicious tirade at them. It got really, really bad."

Concerning the adaptive techniques that Yorke and Radiohead were to employ in the service of reinventing themselves during this trying period then, it's worth first observing that Yorke's aforementioned commitment to the inclusion of "pictures," as an integral part of "what's going on with the record itself," was no longer to extend to printed song lyrics. Becoming weary of the style of endless analysis visited upon the lyrics of *OK Computer*, Yorke discontinued the inclusion of printed lyrics with the band's subsequent recordings until the practice was resumed with *Hail to the Thief*.[7] "There is no point in taking the lyrics alone, apart from the music," he explained to Gabriella of *NYRock*. "That's one of the reasons why we won't have a lyric sheet with [*Kid A*]. You just can't separate it." A listener on BBC Radio 1's *Evening Session* "Interview with Thom, Ed, and Colin" with Steve Lamacq repeated Yorke's sentiments concerning the need for a more holistic interpretative approach, but from the opposite angle. "I think it's definitely important if you are a Radiohead fan to know the lyrics because they are such a huge part of their whole manifesto of being a pop band. . . . If [fans] cannot hear [them] or don't understand [them] I don't think it works as a song or album." Another fan on the show, meanwhile, demonstrated the irony of Yorke's decision, explaining, "It was a pity they didn't put the words in 'Kid A' because it made it harder to understand." Of course, living in the digital age, the lyrics were soon readily available on the internet, but this spatial separation I suspect was still to impair their proper scrutiny for many people.

During the writing of *OK Computer*, Yorke was apparently much influenced by criticism he'd received years earlier. After listening to one of the band's early demos, an old girlfriend apparently told him, "Your lyrics are crap. They're too honest, too personal, too direct and there's nothing left to the imagination." As Yorke went on to say, "She was right. When I first started, I wasn't really interested in writing lyrics. Which is strange in a way because if I didn't like the words on a record, if it wasn't saying anything, I would never bother with it again. But at 16, your own songs are half-formed," he pointed out, "and you don't really expect anyone to hear them, so you don't care what the words are." Working with the rest of the band, he found that if he thought more about the lyrics, they became somewhat less personal. "I suddenly discovered that, if I did concentrate on the lyrics, I'd get much more out of writing and it would be easier to put a song together," Yorke reported at the time. Clarke states in *Hysterical and Useless*, "Now we find that if we haven't got the lyrics to a song, we can't finish it because they dictate where we take the music." Here Yorke offers a clue to the heart of Radiohead's creative process up to and including *OK Computer*, suggesting that the band's work had become highly *lyrically driven*.

During initial efforts to create *Kid A*, however, the group's creative process was turned inside out, apparently deepening what was already a profound crisis, as Ed O'Brien reported to Kent in "Happy Now": "Whenever we'd done a record before, Thom's lyrics were evolving. He'd give you sheets and once you['d] see the words to, say, No Surprises, you['d] immediately think, Ah yes, we need a guitar for this that sounds like a child's musical box." As O'Brien continued, however, "This time, there were no lyrics and therefore no reference points. Phil, Colin and I went through some major dilemmas at various stages. How could we contribute to this new music? We all wondered if it wasn't better to just walk away. It was a very scary thing at first."[8] The band's "reference points" had disappeared, as O'Brien suggests, the words having formerly provided the primary key to the human universe that each song inhabits. In Marvin Lin's *33 1/3 Kid A*, O'Brien notes, "It's the first album that we—as a band—haven't been aware of what Thom's singing about. He didn't talk about his lyrics." Yorke confirms the connection of this reconfiguration of the band's creative process to the post–*OK Computer* experience and describes the newly inverted relationship between performance forces, resulting in the group's work becoming now more musically or *sonically* driven: "The words themselves on *Kid A* are kind of empty because they're leaving room for the music. That's all to do with my reaction against *OK Computer* where the music bashed away behind the words. Whatever emotions I was going through," he explains in Kent's "Happy Now," "I just found it incredibly difficult to write down lyrically. I was listening to us playing and became obsessed with looking for accidents. It was so much about finding accidents— waiting for them to happen. Because that spoke to me more than words. I just had this terrible trouble writing words." In Tom Moon's "Radiohead: Companion to Kid A Sessions," Yorke sheds light on why this may have become so difficult: "I was heavily neurotic about the words being projected back on to me," adding "that interpretation [ticks] me off, it's extremely lazy and dull." Besides employing the removal of the lyric sheets from the new CDs as a method of chastening listeners for being too "print-oriented"—Yorke did likewise with the cover of *Amnesiac*'s limited edition "library book" format. The book originates from the library of "Catachresis College," *katakhrēsis* being the derivative Greek term used to describe "the misuse of words," either in meaning or context.

As noted in Tim Footman's *Radiohead: A Visual Documentary*, Yorke also pointed out another reason for this remarkable change, which related to his pronounced interest in techno music at the time: "All the stuff I've been listening to, almost none of it has vocals. That was one of the things that I was most interested in; that I was so in love with this music, yet there wasn't much vocal interpretation." Regarding *Kid A* he was then to say, "You're not supposed to think about the words. That's the whole point all through the record. That's why I'm not printing the lyrics. Never. Maybe I'll give people clues, but it shouldn't be read like that." Yet another way in which Yorke endeavored to achieve a greater sense of distance and to remove his personality from the equation was in his apparent application of Tristan Tzara's directions for composing a Dadaist poem, which Radiohead had uploaded to their website. The technique involved writing lyrics on pieces of paper, which were then purportedly put into a hat and picked at random.

According to another perspective articulated in *NME*'s "Bright Yorke," Yorke had "articulated big things with *OK Computer* and therefore [was] seen to shun [his] 'responsibility' by not saying anything at all [with *Kid A* and *Amnesiac*]." Yorke's response to this suggestion, however, besides expressing regret, concludes by referencing once again the overemphasis on himself within the critical discussions surrounding the former album, and on his own relationship to dealing with the subject matter of his work. "Well, from my point of view these two records say far more of relevance and importance than *OK Computer* did. *OK Computer* was like flicking channels on the TV and this is . . . um . . . that's a shame. I think that's a real shame people would think that." As he went on to say, "And who the fuck is going to want to sit down and write a bunch of words that that's gonna happen to? Nobody.

You'd end up having some sort of bizarre critical house party going on in your head." Here, Yorke identifies as a key factor in his *OK Computer* crisis the intense scrutiny he underwent, a process he hoped to prevent in the future through recourse to various additional other means.

For example, another primary vehicle of the words—the lead vocal—also came under the knife as part of the re-identification process. "I would start writing a song, stop after 16 bars, hide it away in a drawer, look at it again, tear it up, destroy it . . . I was sinking down and down," says Yorke as James Doheny recounts in *Radiohead: Karma Police*. "I'd completely had it with melody. I just wanted rhythm. All melodies to me were pure embarrassment." One way of transcending this problem was manifested on *Amnesiac*'s penultimate track "Like Spinning Plates," whose melody is the retrograde version to that of the earlier song "I Will," which actually made its official appearance one album later as part of *Hail to the Thief*.[9] Nor was Yorke's vocal timbre spared. "It did my head in that whatever I did with my voice it had that particular set of associations," he expressed as Lin records in *33 1/3 Kid A*. "And there were lots of similar bands coming out at the time, and that made it even worse. I couldn't stand the sound of me even more." The band circumnavigated this by applying all manner of effects to Yorke's voice, and as he was to say, "By using other voices, I guess it was a way of saying, 'Obviously, it isn't me.'" The vocal processing used throughout the recording period, he says, allowed him "to sing things I wouldn't normally sing." For instance, on the track "Kid A," he says, "the lyrics are absolutely brutal and horrible and I wouldn't be able to sing them straight. But talking them and having them vocodered . . . so that I wasn't even responsible for the melody . . . that was great, it felt like you're not answerable to this thing."[10]

A variety of technological means were used to achieve the vocal treatments throughout the recordings, and in this song and others (including *Kid A*'s "The National Anthem" and *Amnesiac*'s "You and Whose Army?") the effect was obtained by playing the vocal through the palm speaker of Jonny Greenwood's *ondes martenot*. "The Palm Speaker is something else that Monsieur Martenot invented, to go with the Ondes," Greenwood explains in Simon Reynolds's "Walking on Thin Ice." "It's a bit like a harp with a speaker in the middle of it. The strings are tuned to all 12 semitones of an octave, and when you play a note in tune, it resonates that specific string and it creates this weird kind of echo that's only on those pitches." On *Amnesiac* the band also employed the vocal processing device called "autotuner" for the tracks "Packt Like Sardines in a Crushd Tin Box" and "Pulk/Pull Revolving Doors," in order to capture the nasally depersonalized and robotic sound sought by its singer. As Yorke recounts in Doheny's *Radiohead: Karma Police*, "You give the machine a key and then you just talk into it. It desperately tries to search for the music in your speech, and produces notes at random. If you've assigned it a key, you've got music."

As Greenwood's recourse to the ondes martenot suggests, the band during this period also reconstituted itself by moving to a significant extent away from its conventional instruments. "I bought a piano after *OK Computer* at a time when picking up a guitar just didn't do anything for me at all," Yorke said to Dave Fanning of *Hot Press* in 2000. "I couldn't listen to guitar music anymore, it was like bloody wallpaper to me. So, you know, I was trying to learn to play piano and trying to learn to program and shit like that." As Yorke's comment suggests, another instrument that acquired a more central role at this time was the computer. "Laptops are the new electric guitar, I reckon," the singer suggested, having used one, for example, on *Kid A*'s opening track "Everything in Its Right Place," a song that was written alongside "Pyramid Song" the same week that Yorke bought his piano.[11] "For 'Everything In Its Right Place' I programmed my piano playing into a laptop," said Yorke to Greg Kot of the *Chicago Tribune* in 2001, "but 'Pyramid' sounded better untreated." The laptop was used to a significant extent throughout the creative process, and as Yorke acknowledged, "It was a bit boring at points . . . staring at laptops all day is only so rewarding. But it was quite liberating to get used to the idea of music on a screen."

We might reasonably ask how the idea of "music on a screen" (along with Yorke's adoption of the piano) can be liberating. Walter Ong explains in *Orality and Literacy* one of the reasons this may be so.

> Technologies are not mere exterior aids but also interior transformations of consciousness. . . . The fact is that by using a mechanical contrivance, [an instrumentalist] can express something poignantly human that cannot be expressed without the mechanical contrivance. To achieve such expression of course, the violinist or organist [for example] has to have interiorized the technology [and] made the tool or machine a second nature, a psychological part of himself or her-

self. This calls for years of "practice," learning how to make the tool do what it can do. Such shaping of a tool to oneself, learning a technological skill, is hardly dehumanizing. The use of a technology can enrich the human psyche, enlarge the human spirit, intensify its interior life.

In addition to this particular existential enhancement that Yorke and his colleagues likely received from "music on a screen," the singer would have gained an advantage by the consequential heightening of the visual sense in his music-making experience. The reason for this is that "music on a screen"—like writing—constitutes a visual enclosure of nonvisual spaces and senses. In this regard, auditory space is very different from visual space, in that we're always at the edge of visual space, looking into it with the eye, but we're always at the center of auditory space, listening out with the ear. In contrast to music that's in written or printed form, however, "music on a screen" does possess an auditory component (as a result of the multimedia capabilities of the personal computer).

This visual extension of music onto the screen introduced a new element into the band's creative experience. "There was quite a lot of not really what you call songwriting in the sense of sitting in a room with an acoustic guitar and plucking at your heartstrings," as Yorke recounts in Fanning's "Here's Looking at You, Kid." "It was much more about editing, getting a bunch of stuff together, throwing a bunch of stuff onto a computer, onto the tape machine and making it coherent afterwards, like you'd edit a film or something. But actually fundamentally what you're ending up with is still songs." It's important to note that sitting in a room with an acoustic guitar and plucking at your heartstrings—like speech—amounts to all our senses being "outered" at once. If this musical moment is re-presented on the page or on the screen, however, it becomes a partial abstraction of the visual from the ordinary sense interplay entailed by Yorke's example of embodied music making. Introduced into the equation, then, is the cultivation of a mode of detachment, a partial withdrawal in one's depth of empathic involvement. With "music on a screen" one is able to see one's musical mind at work, while reflecting on its processes and conferring upon it some type of order. Something similar, of course, became achievable with the introduction of sound recording or disembodied music (i.e., music without the copresence of musicians), a technique following the development of which composers were readily permitted also to *hear* their musical minds at work.[12] Nonetheless, the editing posture that one adopts toward a sonic object is born of the same abstract visual orientation that uses techniques of rational ordering to control space. Yorke corroborates this position in a 2000 interview with Gijsbert Kamer, saying, "What I find interesting in taking on programming and editing and sampling is it stops you trying to emote. There's something I find incredibly exciting about just leaving something to run, just listening to it, not actually playing at the time, not singing along."

As we have seen, in the early stages of adaptation to the band's new media environment, some of Yorke's colleagues were not without their misgivings, given that there were guitarists not playing a lot of guitar on the albums and members of the band not playing anything at all on certain tracks. For Jonny Greenwood the sessions were less of a problem, as a result of his multi-instrumental identity,[13] and since he also had at least a minimal penchant for electronica. "I honestly didn't feel I had a role to play," remarked O'Brien in Kent's "Happy Now?" on the other hand. "My suggestion for *OK Computer*'s follow-up had been to say, Let's go back to the well-crafted three-and-a-half minute song. I came from idolising The Smiths in the '80s," he continued, "and I thought that would be the shocking thing to do. It was really difficult because, as a musician, I express myself more emotionally than cerebrally." Colin Greenwood concurred in "Happy Now?" adding, "I was principally a soul boy and didn't know much about programmed music at the time. A lot of the stuff I'd heard on Warp I didn't like at all. It was really cold. But that was exactly why Thom liked it: there was no emotional baggage attached to it."[14] Things began to work themselves out for the better in the end, nevertheless, as O'Brien was to attest in Doheny's *Radiohead: Karma Police*: "Thom was encouraging and saying, 'Look, this stuff is easy,' and he's right. With all the technology and software available, you can take things and manipulate them in ways that you've never been able to do before. That's definitely something we're going to get more and more into," he continued, "taking guitars and cutting them up, making sounds that have never been made. Everything is wide open with the technology now. The permutations are endless. Completely and utterly endless."

O'Brien was still to observe to James Oldham in the *New Musical Express*, however, that "*OK Computer* was an extremely emotional record," while "*Kid A* is a lot more controlled," and this element of control was extended also to the band's publicity for *Kid A*. "You have to remember that coming back into the lions' den was not easy, especially for me personally," acknowledged Yorke in Doheny's *Radiohead: Karma Police*. "It meant bringing back ghosts that made me shut down in the first place, so a lot of the decisions we made, and what we chose to do, was to avoid the normal giant cogs turning and crushing." Interestingly, Yorke was also to say, as Lin records in *33 1/3 Kid A*, "All my favourite artists are people who never seem to be involved in the industry and I found myself getting involved in it, and I felt really ashamed to be there." Using language reminiscent of Pink Floyd's lambasting of the music industry in "Welcome to the Machine" (from its *Dark Side of the Moon* follow-up), among the usual giant cogs that Yorke and company sought to avoid was the making of music videos. During the *Kid A/ Amnesiac* recording sessions, the group's managers would occasionally come into their new studios for meetings and would express concern about the band's transformed musical direction. "The music's all getting fuckin' weird and we're not sure what's going to happen," they would say, according to Yorke. "And we didn't make things any easier because we didn't do any videos. We did these commercials because we felt videos were just commercials anyway—why lie about it! But then, of course, they didn't get played as commercials because we couldn't afford to get them on TV," he continued, "because we didn't have a product to sell that was ultimately worth that much (smirks). We weren't playing the magazine game properly. We just felt at the time, 'We've earned a licence to do this. Let's just do it.'" Half of these "blipverts," a series of ten- to forty-second animated video "blips," were produced by animator Chris Bran, who created them using the artwork of the band's creative partner and website maintainer Stanley Donwood, while a UK firm called "Shynola" produced the remainder. Of the finished product Shynola director Richard Kenworthy was to say in Paula Carson and Helen Walters's "Radiohead: Modified Organisms," "They're quite political and pessimistic. . . . There's stuff about war and death, death by nature, how we're raping the earth. Stanley has a whole theory about an ice age that's going to come and destroy the world— and that theme crops up in Thom's lyrics. I think Thom shares a lot of his ideas with Stanley, so it's all very inspired by what the songs are about." To this Donwood would add there as well, prior to learning about their unfeasibility as television commercials, "they go from Blair Witch to Captain Pugwash. . . . Some of them are stupid—but the important thing is they're meant to be throwaway, not works of art . . . they'll just be on between Jif Micro Liquid and Volvo."

In the end the blipverts were instead to be used primarily on the internet, where the band's U.S. record company, Capitol, faced with "the challenge of marketing the seemingly unmarketable," turned the promotion of *Kid A* over to the band's legions of dedicated web-savvy fans. It did so by setting up a special website that included an instant "messaging buddy" that connected international Radiohead fans, and acted as a bridge to over a thousand unofficial websites dedicated to the band, and by steadily releasing pictures, the blipverts, music, and other information that fans were then permitted to incorporate into their own sites.[15] Moreover, three weeks prior to the album's official release, both the band and the record company encouraged fans to circulate free bootlegs and to stream the new album off Capitol's website. "As groundbreaking as the music of *Kid A* undoubtedly was for a hitherto 'front-line' rock act, the way its audience had first encountered it was without precedent, and yet as a marketing strategy could not have been more successful," James Doheny wrote in *Radiohead: Karma Police* with regard to all this frenzied activity. "Without radio airplay, hit singles or videos, *Kid A*, when released in October 2000, went straight to the top of the charts on both sides of the Atlantic. The band, their music, their methodology and their faith in their audience," he continued, "had been completely vindicated in both artistic and, still more remarkably, commercial terms." The band did not release any singles for the album either, and its members dramatically reduced the number of interviews they chose to give. As O'Brien remarked to Oldham in *New Musical Express* with regard to Yorke, "He's got quite a legacy with the music press. I think in 1995 his face was on the cover of a magazine with the words: 'Is this going to be the next rock 'n' roll suicide?' Why do you think he doesn't want to talk to people? I think he's got better things to do with his time." As O'Brien added, "We haven't cut ourselves off, because of our website. We correspond with people through that. That's our outlet." Yorke also increasingly opted to do interviews via email, or with alternative internet-based radio stations such as WHFS out of Washington.[16]

Another of the band's efforts to avoid the music industry's "normal giant cogs turning and crushing" manifested itself in what became known as its "No Logo" 10,000-capacity tent tour, undertaken following the release of *Kid A* and named for the previously mentioned book by Canadian journalist Naomi Klein. Defiantly unsponsored, as Doheny notes in *Radiohead: Karma Police*, the tour had the band taking "a specially designed and acoustically optimised tent to as many interesting and non-standard places as possible,"[17] and the concerts sold out within minutes of tickets going on sale. But they managed to do so without the help of a single poster, flyer, or newspaper advertisement, and again, it was creating a buzz on the internet that achieved this. This increasing "disintermediation" (or cutting out of the middle man) garnered for the band the attention of people like Andrew Blau, a New York consultant on digital technology, who was presciently to observe to Ed Vulliamy in the *Observer*, "Radiohead stands on the cusp of something entirely new in the relationship between the producers and consumers of music."

The group's efforts were to be stymied to some degree in the United States, however, as Yorke explained to Greg Kot of *CD Now*:

> There are a couple of well-known cartels (Clear Channel Entertainment, formerly SFX, and Ticketmaster) that now operate the entire live music scene in America, and we find it extremely surprising that no action has been taken by your government monopolies people. Even brave independent promoters have to bow down to the brethren. It is no longer a case of a certain ticket-selling company, the whole thing is sewn up as we found when we were doing our research into taking out our tent. . . . SFX and Ticketmaster have come against every step of the way demanding a piece of the action— utterly bent if you ask me. Suffice to say, us suggesting playing in a tent didn't fit the scenario they might have had in mind.

Where the group was told the tents weren't "feasible," the band members attempted to assert as much control as possible to ensure they were performing in interesting outdoor locations such as Chicago's Grant Park or on the bank of New York's Hudson River. "In some places we have just had to be cool about it, given 10 months of research and finding no solution," Yorke admitted. "As far as we were concerned, it got so bad at one point that we talked about forgetting touring in the

U.S. until we could find a way to do it completely on our terms. But then they really would have won and a lot of people other than us would have been upset."

In any case, in the process of producing *Kid A* and *Amnesiac*, Radiohead was able to re-create themselves through various means as we've seen, and perhaps the biggest clue that the band's identity crisis had been successfully resolved was when they gave their only UK performance of 2001 in a homecoming festival–style concert in Oxford's South Park, where, for the first time in three years, the band was to perform "Creep." Of their new work Yorke was to say on BBC Radio 1's *Evening Session* with Steve Lamacq, "'There you go, we've burst the bubble now, so let's start over.' That felt quite good. The pressure was so stupid, and the level of scrutiny, so it's good to not have that anymore, because it's never going to be like that again. That is all over now. We are just carrying on."

6

CRAZY, MAYBE?

Kosovo and the First Human Clone (1999–2001)

For the last six months of 1998, Radiohead was to remain completely out of the public eye, the longest period for which they had done so since the band had been signed to EMI. During this time a lot of things occurred, however: they released Grant Gee's *Meeting People Is Easy*, Colin Greenwood became the third member of the group to get married, Thom Yorke bought a house by the sea in Dorset, and the band interrupted its sabbatical with a December performance at the Amnesty International concert in Paris that commemorated the fiftieth anniversary of the United Nations Declaration of Human Rights. With regard to the difficulties that the band had at this trying time, Ed O'Brien was to suggest in Andy Greene's "Oral History" of *OK Computer* that they complicated their problems because they didn't take sufficient time off: "We finished touring in the middle of '98. By the fall of '98 we were rehearsing for *Kid A*. We were at Canned Applause, rehearsing. So we did end up back in the studio in January '99. And we were still reeling. We were having growing pains."

Another reason for these difficulties, as we have seen, was the fact that Yorke had rediscovered his penchant for techno music, a genre that resonated with him, especially as a result of its de-emphasis on melody and vocals. He bought the whole back catalog of Sheffield's Warp Records, and the work of Aphex Twin, Autechre, and Boards of Canada he found particularly compelling. Over the course of a few months recording demos, Radiohead moved from Paris to Copenhagen, and in April, they then set up at a mansion in Gloucestershire called Batsford Park. As Nigel Godrich was to explain in Mac Randall's *Exit Music*, however, with regard to the band's limited progress until this point, "There was a lot of arguing. . . . People stopped talking to one another," to which he added, "Thom really wanted to try and do *everything* different and that was . . . bloody difficult."

As O'Brien was to explain, this consisted more or less of "splitting the band up and reforming it with the same five members," as well as learning "how to be a participant in a song without playing a note." As Phil Selway was also to clarify, this involved "working more like producers than musicians," though Colin Greenwood was to say that he also spent this year of adaptation learning how computers work. Another problem for the ensemble turned out to be simply the inability of bringing anything to fruition: "To be perfectly honest," said Yorke to Dave Fanning of *Hot Press*, "if it had been me I would probably never have finished any of it, 'cos for a long time I was like 'Yeah you know we can finish that some other time, let's do something else today.'" As he further explained, "I was doing that for about six months because I really didn't want to finish things and have to put them out to people and have to deal with all that crap that I'd essentially forgotten about."

Things were put aside briefly in June, when Phil Selway and his wife had their first child, and when Yorke and Jonny Greenwood set off to Amsterdam to perform their acoustic duo at the annual concert for Tibet. Around this time, Yorke also began advocating for the aforementioned organization known as Jubilee 2000 and its Drop the Debt campaign at the G8 meeting in Cologne, Germany. And in order to update fans on the band's progress in the studio, O'Brien, through the band's website, and with the word "blog" not in common usage yet, began to keep a diary, which he was to maintain over the next year, as Radiohead worked through the material for *Kid A* and *Amnesiac*. By the end of the summer, the band's studio was finally equipped, and before breaking for their December holidays, Yorke and Jonny Greenwood executed the band's first webcast, performing a rendition of their new song about "cannibalism": "Knives Out."

Reconvening in January, Radiohead continued recording, and because the band had so many songs completed by this point, a decision had to be made regarding whether they ought to release a single or double album. In April, meanwhile, O'Brien marched in protest against the World Bank and the International Monetary Fund (IMF), and around the same time, the band introduced its W.A.S.T.E. online merchandising operation (its name referencing Thomas Pynchon's second novel *The Crying of Lot 49* and its subversive underground postal system). "We've also opened our own store, called w.a.s.t.e. on-line," Colin Greenwood wrote in the operation's first email to subscribers as Marvin Lin notes in *33 1/3 Kid A*. "We're doing this because we want to try and use this amazing communication thingie to matter directly to you and not via any corporate third party bollocks with spinning car ads."[1]

As things were to progress, the group decided to release two single albums rather than a double, and all the mixing and mastering for *Kid A* was finished by the beginning of June. The band embarked on nearly a monthlong tour of old theaters and amphitheaters throughout Europe, concluding with a performance in Israel. Following the album's completion, Yorke also found the opportunity to perform guest vocals on tracks by Björk ("I've Seen It All," from the album *Selmasongs*) and P. J. Harvey ("This Mess We're In," from the album *Stories from the City, Stories from the Sea*).

Kid A was finally released in October 2000, but since the emergence of *OK Computer*, the digital file-sharing service Napster had also arrived on the scene. Thus, at least fourteen songs from the *Kid A/Amnesiac* sessions had been circulating as live bootlegs and were already known to many fans. Not only that, the completed album was leaked to Napster three weeks prior to the official release, iTunes not having emerged as the first monetized site until three months later. Meanwhile, at the beginning of September, Radiohead was to embark on another five-week tour of Europe, their so-called No Logo tour, for which the band employed their two sound-optimized traveling tents in order to facilitate getting around. Recalling how they were unable to put their plans into effect in North America, that October saw three instantly sold-out shows in New York, Los Angeles, and Toronto. The latter I was able to attend myself but experienced the same disappointment as one reviewer, who noted to O'Brien that the band had played the previous night at the Air Canada Centre's Sears Theatre in Toronto—a venue plastered with logos: "The Air Canada Centre we HAD to play. It was the only place we could get enough people into," said O'Brien to *Access Mag*. "But if you want an honest reaction to it, the place sucks. [It's] fucking everything we hate. . . . It's a bloody sports arena, and it's not a place where bands should be playing music. It's very demoralizing for bands to see that shit, for our band it is. Everywhere you look it's a corporate logo." Performing also for the first time on the American program *Saturday Night Live*, Radiohead played "The National Anthem" and "Idiotheque." During the credits at the end of the program, when the show's cast and guests typically wave goodbye to the audience, Yorke held up a "Let Ralph Debate" sign, in reference to the media's exclusion of then Green Party candidate Ralph Nader from the 2000 U.S. presidential election debates. "The highlight of the whole *Kid A* thing was our *Saturday Night Live* performance," explained Yorke in Trevor Baker's *Thom Yorke: Radiohead and Trading Solo*. "I was so proud of that. I was walking on water for a week after that—I felt so good."

Despite being what *Village Voice* famously called "the biggest, warmest recorded go-fuck-yourself in recent memory," *Kid A* debuted at number one in both the UK and the United States. But not having the longevity of either *The Bends* or *OK Computer*, it disappeared quickly from the charts, given that the band didn't conduct the same kind of extensive promotional tours in support of the album. Nor, again, did they produce videos or singles, and the album received little airplay accordingly. In the new year, however, the band did secure another Grammy for Best Alternative Rock Performance, and attending the ceremony this time were Colin Greenwood, Selway, and O'Brien, with the latter apparently having taken magic mushrooms prior to the event.[2] By February 2001, Yorke had his hands otherwise full with the birth of his first child Noah, while O'Brien and Selway joined Neil Finn in Auckland, New Zealand, at the beginning of April for charity performances on behalf of Finn's *7 Worlds Collide* project.

Radiohead somewhat returned to business as usual with *Amnesiac*, releasing the first official single and video outside the United States that May for "Pyramid Song," which in the UK reached number five but was soon to drop off the chart. Meanwhile, "I Might Be Wrong" was released in early June as a video and radio-only single in America, quickly followed that month with the release of the album, which was to appear at number two, though on the UK chart it was to debut at number one. A third video and single from the album, "Knives Out," was then released in August, attaining in the UK only number thirteen but reaching number one in Canada. Meanwhile, the special limited edition of the album was to win them another Grammy for Best Recording Package. Among the eight B sides were the songs "Cuttooth," "Trans-Atlantic Drawl," "Kinetic," "The Amazing Sounds of Orgy," "Worrywort," "Fog," "Fast-Track," and a full-length version of "Life in a Glass House." Over the spring, summer, and autumn the group were to perform thirty-four concerts in twelve countries. And as previously, Radiohead chose to host its performances in unusual locations such as parks, with the band reserving large blocks of tickets for fans, sold on the internet via their website, a technique that enabled them to partially get around dealing with companies like Ticketmaster and Clear Channel. In addition to their celebrated homecoming performance in Oxford's South Park, the group likewise made an amusing appearance that summer on the animated U.S. program *South Park*. November also saw the release of *I Might Be Wrong: Live Recordings*, which included a number of isolated tracks taken from four separate concerts. Unlike a real Radiohead concert, however, the album included no pre–*Kid A* tracks and was intended rather to represent the band's conversion of their most recent recordings into performance pieces. Notably, the album included a version of "True Love Waits," a song that was not to be included on a studio album until a decade and a half later with the release of *A Moon Shaped Pool*.

KID A

Since they were essentially products of the same recording sessions ("Life in a Glass House" being the only *Amnesiac* track left to be recorded following the release of *Kid A*), it makes sense given this interconnectedness to consider the albums in combination. "I'm not sure they are two records," Colin Greenwood remarked as James Doheny records in *Radiohead: Karma Police*. "*Amnesiac* is more conventional, perhaps, but also more dissonant . . . it continues on from *Kid A*. It was all done in the same recording period. It is all a whole." As Yorke was to add, "In some weird way I think *Amnesiac* gives another take on *Kid A*, a form of explanation,"[3] while explaining in Doheny's *Radiohead*, "I think the artwork is the best way of explaining it. . . .The artwork to *Kid A* was all in the distance. The fires were all going on the other side of the hill. With *Amnesiac* you're actually in the forest while the fire's happening."

Using ARText paint, Stanley Donwood painted ten large six-by-six-foot canvases for *Kid A*, and these were then photographed, scanned, and combined with computer graphics. In 2007, Donwood and Dr. Tchock were to release "a picture book" called *Dead Children Playing*, which chronicles the artwork that they'd collaborated on up to that point, and that had accompanied the duo's art exhibit at the Iguapop Gallery in Barcelona toward the end of 2006. Apparently inspired by accounts of the snow-capped Kosovo mountain range appearing to be on fire, Donwood was to write in this book, in relation to the artwork for *Kid A*,

> The news is dominated by the concurrent wars in Kosovo. The Racak "incident" has recently taken place. I'm a pampered UK citizen, but I recognise the logos on the clothes of those pulled from rubble, I recognise the types of trees around the burning villages, and guiltily I realise that this conflict is affecting me like none has before. This feels as if, with a little bad luck, it could be me in the news. My girlfriend. My kids.

Referring to the reported massacre of forty-five people in Racak on January 16, 1999, most of the international community pinned the massacre on government security forces, which were battling terrorists from the Kosovo Liberation Army; later that year, two days following the release of *Kid A*, the president of Serbia was forced to resign. Much like Donwood, Yorke was to refer to a sense of guilt, suggesting with regard to Radiohead's work that it's "difficult to ignore wider issues . . . it's difficult to live with a bad conscience." In Lin's book Yorke was to express similar concern in relation to *Kid A* for "the generation that will inherit the earth when we've wiped everything out," a sentiment that ties the two new albums strongly to the dominant apocalyptic character of *OK Computer* and of earlier segments of the band's work. In this regard, Donwood originally intended to use an image of the 1950s children's book heroes, Peter and Jane, surveying the bleak landscape of destruction. But the publisher, Ladybird, purportedly refused permission to do so, out of concern that such young, innocent characters—typically employed as a learning resource—should not be witness to such horrific scenes. Their response was, in part, certainly ironic, particularly given that this is precisely the album's overriding message.

By the middle of 2000 the front page of Radiohead's website featured five highly stylized bears (presumably one representing each member of the band), and this imagery was to become prominent across both albums. Some of the blipverts that were used to promote the recording were also to include flying bears, sporting "the look and atmosphere of a children's cartoon highjacked by a twisted horror film." The creatures apparently originated in a bedtime story that Donwood used to tell his daughter about teddy bears that rise up and eat the adults. Living happily with the children, the toys then likewise begin to look at the children with hungry eyes. The bears were first officially featured in Donwood and Dr. Tchock's online cartoon strip called *Modified Organisms*, which Yorke also refers to in Lin's *33 1/3 Kid A* as "Test Specimen":

> Early on, Stanley Donwood . . . and I started doing this thing, Test Specimen, a cartoon about giving birth to a monster, the Frankenstein thing. For example, the bear logo—that is a test specimen, the first mutant. The idea was loosely based on stuff we were reading about genetically modified food. We got obsessed with the idea of [a] mutation entering the DNA of the human species. One episode was about these teddy bears that mutate and start eating children.

It's in this way that Donwood was to suggest that Yorke was dedicating the album to the first human clone, and we ought briefly to note how concerns arose over the uncertainties associated with genetically modified organisms (GMOs), which, in terms of food, the majority of North Americans were eating before even being aware of their existence. Unlike those living in other states, South Korea, for example, the NAFTA bloc countries have yet to win the right to mandatory labeling of products that contain ingredients that have undergone genetic modification. In the agricultural sphere it's feared that the world risks becoming dependent for its foodstuffs on nonrenewable seeds—the legal property of a limited number of mammoth private organizations, some of which, including Monsanto, have busied themselves securing the patent rights on ancient traditional herbal remedies transmitted over millennia in the agricultures of so-called developing regions.

As per Yorke's comment, many have also raised concerns regarding the prospects of applying genetic modification and cloning technology to human beings. The Canadian medical ethicist Margaret Somerville, in this relation, points to the enormous difference that exists between our *never* cloning a human being and our cloning just one, highlighting that the effects of such an act would be irreversible. She outlines the implications of some of the astonishing and unprecedented powers that the new technology has put in the palm of our collective human hand, and reminds us, too, of the old adage that "along with great power always comes great responsibility." Among these recent powers is the ability to alter the very essence of life, including human life and, similarly, to alter the nature of the transmission of life, again including that of humans. Her observations in CBC Radio's "Reflections on an Ethical Society" demonstrate some of the concerns encapsulated within *Kid A*:

> What about designing our children? And not just them, but every one of their descendants changed in the same way that we change our child. This is possible by intervening on what is called the human germ-cell line, the genes that are passed from generation to generation. What ethics should govern this and how we go about deciding that? Should we, as some American scientists believe we should, just leave this to the so-called "ethics of the marketplace"? The basis of this theory of ethics is that consumers are ethical, and will not buy unethical products, which therefore will not be commercially viable. . . . Some of these scientists . . . say, totally seriously, that genetic enhancement of embryos makes good economic sense for future parents. It will cost much less [they say] to use genetic enhancement to improve your future child's intelligence, give them a photographic memory (which we have just done with fruit flies), make them really good at sports and music—than to pay for private schools and tutors, sports-coaching, and music lessons.

Radiohead reproduced this ethic when they presented computer-manipulated photographic images to publications such as *Q*, where band member facial features were drastically altered and embellished (in part, also, an effort to resist their celebritization). But the band also submitted a composite image they called "Kid A Mutant Specimen." "That's Phil's head, obviously, Jonny's eyebrows, my nose and mouth," Thom was to say in Lin's *33 1/3 Kid A*. "It's like a human mutation, not a comment on the GM [genetically modified] thing as such, though you can't really ignore the GM issue. It's everywhere, innit?" Amusingly, these techniques were also employed for a *Spin* article containing photo portraits of each member of the band, pictured holding up a cardboard sign in front of him, sporting a handwritten list of all the digital manipulations and touch-ups that had been carried out in order to "improve" their photos. "Make my eyes the same" is one of the instructions held up by Yorke, referring to his lazy left eye, which in the portrait edit is set perfectly straight. The intended superficiality is expressed through Yorke's "spotless" and "heroic" face, smiling beamingly "with a healthy glow."

Surely the argument that Somerville recounts above must be the defining orientation of the thought-world that gives primacy of place to "Homo Economicus." At the very least, it's a far cry from the ideas expressed by Mary Shelley in her impressively prescient 1818 book *Frankenstein* to which Yorke alludes above. Recovering the ancient concept of *hubris* in relation to "a modern-day Prometheus," Shelley observed in the novel's original preface that "supremely frightful would be the effect of any human endeavour to mock the stupendous mechanism of the Creator of the world." Nevertheless, early in 2001 the world learned that an international team of scientists with "unlimited funds" provided by anonymous private donors were working to produce the first human clone, and that between six and seven hundred couples had volunteered for experimentation purposes. "Now that we have crossed into the third millennium," suggested the consortium's spokesperson, an American doctor named Panayiotis Zavos, "we have the technology to break the rules of nature." Zavos added in his comments to Reuters in 2001 that his experiments should not be subject to government scrutiny: "We don't want the government involved in this project. . . . This is a high-tech, serious project and we're not going to bring in the technocrats if they are not needed." As Somerville points out, however, it's not merely an individual choice by a parent, a scientist, or a research facility whether we clone a human being; that single act is not just an act with impact on individuals and thus ought to be a societal choice at the broadest level. Nonetheless, she observes how the British had already established what are called "Human Embryo Manufacturing Plants"— the British Patent Office already having granted that human embryos could be patented for the purposes of therapeutic cloning.

In the United States, meanwhile, technology critic Jeremy Rifkin and medical school professor Stuart Newman led an effort to provoke the first test of what officially constitutes a human being in the age of biotechnology. Seeking a patent on a "humouse," a creature half-human, half-mouse, the U.S. Patent and Trademark Office did not permit Rifkin and Newman to patent their idea, on the grounds that it contravened the spirit of the Thirteenth Amendment against slavery (it's been illegal in the United States to buy and sell human beings since 1865). But for over a quarter of a century, patents have been granted for a wide array of living organisms and elements of life (among which are human genes, human cells, and animals that contain human DNA). This is a reality reflected in the cover art of *Amnesiac* and in the concealed booklet found beneath the jewel case of early pressings of *Kid A*, where all sorts of little critters bear the copyright or trademark symbols. In practice, such forms are used in research on cancer and other diseases, and as long as certain administrative rules are followed and no taxpayer monies are used, all procedures are legal. Rifkin and Newman's application was put into effect in the hope of delaying or preventing such a technological excursion in the United States for at least twenty years, something they managed to achieve in 2005. At the very least, they've forced tighter limits on what can be made and patented, while forcing Congress and the American people into a renewed debate over what constitutes a human being within the new technological age.

The hidden booklet also includes many words and phrases, mixed in with excerpts from song lyrics, and thus appears to represent something like the overall product of Yorke's hatful of lyrics. Many of the phrases are violent, and the booklet's first page includes the German title "Theater des Todes," which translates into English as "Theater of Death," a title likely derived from a 1987 Italian slasher film. We also see the head of a bear apparently being served for dinner, conjuring the tracks "Hunting Bears" and "Knives Out" from *Amnesiac*. But bears are also otherwise pictured with automatic weapons, and inside the booklet, they're portrayed in the form of a fashion magazine cover or poster headlined "Glamor," suggesting some kind of glamorization of violence. Another recurring image throughout the pages of the CD's actual sleeve is that of a red swimming pool. As Donwood writes in *Dead Children Playing*, "Another Memory; a comic by Alan Moore and Bill Sienkiewicz called 'Shadowplay: The Secret Team,' in which the number of the dead were tallied by images of red swimming pools. The average human body holds a gallon of blood. The average swimming pool holds 50,000 gallons of water. The maths, and the graphic, were inescapable." What Donwood leaves out here, however, is that this technique was one that belonged to the CIA and, moreover, that the comic strip generally consisted of probing the agency's controversial involvement in the Vietnam War, the Iran-Contra affair, and its relationship to individuals such as Augusto Pinochet and Manuel Noriega. In any case, all of this imagery appears presciently to evoke the forthcoming War on Terror, and what was to be the CIA's illegal systematic adoption of drone warfare and methods of torture.

In addition to this evocation of frightening forms of violence, Yorke was to suggest that a fear of dying also animates *Kid A*. "I have this house down by the sea and the landscape around it is really harsh, brutal. I used to just go off for the whole day, walking, and just feeling totally like nothing. Thinking I'll be back in the ground as soon as I know it." The singer additionally suggests that this fear was to manifest itself in various ways. "I had this thing for a while where I was falling through trapdoors all the time, into like, acid flashbacks," he remarked to Lorin Zoric of *Juice Magazine*, providing a hint to the character of the transitions between the various scenes that comprise the songs of the album. "I'd be talking to someone and then I'd be falling through the earth, and it went on for months and months, and it was really weird," he continued. "And that was all happening towards the end of *OK Computer*. And that was all linked in with death. Seeing people dead, like, as I'm talking to you."

The fact that the group continued to take considerable pains in the sequencing of album tracks is worth noting. As Colin Greenwood was to attest, noted in Baker's *Thom Yorke: Radiohead and Trading Solo*, "I can assure you it's hell. We have meetings that take hours—often from 4pm until midnight—only about the order of the songs." Keeping in mind, however, Yorke's suggestion that we're not intended to listen so much to the words of *Kid A*, given their "secondary" status, we shouldn't be surprised that it's difficult for one to say anywhere near as much about the album as compared with *OK Computer*.

The recording begins with "Everything in Its Right Place," and we soon notice that we're in a purely laptop electronic environment. The programmed nature of the keyboard part reinforces the sense of high technology, as does Yorke's sampled and manipulated voice, which is cut up and reinserted into the song, using a Korg Kaoss Pad (a small touchpad sampler, MIDI controller, and effects processor). Using this technique, the song immediately provides us with a verbal link both to the album title and to the second track, which shares the album's name. A narrow and claustrophobic melodic and harmonic range characterizes the song, a characteristic sense that accrues to its protagonist, who sings mechanically four times, "Yesterday I woke up sucking a lemon." While Yorke was to indicate that this is "the face you pull because a lemon is so tart," he was also to share that this phrase is the best way to characterize his attitude throughout the promotional cycle for OK Computer, confessing, "That's the face I had for three years." When the character also sings, "There are two colours in my head," one imagines that these refer to the colors black and white, and to a perspective that tends toward framing things in an oversimplistic way. Communication is likewise a problem, as is apparent when the protagonist sings, "What is that you tried to say?"; and, of this time period, Yorke was to remark to Zoric of Juice Magazine, "I didn't trust people at all, not even the people closest to me for ages and ages, and that means you really have nothing to hold onto. 'Everything in Its Right Place' is about that. You're trying to fit into the right place and the right box so you can connect." That this issue is ongoing is evident throughout the album, and in the fact that the song doesn't come to any harmonic resolution but fades out on its repeating, unresolved chord progression.

The trap door opens into another wholly electronic environment, this time a kind of "Kid A" laboratory-nursery, where test specimens are created. The track's bright, major tonality creates a pleasant and relaxed atmosphere, particularly in combination with the gentle sounds that resemble train set bells, digital toy pianos, and flying bear angels (or perhaps a kind of spacecraft landing?). This positive atmosphere likewise reflects the vapid naïveté with regard to the lack of consideration of future possible problems surrounding the procedures underway. Yorke's voice enters and is electronically superimposed through a vocoder onto the "artificial" pitches of the ondes martenot, the early electronic instrument that Jonny Greenwood adopted through his interest in the twentieth-century French composer Olivier Messiaen and was then to use throughout much of the album. As Yorke was to say to Fanning of Hot Press, "I didn't write the melody, all I did was talk into a mike and Jonny played the melody. So it's like a vocoded thing, where the keyboard's singing and all I'm doing is mouthing words that I'm picking out of a hat."

The lyric begins in reference to slipping away, with the protagonist articulating, "I slipped on a little white lie." This line establishes a connection with the album's final song "Motion Picture Soundtrack," a selection associated with old Disney films, in which we find out that "they fed us on little white lies," imagery that refers beyond "technological theology" to the powerful propaganda influence of the entertainment industry. Making reference to the lines "We got heads on sticks— you got ventriloquists," Yorke was to describe the words to "Kid A" as "the most vicious I've ever sung." The character creates a sense of us and them, aligning himself with the former's violent savagery and associating the latter with the powerful purveyors of "little white lies" through their employment of "ventriloquists." With its use of synthesizer keyboards, musically the song takes on an even more dreamlike character, appropriately following repetition of the line "Standing in the shadows at the end of my bed." Its fairy-tale quality is also reinforced toward the end of the piece, by way of its reference to the legend of the Pied Piper of Hamelin, who, after he led the rats out of town and didn't receive compensation for his services, did the same with the town's children, singing, "Rats and children follow me out of town . . . come on kids." This, of course, again invokes the idea of our providing inadequate direction to our younger generations and, instead, leading them into the direction of harm.

Falling through the next trap door we arrive in the context of "The National Anthem," the first time that we hear the typical rock instrumentation of bass guitar and drums. Built on a repeated bass figure, the drums help create tension at a couple of junctures in the song, when their fast pulse briefly drops out, only to reenter immediately. The first minute and a half features some haunting ondes martenot and electronic sound effects heard over the repeated bass figure, the outline of which repeatedly signals a somewhat unsettling shift from major to minor. Perhaps among the most remarkable aspects of the piece is its inclusion of horns, the style in which they're arranged and performed indicating the influence of the iconic jazz bassist Charles Mingus. Yorke was to say with regard to *The Complete Town Hall Concert*, "It was the most formative record of the whole time that I was 'away.' I got absolutely obsessed with this record . . . I started seeing things, it was really freaky. It's not happened to me very often, but it was immediate." Strangely, as Yorke was to add in conversation with Fanning of *Hot Press*, "I couldn't even see where I was, barely. It was fucking weird."

When the vocal finally enters, Yorke's voice is endowed with an eerie quality, as through a ring modulator he sings, "Everyone around here, everyone is so near, what's going on?" Foreshadowing the impending launch of the War on Terror, to the second verse he adds the line, "Everyone has got the fear, it's holding on," paranoia soon to be no longer the preserve of those unable to count themselves among the inno$ent. Following the second verse, the horns enter more prominently, and the band was to set up eight musicians in the same way that they appear on the Mingus album. Once again employing travel imagery, Yorke explained to Zoric of *Juice Magazine*, "On the day I said to them, 'You know when you've been in a traffic jam for four hours and if someone says the wrong thing to you, you'll just kill 'em, you'll fucking snap and probably throttle them?'" Holding his hand mere millimeters from his face he continued, "'You're like this—with everybody and any tiny spark and you're going to go off, and you're in the midst of two or three hundred other people who are in exactly the same thing. I wanted them to play like that, like, this fucking close to going off, lynching or killing, it's like a mob just about to spark off.'"

At first the musicians had difficulty, given there was no proper score, and so it was suggested that Yorke and Jonny Greenwood conduct the ensemble, to give the musicians more guidance on how to approach their parts. As Yorke was to say again to Fanning, "The bit at the end was my favourite bit, because they said, 'Well, what are we going to do at the end?' And I said, 'I'll go, 1–2–3–4 and you just hit whatever note's in your head as loud as you possibly can.' And that was just the best sound you've ever heard." Yorke was so enthusiastic during his conducting, in fact, that through his jumping up and down, he broke some of the bones in one of his feet.

Following the short sample of what sounds like an excerpt from Elgar, "National Anthem," concludes with a dreamlike transition into "How to Disappear Completely," a song that was apparently based on a dream that Yorke had as recorded by Mark Paytress in *Radiohead: The Complete Guide to Their Music*. "I dreamt I was floating down the Liffey [the river that flows through Dublin] and there was nothing I could do. . . . The whole song is my experience of floating." Among the oldest songs on the album, it was written in 1997, in the midst of the fallout from *OK Computer*, and just prior to the band playing in front of its largest audience yet. "We were about to do some big festival in Ireland," Yorke said to Fanning. "I was up all night, having the most terrible dreams, I was so shit-scared. And I had one of those really, really vivid dreams and the Liffey was really, really muddy, like a mud river, and I was drifting down to the sea." Clearly the "strobe lights and blown speakers" evoke this pending concert experience, and some of the lyrics were derived from a telephone conversation that Yorke had with REM's Michael Stipe as Paytress records in *Radiohead*: "I said, 'I cannot cope with this.' And he said, 'Pull the shutters down and keep saying, "I'm not here, this is not happening."'"

When the song begins, it's the album's first instance of an identifiable guitar sound, let alone that of an acoustic guitar, and concerning the intersection of technology and musical aesthetics, it's interesting to consider Jonny Greenwood's thoughts from the time as recorded in Lin's *33 1/3 Kid A*: "The whole artifice of recording. I see it like this: a voice into a microphone onto a tape, onto your CD, through your speakers is all as illusory and fake as any synthesizer—it doesn't put Thom in your front room. But one is perceived as 'real,' the other somehow 'unreal.'" Greenwood continued, "It's the same with guitars versus samplers. It was just freeing to discard the notion of acoustic sounds being truer." The question Greenwood raises is interesting and certainly relevant, though I'd maintain that the band doesn't here discard that notion in terms of musical significance. I've alluded to the acoustic guitar's connotations of honesty and intimacy, and the same can be said of orchestral strings in certain contexts, including this one. The strings were recorded in Dorchester Abbey, which would appear to indicate that there was, indeed, something "more true" that the band wanted from its instrumentation—mainly, its resonance with that particular kind of acoustic space. It's worth noting that Greenwood was to take two weeks away from the band to complete his work of scoring the various string parts.

Recalling the identity implications of Radiohead's transformation in relation to their mass success, as well as the adaptive techniques of remediation they employed in their efforts to re-create themselves, it's worthwhile to note that the song's title is taken from Douglas Richmond's 1985 book *How to Disappear Completely and Never Be Found*, a self-help guide concerning how to create a new identity. The alienating, vast sense of space created by the use of reverb communicates the disorienting and grueling nature of this process. The same effect is created through the polyrhythmic effects of the melodic synthesizer parts that enter in the latter half of the song, along with the dissonant clusters heard in the string parts, first very subtly at the beginning of the piece, but sounding ever more sickly, during the repeated string slides toward the end of the song, where Greenwood impeccably exhibits the style and influence of Polish composer Krzysztof Penderecki.

The trapdoor opens once again, this time into "Treefingers," an instrumental, which was also used in Christopher Nolan's neo-noir psychological thriller film *Memento* (2000). We are returned to a predominantly electronic environment that removes any emphasis not only on Yorke but also on the personalities of the other band members as well. Apparently, what we hear is a slowed-down, transposed sample of O'Brien's guitar, whose overtones begin to separate and sound more like a chord than a single line melody. The "treefingers" conjure the treelike beings known as Ents in Tolkien's *Lord of the Rings* and would seem in this context to relate somehow to the Cotswolds, as well as to the Kosovo mountain ranges that inspired the album's cover art. While the piece provides an ambient and atmospheric sonic experience, there isn't any sense of threat or foreboding, although the soundscape certainly does create an overwhelming sense of strangeness in its complex harmony and lack of harmonic direction.

With the beginning of the next song, "Optimistic," we return to more of the hard rock musical setting we're accustomed to with Radiohead, and with the next four songs merged together, we enter a nonstop sonic stream that takes us to the album's final track. The main riff of the song, with its repeated movement from the tonic minor to the tonic major, articulates the constant struggle to remain optimistic within the cultural conditions reflected in the band's work, here portrayed as a kind of Hobbesian wasteland, with flies buzzing round the protagonist's head, "vultures circling the dead," and the big fish eating the little ones. The environment of self-interest is reflected, also, when the character sings of this situation, "not my problem, give me some." The second verse endows the song with a twisted, fairy-tale quality, primarily by way of its reference to the nursery rhyme "This Little Piggy," through its repeated verbal structure and the line "this one goes to market." Combined with the objects found on the back cover of the American version of the *Kid A* sleeve that James Doheny suggests look much like U.S. Air Force stealth fighters, when the character sings "this one dropped a payload," the work evokes the military-industrial complex, especially with the accompanying lines "fodder for the animals living on an animal farm." The reference to Orwell's 1945 book of the same name, *Animal Farm*, a pastiche of all the major modern political revolutions up to and including the Russian Revolution in 1917, likewise raises the specter of totalitarianism. The predatorial imagery is evident, too, when the character sings of "dinosaurs roaming the earth." According to Donwood in Paula Carson and Helen Walters's "Radiohead: Modified Organisms," "The dinosaurs roaming the earth are like these rapacious corporations storming over the planet and chewing it up," and Yorke recounted, as Doheny notes, "I can see the dinosaurs stepping over the mountains every time I sing that song . . . Monsters . . . Out of control monsters roaming the earth. All powerful, utterly invisible, wreaking destruction. Faceless. Nameless." In this regard, Yorke was to cite the noted journalist and author George Monbiot's book *Captive State: The Corporate Takeover of Britain* (2000) as a significant influence on the album. "A lot of the time, now, it would seem that the power doesn't reside with politicians. So much power has been given over to corporations," as O'Brien was to say as noted in Lin's *33 1/3 Kid A.* "I think a lot of people are finally waking up and realizing that we don't live in a democracy."

A week prior to the release of *Kid A*, protestors brought the IMF and World Bank summit in Prague to a halt on its final day, but it was in excess of a year prior to this, in June 1999, that Yorke, along with U2's Bono and Bob Geldof, went to Cologne on behalf of the organization Jubilee 2000 and its "Drop the Debt" campaign, which highlighted the crippling burden of debt faced by the developing world. Among other high-profile supporters of the organization were the fourteenth Dalai Lama and Pope John Paul II. Having its beginnings as an ecumenical organization, the group took its name from the biblical concept of the year of Jubilee. Found in Leviticus 25:8–55, the Jubilee Sabbath occurred every fifty years and consisted of freeing those enslaved by debt, returning lands that were lost because of debt, and thereby restoring community that had become torn by inequality.

In regard to his work for Jubilee 2000, Yorke explained that he was pleased to get involved with the group because it was an acceptable, mainstream face of resistance against corporate globalization. "But equally, I'm interested in the unacceptable face of it, the disruptive elements, the anarchists," he pointed out to Zoric of *Juice Magazine*, "because I don't really care what methods are used to make the IMF and World Bank so incredibly unpopular that they dismantle it. I don't really care how it happens, as long as it happens. That's the point." In this department, however, Yorke was also to say to Sylvia Patterson of *NME*, "I know some stuff about MI5 that would shit your . . . but I can't tell you. Cos they'll do it to me, too. Seriously. And I'm not winding you up, either. . . . Put it this way," he continued, "last year at the May Day protests, there were policemen with bulletproof jackets and machine guns, and a photographer with a bulletproof jacket, walking through the crowd taking photographs of all the main people and putting them on file. And that's all you need to know." Shortly after, Yorke was to include a "hidden message" on the "links" page of their website, which read: "RECKON I MAYBE DESERVE A FILE AT MI5 NOW TONY WHAT DO YOU THINK?"

While Yorke was in Cologne, there were simultaneous protests in London that had turned violent, and which the media, in their coverage, were lumping together with Jubilee 2000, as the singer was to protest in conversation with Patterson. "All these pretty respectable-looking, middle-class people in Cologne, tens of thousands of them, are being associated by the fucking BBC, even by Channel 4, as somehow part of this violence in the City Of London," he said. "Something that I thought was pretty cardigan-wearing and so on was actually turning out to be, as far as the mainstream media was concerned, unfortunate, radical and naive. And not one motherfucker among them talking about the issue of debt. Not one." Rather, all they had was a chintzy photo of the British prime minister, Tony Blair, shaking hands with Bono and Bob Geldof, and of course a caricature of Blair appears on one of the pages of the *Kid A* CD sleeve. As Yorke was to say to Fanning of *Hot Press*, "all the stuff going on behind the scenes, all the political wranglings, all the point scoring, being done by Blair and his cronies—it was mad," adding, "I'd never, ever seen the workings of the whole man. It just left me with total, complete, 100% contempt for the Labour Party, and Blair in particular." Observing that nothing appeared to change on account of their actions, Yorke was more hopeful the following year, given that UN secretary General Kofi Annan was, by then, also advocating for debt cancellation. Nevertheless, as Yorke was to point out, again in *Hot Press*, "still they ignore it. And it just totally does my head in, that the leaders of the G8 believe that they can do that. . . . I kinda saw the light in a certain way, but in another way it was incredibly disillusioning." In reference to coping with such disillusionment, Yorke's partner Rachel Owen was to inspire and provide the words for the chorus of "Optimistic," which is consistently accompanied by a hopeful and dynamic, ascending guitar line—"if you try the best you can, the best you can is good enough."

Over time, cities around the world were to become leery of hosting the international institutions, particularly due to the enormous costs associated with providing security for their meetings, and as a result of the significant property damage that often took place alongside the demonstrations. In this regard, during the July 2001 protests against the G8 in Genoa, as with some of the earlier events, it was common to see masked individuals hurling rocks and smashing cars. But the police responded using excessive force, leading to the injury of more than two hundred protesters and to the untimely death of a twenty-three-year-old man—to whom Yorke dedicated "Optimistic," during the band's Madison Square Garden performance the following month, because the young man had "tried the best he could."

"That's how it's always dismissed in the mainstream media," said Yorke to Simon Reynolds of *Wire* in July 2001, defending the global protest movement from accusations that it was reactive and ideologically incoherent—"but that's because it's this coalition of disparate interest groups who are all pissed off because they've been disenfranchised by politicians who are only listening to corporate lobby groups or unelected bodies like Davos [the World Economic Forum]." Referring to the reinvention of the political spectrum, and suggesting of our emerging technological theology, Yorke was to say of the movement, "It's not based on the old left/right politics, it's not really even an anti-capitalist thing. . . . It's something far deeper than that: 'Who do you serve?'"

Such demonstrations resulted from the broad-based coalition work of various organizations and individuals—a "network of networks," many of which being "directly or indirectly 'hyperlinked' to each other," their deficiency of means and central authority being remediated by the internet. According to a 2000 Canadian Security and Intelligence Service (CSIS) study by Peter Van Aelst and Stefaan Walgrave called "New Media, New Movements?" Canada's answer to the CIA, the new communication environment enabled such groups "to identify and publicize targets, solicit and encourage support, organize and communicate information and instructions, recruit, raise funds," and generally functioned "as a means of promoting their various individual and collective aims." In fact, it was the posting online of a leaked copy of the draft of the Multilateral Agreement on Investment (MAI) in February 1997 by Ralph Nader's group Public Citizen that sparked a successful and unprecedented worldwide campaign against the secretive agreement, and which also provided much of the momentum for the long string of demonstrations that were to ensue.[4] Speaking of the important links to information sources and organizations such as Jubilee 2000, Indymedia, and CorpWatch that were to be found on Radiohead's website, Yorke remarked to *NME* in "Thom for Peace, Love, and Understanding" at the end of 2001, "A quarter of a million people come through the site every month and maybe one or two will be curious and go and have a look. They don't have to believe it—who's saying we always believe it?—the point is just having access to other sources of information," recommending, "You're not gonna get the other side of the story most of the time."

During the song's last verse, the character sings, "I'd really like to help you man," presumably referring to the "nervous messed up marionette floating around on a prison ship." Evoking Coleridge's "Ancient Mariner," certain lines on the back page of the concealed booklet pertain: "Packt like sardines in a crush tin box / puppets on strings / invisible forces / speaking in a tongue / that dribbles and lashes / salivates in the ashes / of the gap in between you and me." With the initial line looking ahead to the first song on *Amnesiac*, the excerpt reflects the marionette imagery, as well as the difficulties in connecting with others that were cited during the album's introduction with "Everything in its Right Place."

As we segue from "Optimistic" through Yorke's inventive playing on the Fender Rhodes, we arrive "In Limbo" where this theme continues, as we reencounter the inability to connect. Indeed the issue is now our own, as it's highly difficult to hear the character, who sings, in the introduction, "I got a message I can't read, another message I can't read." As we're soon to learn, he's "lost at sea" (the song's original title), sustaining the nautical imagery found in "Optimistic," as does the song's opening line, a direct quote from the UK shipping forecast ("Lundy, Fastnet, and Irish Sea"). That the character is himself now in the Irish Sea also connects him to "How to Disappear Completely" and its protagonist, who floats out to sea down the River Liffey. Yorke was to give words to the song's oceanic, "disorientating, floaty feel [that] comes from this really peculiar place," which is reflected in the irregular rhythmic groupings found in each of the song's two alternating sections (4+2 and 5+3). A song whose lyrics refer directly to the trapdoors to which Yorke earlier referred, the protagonist finds himself spiraling down, suggesting to his addressee that there's "nowhere to hide," and thus creating a sense of apprehension for his listener. Though the character reassuringly sings, "I'm on your side," he appears to demonstrate inconstancy when he later adds, "don't bother me." We learn that he's lost his way, and these lines are sung over meandering arpeggios, the harmonic progression of which sounds directionless, with its narrow and dissonant chordal range. This section constitutes a different harmonic environment to the refrain, where the addressee is told, "You're living in a fantasy world—this beautiful world." Meanwhile, toward the end of the song as Brent Sirota so effectively articulates in "The Ministry of Information," "The vocals rise and morph into a pure white noise, as all the instruments phase into a singular turbine howl before dissipating into tremulous silence."

The silence is brief, however, as the trapdoor opens again into the driving and frantic environment of laptop electronics with "Idioteque." The song makes use of samples taken from two pieces by composers Paul Lansky and Arthur Kreiger that Jonny Greenwood procured from a 1976 album *First Recordings: Electronic Music Winners*. A French-inflected name that would appear to mean either just "idiotic," as a form of wordplay, or "idiot repository," "Idioteque" appears predominantly to be a critique of our collective inability to address climate change, an issue whose understanding has been as problematized by fossil fuel and agricultural interests, as the effects of smoking previously by the tobacco industry. The character's inconstancy returns, first singing "I've seen too much" and then, immediately following, "I haven't seen enough / You haven't seen enough," reflecting the difficulty for public decision making in the context of this potentially grave phenomenon, especially in a milieu where deliberate, ongoing, and commonplace attempts are made to feed people on "little white lies" (what was in part later to become better known as "fake news" or "alternative facts" during the Trump era). While the full page of statistics for glacier melt included as part of the U.S. CD sleeve evokes climate change, the protagonist sings, "Let me hear both sides," and "we're not scaremongering, this is really happening." One of the band's blipverts featured "an oil fire burning furiously on a freezing white glacier" (adding reference to his apparent command to "throw me in the fire"), and the lines "glaciated autoinferno / lovingly scraping the bottom of the oil barrel" appear in the recording's concealed booklet. The "ice age" imagery is portrayed on the *Kid A* album cover, and in a 2006 interview with the *Guardian*, Stanley Donwood was to point out the profound influence that a *Guardian* front-page photograph had on him when it appeared during the Kosovo War. "It was of a square metre of snow and it was full of the detritus of war, all military stuff and fag stains," he explained, noting again the personal profundity of this event for him: "I was upset by it in a way war had never upset me before. It felt like it was happening in my street."

Hence the character's frantic-sounding question "Who's in a bunker?" and the imperative to make room for "women and children first." Meanwhile, the image of scraping the bottom of the oil barrel seems to relate closely to the refrain, and its idea of living in a society where, "Here I'm allowed everything all of the time." Moreover, the mobiles are heard chirping not so much in the service of rescuing or protecting people but rather to "take the money and run." While the issues addressed are certainly serious, a childlike quality is again expressed in lines such as "I laugh until my head comes off" and "I swallow till I burst." But the protagonist appears to be ushering the youth toward their doom by the end of the song, where he's heard singing rhythmically in conflict with the rest of the performing forces, "The first of the children," which is heard quietly in the background, while the song transitions to "Morning Bell."

Though with different musical settings, "Morning Bell" has the distinction of being a song that appears on both *Kid A* and *Amnesiac*, thus significantly linking the albums. It too appears to allude to a nursery rhyme, this time "Frère Jacques" and its twice-repeated "morning bells are ringing." Although the English version refers to "Brother John," the repeated line "are you sleeping?" and the original French title seem to correspond to the character's decision to "sleepy Jack the firedrill." Appropriate to the original nursery rhyme's ritual environment of the monastery are the missives to "light another candle" and "release me," with the latter pointing ahead to the album's final song "Motion Picture Soundtrack." The "round and round and round and round and round" endows the track with a sense of childish play, and considerable resolution occurs when the shift between the two unrelated minor chords is followed by the repeated shifts between two major ones. The overall tenor of the piece, however, is minor, and among the practically inaudible lines heard toward the end of the song is "nobody wants to be a slave," a lyric complemented by another from the concealed booklet that reads, "For Christmas I got you a prepacked newborn slave to serve your every need." When considering the rest of the lyrics, it's hard not to draw the conclusion that they describe a break-in by criminals, in order to kidnap and sell the kids, either for slavery or for food, the latter suggested by the character disturbingly singing, "cut the kids in half," and by the following lines from the concealed booklet: "The innocenty have been used to thicken the soupy / the soupy can be used to feed the troopys from tin cans / honey from the honey bears / nervous messed up marionettes / food is food." Yorke was to describe the song as "extremely violent," and in yet another sense, it again points ahead to the final track, with its inaudible line toward the end, "the lights are on but nobody's home."

In "Motion Picture Soundtrack," the last and oldest song on the album, hailing from the early 1990s in fact, this translates into the more tentative "I think you're crazy, maybe," a remark that the protagonist directs toward an apparently estranged romantic partner. The song has an overall sense of sadness, which the addition of harp glissandos in the second verse doesn't serve to alter, nor does the singer's admonishment to cease sending letters that always end up being "burned." "It's not like the movies," he sings; "they fed us on little white lies," referencing the propaganda complex of which Hollywood and even Disney, of course, form significant parts. "I love the sound of harps, the atmosphere we were trying to get was one of Disney films of the 50s where the colour fades slightly," Jonny Greenwood remarked on BBC Radio 3's *Mixing It* in January 2001. "I think one of the regular introductions included the fairy spinning around—a Blue Jay—and the sparks coming from behind. It was all a bit faded and watery—that was the kind of music we wanted to copy." For Yorke's part, the song particularly reminded him of "Zip-a-Dee-Do-Dah" from Disney's *Song of the South*.

Returning to the focus on death, the religious connotations of the harmonium, the harp, and eventually the angelic, choral-sounding voices of the ondes martenot mark the beginning of his release, as he sings, "I will see you in the next life." In this regard, it's worth referring to Yorke's suggestion that we don't collectively spend much time addressing death and other weighty topics: "If you're accused of being morbid or bleak, then you're onto a good thing," he suggested to *NME* in "Thom for Peace, Love, and Understanding." "Cos our culture is the most fucking desperate culture, desperately trying to avoid anything vaguely depressing, which is alarming. We're at a time when we are being presented with undeniable changes in the global climate and fundamental issues that affect every single one of us," he continued, "and it's the time we're listening to the most hokey shite on the radio and watching vacuous bullshit celebrities being vacuous bullshit celebrities and desperately trying to forget about everything. Which is fine, you know, but personally speaking, I can't do that."

AMNESIAC

"Since I started drawing little weeping minotaurs I've been trying to find the maze," Donwood writes in *Dead Children Playing*. "Hours of study and several journeys to famous mazes have ultimately led me here; to London. London is the labyrinth, the miz-maze, the original troy town. My 1911 guidebook takes me all over the city, seeking markers and signifiers." Donwood's curious use of this historical artifact no doubt relates to the line "history is dying" from the *Kid A* concealed booklet, and if history is conceived of as "collective memory," part of the significance of the *Amnesiac* title begins to become apparent. Cultures like our own, in this respect, think of history as "recorded history," in contrast to low-technology cultures, which preserve their history orally, because they have neither invented a system of writing nor borrowed one from another culture. Such cultures continue to exist in the world, though are generally remote and dwindling, and their history and collective wisdom is preserved only in their poetic songs and aphorisms. That is, their history is ultimately only preserved in their minds to the extent that these are both taught to the young and reproduced by them. If they forget these songs and aphorisms, they forget their history.

Writing, on the other hand, is a technology by which we extend our memory, so it can be not only preserved but also shared with others, and when the writing of Europeans was committed to print, beginning in the fifteenth century, it allowed their extended memory to be mass produced as never before. Consequently, it vastly facilitated the development and sharing of knowledge, in all areas, leading eventually to the eighteenth-century Enlightenment—the so-called Age of Reason, during which our modern democratic societies were also brought into being. The subsequent emergence and development of electronic modes of communication, however, beginning in the nineteenth century with the telegraph, ended the printed word's four centuries of uncontested monopoly in communications—simultaneously ushering in what some refer to as the postliterate age. The most common and enduring of these technologies in our contemporary experience, the telephone, the sound recording, radio, "talkie" movies, and television, are oral/aural in nature; that is, we process their spoken languaging *acoustically*. And after more than a century and a half of exposure to the electronic mode of information shaping and movement, such experience now predominantly forms the sensibilities of the young. Some have thus suggested that we in the present day are therefore oriented more toward the tendencies of an oral rather than a literate culture, particularly as these forms have largely come to monopolize our perceptual activity to the considerable detriment of reading. We should recognize, however, that truly widespread advanced literacy didn't exist in Western countries until the expansion of access to higher education following World War II, and so it's noteworthy how Donwood includes the observation that his 1911 guidebook contains "mostly monosyllabic words."

That the Radiohead band members value literacy is apparent in the plentiful allusions to literature in their work and in Yorke's constant references during interviews to books he's recently read. Indeed, when Radiohead toured in 1993 with the band Belly, the two groups held a book party at the end of the tour. "Everyone in our band bought books for everyone in their band, and they all bought books for us," according to Belly guitarist Tanya Donelly in 1995, as recorded in Randall's *Exit Music*. "Someone gave me *Geek Love*, which is a great book. [Belly guitarist] Tom [Gorman] and Ed [O'Brien] still mail books to each other." We could also refer again to the book on the cover of *Amnesiac*, for which the band's special limited edition actually came in the form of a red book, which contained references on library slips and date stamps to Ray Bradbury's classic and prescient 1953 novel *Fahrenheit 451*, a work the group also referred to with visuals during their performances in support of the album. In *Fahrenheit 451*, the job of "firemen" is to set fires, not put them out—specifically, to burn books and the cultural life they contain. As Bradbury clarified in 2007 in Amy E. Boyle Johnston's "Ray Bradbury," the book is not about government censorship, and nor was it a response to the witch-hunts that Senator Joseph McCarthy was busily conducting at the time of its writing. Rather, the science-fiction author was to suggest it's "a story about how television destroys interest in reading literature." Of course, the computer retrieves all previous media forms, including television, and nowadays many of us do considerable reading on our various devices; but whether this development can at all emulate the type of literacy associated with centuries of newspaper and book reading is the million-dollar question, and one whose answer may largely depend on what we do with it.

Also in question, especially given the constant change in formats, is how successful we'll be in preserving our digital information as, according to recent reports, much scientific data produced in the 1990s is no longer available. In this respect, in conjunction with the release of *Amnesiac*, the new media department at Capitol Records, working with a digital technology start-up called Active Buddy, launched GooglyMinotaur, which was to be active only for the following ten months. This was an automated online interactive agent that Radiohead fans, predominantly those who were also AOL, Yahoo, or MSN users, could add to their instant-messaging friends and chat with, just as they would their friends or family. The "chatbot" specialized of course in questions about Radiohead and functioned as the primary means of diffusing the group's digital promotional content.

Continuity is established between *Kid A* and *Amnesiac* through the inclusion of various images of patented modified organisms on the latter's booklet, while one particular image of the weeping minotaur aligns him with us—the comic-book-style thought caption illustrates him imagining a hostile bear. "The figure of the weeping minotaur, a cursed monster condemned to live and die in a subterranean labyrinth, is my guide," writes Donwood in *Dead Children Playing*. "All I want to do is make representations of the walls that imprisoned the minotaur, the child of Queen Pasiphae and the white bull, gift of Poseidon. . . . I want to make the walls of the maze, to daub and scratch the frustrations of the monster in the cage." As Donwood was to put it to Evan Pricco in *Juxtapoz*, in terms of what the artwork for *Amnesiac* is all about, the weeping minotaur is intended to be representative of everyone: "London as an imaginary prison, a place where you can walk around and you are the Minotaur of London, we are all the monsters, we are all half human half beast. We are trapped in this maze of this past."

"*Amnesiac* is packaged like a closed book," according to Yorke, who, echoing Donwood's pilgrimage above, goes on to say to Kent in 2001, "we had this whole thing about [its] being like getting into someone's attic, opening the chest and finding their notes from a journey that they'd been on. There's a story but no literal plot, so you have to keep picking out fragments. You know something really important has happened to this person that's ended up completely changing them but you're never told exactly what it is." Elsewhere, Yorke suggests that the notes also include "maps and drawings and descriptions of going to a place you cannot remember," and, as Donwood was elsewhere to add, "visually and musically the album is about finding the book and opening the pages."

These pages begin, of course, with "Packt Like Sardines in a Crushd Tin Box." As Doheny observes in *Radiohead: Karma Police*, the song opens with the sound of a gently modulated Indian water drum, which conjures the spiritual heritage of India. So do the song's lyrics, whose singer intones to his addressee, "After years of waiting nothing came," something only realized "as your life flashed before your eyes" and as you discovered that you've been "looking in the wrong place." The song is about the "road rage psycho from Hell," its title bringing to mind *Kid A*'s "National Anthem" and particularly Yorke's image of the congested traffic mob just about to "spark off." In response to the mob, however, and perhaps also having in mind past charges of "scaremongering," the protagonist recommends, "I'm a reasonable man get off my case." He then aligns himself with his addressee against someone else, singing, "You're a reasonable man get off our case." Fittingly, given the numerous repetitions of these lines, as Yorke has said, "Most of the stuff on *Amnesiac* is about being trapped in one particular lock in your heart or your head." And apart from the water drum and the backward electric guitar heard in the middle of the song, we are back to the realm of laptop electronics, much in the manner of Kraftwerk. Combined with Yorke's vocal, the nasal effect of which is achieved using autotuner, this evokes a sense of dehumanization, particularly with the audio allusion to *Animal Farm* toward the end of the song, where the sounds of bleating sheep are heard.

"Pyramid Song," in contrast, is about rehumanization, as indicated by its use of acoustic piano and strings. Originally known variously as "Nothing to Fear" and "Egyptian Song," the piece was written after Yorke spent a day looking at Egyptian figurines in a museum. "The Egyptians have these rowboats that when they die they go through the Milky Way in," Yorke was to say of the song. "It was based on that and a fusion of experiences that I had dreamed. . . . I was reading the Tibetan Book of the Dead too," which "freaked the living crap out of me." Apparently, Mingus also influenced "Pyramid Song," with Yorke suggesting as Doheny records that the song "is me being totally obsessed with . . . 'Freedom.'. . . I was just trying to duplicate that really," adding, as well, that the first version of the song even included handclaps. Mingus's "Freedom" was adopted as a symbol of black suffering, and thus the song also evokes the plight of Moses and the Israelites in Egypt, while its opening line "what did I see?" seems to hearken to the celebrated Afro-American spiritual "Swing Low Sweet Chariot."

Amnesiac's title was purportedly inspired by a passage that Yorke was to read in a book about gnosticism. "I read that the gnostics believe when we are born we are forced to forget where we have come from in order to deal with the trauma of arriving in this life," he pointed out in *NME*'s "Bright Yorke." "I thought this was really fascinating. It's like the river of forgetfulness," his reference suggesting that this is likely the river we encounter in "Pyramid Song." Elsewhere, he was to say of the title, "It's about . . . the things you forget. And remembering." When he sings of the black-eyed angels that swam with him, it thus brings to mind the angelic choir simulated by the ondes martenot in the second chorus of "Motion Picture Soundtrack," where the protagonist sings of seeing his addressee "in the next life." Here, with all his lovers past and present in tow, he sings, "And we all went to heaven in a little row boat," a line probably taken from Tom Waits's "Clap Hands," which itself quotes the 1960s American soul singer Shirley Ellis's "Clapping

Song," which in turn took its words from a 1930s song titled "Little Rubber Dolly."

Apparently buttressed by a traditional narrative, the protagonist sings that "there was nothing to fear and nothing to doubt." Describing some of what he'd understood from Stephen Hawking's celebrated 1988 book *A Brief History of Time*, which outlines the cyclical nature of Hawking's topic, Yorke was to say on *VHS* in July 2001, "It's always doing this °spins finger around in circles°. It's just a factor like gravity. And it's something that I've found, sort of, in Buddhism too." And he added, "It's not a desperate attempt to avoid death. . . . It's not a desperate attempt to avoid life passing you by . . . getting old, all that sort of stuff. That's all just bollocks. It's great. It's just this really beautiful thing that's just going 'round and 'round."

Although this could easily describe the hypnotic and circular chord progression of "Pyramid Song," it could equally do the same for the next track, "Pulk/Pull Revolving Doors," a piece composed using a Roland MC-505 groovebox that consists largely of loops that sound like they're moving in circles. In *Radiohead: The Complete Guide to Their Music*, Paytress refers to the piece as some kind of sonic claustrophobia, not least of which because of the strange vocals being again articulated through autotuner. The song is about doors and, among others, "there are barn doors" in relation to the *Animal Farm*, "doors on the rudders of big ships" hearkening back to the second half of *Kid A*, and "trap-doors that you can't come back from." Also noted by Paytress, the song, according to Yorke, derived from a scene from *Alice in Wonderland*, "where she walks down the corridor and there are lots of different doors. And I was in that corridor, mentally, for six months. Every door I opened, [I] was like dreading opening it, 'cos I didn't know what was gonna happen next."

The next page of the *Amnesiac* book opens to "You and Whose Army," a song whose style conjures the work of World War II vocal groups such as the Ink Spots, apparently a Greenwood family favorite. In their effort to re-create this style, the band ran Yorke's voice through the speaker of the ondes martenot, while also using an egg box to cover his microphone, and since they were recording live off the floor, all the track's instrumentation is heard through this microphone as well. The protagonist and his entourage take on British prime minister Tony Blair and his cronies, "Tony's cronies" being a formulation in common usage by the UK media at the time. The character taunts Blair, and the reference to the Holy Roman Empire conjures wording found in the *Amnesiac* booklet that reads "THE DECLINE AND FALL OF THE ROMAN EMPIRE." Also the title of a book by the English historian Edward Gibbon, the phrase is superimposed on an aerial vision of a contemporary city, suggesting the idea of an impending collapse of the American empire. As Yorke was to articulate to Fanning of *Hot Press*,

> The song's ultimately about someone who is elected into power by people and who then blatantly betrays them—just like Blair did. At the same time, I think he couldn't help betraying this country. I think the man's a fool. He's just a product of his time, like any important public figure. I've become slightly more charitable toward him of late. Anyone who's put into that position just immediately becomes like all the people surrounding him. He can't help it—that's just who he is. So it's never been a personal thing. When we put that image of Blair in the *Kid A* booklet, it was just us saying, "He's just a public figure. He's fallen from grace and he's useless like everybody else." The problem with Blair is that he's surrounded by all this other stuff that will end up destroying anything worthwhile he as a human being might want to achieve. That's why I call him "a fool," because a fool is just someone who plays to the court; he's a court jester, in other words, and that's all he is.

Regardless, toward the end, the minor tonality of the piece transitions to the major, and the song's conclusion is heard as a kind of rallying cry (particularly with the dramatic entries of drums and piano). Meanwhile, the "ghost horses" upon which they ride invoke a kind of mythical cavalry of apparitions joining the cause.

Appropriately, of the next song "I Might Be Wrong," Yorke was to say, thus, as Doheny records, "It's a document of a complete crisis point, basically. I live on a beach and one night I went on my own and looked back at the house and even though I knew there was nobody there, I could see a figure walking about inside." Yorke then returned to the house and recorded the track "with this presence still there." Though allowing that he might be wrong, the protagonist sings, "I could have sworn I saw a light coming on," and talks about having in the past considered that there wasn't really any kind of future. But the song, according to Yorke, represents an overall more positive engagement, as noted in Baker's *Thom Yorke: Radiohead and Trading Solo*: "The song really comes as much from what my long-term partner Rachel was saying to me, like she does all the time, 'Be proud of what you've done. Don't look back and just carry on like nothing's happened. Just let the bad stuff go.'" As the singer continued, "When someone's constantly trying to help you out and you're trying to express something really awful, you're desperately trying to sort yourself out and you can't—you just can't. And then one day you finally hear them, you finally understand, after months and months of utter fucking torment: that's what that song is about." Fittingly, therefore, the song's narrator sings to his addressee, "What would I do if I did not have you?"

Returning us to the theme of violence, we move from this fragment to the imagery behind "Knives Out," which Yorke was to introduce as "a song about cannibalism" and which begins a sequence that returns us to the twisted fairy-tale character of *Kid A*. The overall tonality of the piece is minor and, in combination with some of its dissonant harmonies, creates a general sense of unease. This, of course, is heightened by the desperate scene painted of individuals being reduced to eating mice for their survival, along with the apparently treacherous conditions indicated by the warning "don't look down." The song is about abandonment, and Yorke was to say to Patterson that it's in part the idea of the businessman leaving his wife and kids and never coming back. "It's also the thousand yard stare when you look at someone close to you and you know they're gonna die," he submitted. "It's like a shadow over them, or the way they look straight through you. The shine goes out of their eyes."

Accordingly, *Amnesiac*'s next page opens upon a reprise from *Kid A* of "Morning Bell/Amnesiac," which again concludes with the threatening instruction to "cut the kids in half." As Yorke was to say of the piece in this context, "It sounds like a recurring dream," and we should note that it represents the first explicit reference to the "children" that we hear on *Amnesiac*. Constituting the album's title track, its inclusion here points to the centrality of the ideas that the major consequences of our forgetting the past are handed over to our children and that *this* is the most profound thing we've collectively forgotten.

Set not like the *Kid A* version in 5/4 but instead in 4/4 time, its twisted nursery rhyme character is accentuated, in part since it has been considerably slowed down and because its dark flavor is reinforced by its minor key and sinister fairground-like instrumental connotations. *Kid A* is dedicated to Phil Selway's first son Leo, and *Amnesiac* is dedicated to Noah and Jamie (Yorke's first son and Selway's second). While also recalling the concerns about climate change expressed on the previous record, it's relevant to consider comments that the singer was to make as part of an interview to promote the environmental organization Friends of the Earth: "You wake up in the middle of the night thinking about it. You look into the eyes of your children and hope that they don't grow up in a future that has riots for fuel or constant floods and infrastructure collapse." As the song fades out, the protagonist repeatedly sings "release me," and this is heard, as the song's four-chord harmonic sequence retires its first two haunting minor changes, perpetually by way of the fade-out of the song, in order to repeat the second progression, which satisfyingly alternates between two major chords. Again, as Yorke was to say to Patterson of *NME* of both *Kid A* and *Amnesiac*, in this regard, "There's an unhealthy obsession with death going on, and also the absolute opposite of hopeless."

Recalling Donwood's comment that he wanted to draw the walls of the weeping minotaur's London labyrinth and capture the frustrations of the monster in its cage, his description invokes the violent London protests that occurred in conjunction with the G8 meeting in Cologne. This event is likewise conjured by the following track, "Dollars and Cents," some of whose words, under the label "corporate strategic marketing initiative," were included in episode 15 of Donwood and Dr. Tchock's online cartoon strip *Modified Organisms*. The image of a mutant bear in suit and tie, with a dollar sign pictured above his head, includes the caption "The bears begin to use a hidden code of symbols and numbers implanted in news items on CNN . . . International Bizniz Hotel Channel." Moreover, playing on the City's historic role as the planet's financial capital, available on the band's website were pages titled "SOUTHSEABUBBLE" and "INVESTMENT OPPORTUNITIES," which contained slight variations of the following text:

> we are the dollars¢s£the pounds$the pence&were gonna crush you little skulls. witless helpless eurokids you will learn eventually. all one big happy village complete with slaves. look after the pennies and fuk evrybody else. be constrictive in your analysis. we want none of your cnspircy shit here. quiet down. why dont you quiet down $$$$$$££££££££££££££££££££££?

Many of these lyrics that address the "eurokids" found their way into "Dollars and Cents," reflecting the authoritarian "high priests of globalization" and crass self-interested materialism encountered earlier in *Kid A*'s "Optimistic." Bemoaning how the world was run by "a bunch of old miserable motherfucking economists," in this respect, Yorke was to articulate to Patterson,

> I read some journalist recently lecturing the anti-globalisation lobby, saying, "This is the way capitalism works, all capitalism is exploitation and to make it try and do something else, it's never gonna happen." And it's like, yeah, but where does that leave us? This is somehow God's will? All this? It's God's will that we sit in traffic? It's God's will that millions of people are gonna die this year because of some outmoded economic policies? No, it's not! It's like some deranged sacrificial altar, the high priests of the global economy holding up these millions of children each year, like (Arms aloft) "We wish to please you! Oh Gods of free trade!" It's like . . . give us all a fucking break!

The voice or perspective within "Dollars and Cents" is unstable and shifts. But the positive sense established in the introduction indicates that the song begins with the perspective of those interested in the global "pro-democracy movement." Among "the weapons" to be used—being "constructive with your blues"—inherent in the song is how it moves for its entire duration in a blues style, back and forth between a tonic minor and major chord. This connotes an inability to break out of the labyrinth, but judging from the website excerpt above, we're hearing the voice of globalization's "high priests" when we hear, "Why don't you quiet down?" Responding to this directive, discernible in the background vocals, are "maybe I want peace and honesty," "I want to live in the promised land and maybe wander the children's land," and "there we can [be] free." This perspective continues to sing about our goals being won "in a liberal world, living in times when I could stand it," but then announces, "all over the planet's dead . . . so let me out of here." Taking the website excerpt again as our guide, it would appear the high-priest technocrats return at the end, simultaneously singing "quiet down" while declaring that "we are the dollars and cents" and "we're gonna crack your little souls."

When in 2001 Nick Kent told Yorke in *Mojo* that he couldn't make sense of the song's words, the singer explained, "The lyrics are gibberish but they come out of ideas I've been fighting with for ages about how people are basically just pixels on a screen, unknowingly serving this higher power which is manipulative and destructive, but we're power-less because we can't name it." In the tradition of Christian doctrine, the individual is warned of money's spiritual snares, along with the incompatibility between serving Mammon and God, and it's worth not-ing, too, that not only did Christianity once forbid the practice of usury but so did Judaism and Islam. Clearly, Yorke has sought to raise aware-ness of money's role as debt within the international political sphere, and referring to the involvement of mass media systems in the multina-tional consolidation of the banking interests, he was to observe to Adam Rivera that "we live under a world banking system and media that make it almost irrelevant who is in power." In this relation, significantly, the powerful European banker Anselm Rothschild is purported to have said, "Give me the power to issue a nation's money, then I do not care who makes the laws."[5]

In its acknowledged homage to Alice Coltrane's 1970 album *Journey in Satchidananda*, "Dollars and Cents" is characterized by its shared bluesy and meditative Indian religious flavor, a description that can perhaps be said to apply just as well for the next instrumental piece, "Hunting Bears." Referencing the American children's folk song "We're Going on a Bear Hunt," as indicated by the scrawling of the song's refrain, "I'm not scared," on the concealed *Kid A* booklet and in *Dead Children Playing*, the piece consists of an overdriven electric guitar, accompanied by reinforcing computer bass parts. True to form, there are no fearful moments communicated during the course of the bear hunt. Rather, such moments are reserved for the lyrical imagery of the unique and next-to-last track "Like Spinning Plates," where the protag-onist is "cut to shreds" and fed to the lions as part of the ongoing sacrificial activity of the high priests, who meanwhile, along with Tony Blair and his cronies, "make pretty speeches." The piece was composed by playing backward another song they'd been working on called "I Will," which wasn't to see release until the band's next album *Hail to the Thief*. Yorke wrote new words for the backward melody and sang it against the throbbing and ominous keyboard soundscape: "I sang each line. Then they cut it up [via computer program], and spun every word backwards, and pasted it back together," the singer was to say as noted in *Exit Music*. "Then you got an entire line in reverse, but with the words in the correct order. And then I spent a couple of hours singing along to my own singing in reverse, until I could copy that weird reverse singing pretty well. And then I sung the reverse bit myself," he continued, "which sounds ghostly, like speaking in tongues during some religious African ritual as if a ghost speaks through me." The song alludes to the "crazy maybe" of "Motion Picture Soundtrack," in its references to "living in Cloud Cuckoo land" and to "Pyramid Song" and the River Liffey, with his body "floating down the muddy river." It notes the amnesiac's remembrance, as well as forgetting, and the expression "spinning plates" is similar to the idea of a juggler having many balls in the air—hence, the protagonist's sung reference to "a delicate balance."

But as Yorke was sagely to articulate some years later to Brian Draper, just ahead of "the great recession" of 2008, and in reference to the contemporary idolatry to which he earlier referred,

> For the most part in the West we worship a certain type of economics, which is like worshipping a false god. It's like the Incas sacrificing children to try to get immortal life: politicians are willing to sacrifice the well-being of the people in their country in order to fit into this economic straitjacket which doesn't actually benefit anyone. . . . It's a theory about economics which will collapse, and the sooner people realise that, the quicker they will be able to understand how we should be engaging with the world around us. Hopefully they will realise it before it collapses. To me, it's like spinning plates: I'm not sure how long we can keep this trick going.

Employing the "spinning plates" expression here, it was to become clear to everyone in a few more years that the trick was not to be kept up for much longer.

In this regard, the New Orleans funereal quality of the album's final track, "Life in a Glass House," is thus appropriate and was achieved with the assistance of legendary British trad jazz trumpeter Humphrey Lyttelton and his Dixieland band, whom Colin Greenwood had booked at his Cambridge University college back in the day. As Yorke was to say of the song, as Doheny records in *Radiohead: Karma Police*, "It began after I read this interview with the wife of a very famous actor who the tabloids completely hounded for three months like dogs from hell."

Referencing the first verse specifically, he said, "She got copies of all the papers with her picture and she pasted them up all over the house, over all the windows so that all the cameras that were outside on her lawn only had their own images to photograph. . . . I thought that was brilliant." Starting as "a complete rant" on the subject of tabloid journalism, Yorke was to observe that such activity "seems to be particularly rife in this country [the UK]."

The second verse, with its imagery of being "packed like frozen food and battery hens," conjures both "Packt Like Sardines in a Crushd Tin Box" and "The National Anthem." It also brings to mind Yorke's experience with Jubilee 2000, in its reference to "the starving millions," its imperative to "don't talk politics and don't throw stones," and in addressing its priestly listeners as "your royal highnesses." The chorus then expresses the protagonist's interest in continuing to communicate with his addressees, but he claims he can't because "someone's listening in." This both reflects lines from the concealed *Kid A* booklet, including "Zoom lens in the trees" and "CCTV in every room," and what Donwood records in *Dead Children Playing* as the experience of he and his hastily assembled film crew nearly being "arrested by the City of London's private police force (having been surveilled by CCTV since we began filming)."

But the song possessed considerable foresight in pointing to the much larger sphere of increasing state surveillance. For instance, Canadians learned in their privacy commissioner's 1999–2000 annual report that they should be concerned about the existence of a de facto citizen profile compiled by the government's ministry of "Human Resources" and known as the "Longitudinal Labour Force File." Purportedly dismantled shortly afterward, this database compiled approximately 2,000 pieces of information on each of the nation's citizens. Americans learned in the middle of the year 2000 that the FBI had been using internet eavesdropping tools to track criminals. Originally known as Carnivore, in early 2001 these tools were refashioned DCS1000 for "digital collection service." Also in 2001, French intelligence accused American secret agents of working with computer giant Microsoft in order to develop international spy software. And the following month, the week before the 9/11 attacks in the United States, the European Parliament confirmed rumors about an American-led automated global interception and relay system operated by the intelligence services of the major Anglophone powers—the United States, the United Kingdom, Canada, Australia, and New Zealand. Known as "Echelon," later it was to become more colloquially known as the "Five Eyes."

Half a year earlier, a senior British official in the European Commission's cipher unit had fueled concerns with his claim that this superior technology meant there was little Europe could do to prevent interception of its most sensitive electronic satellite-bounced communications, email, phone, or fax, unless it was constantly to encrypt them. Such concerns increased considerably following the 9/11 attacks, especially after the passing of the U.S. Patriot Act (2001) and with the rise of suggestions that nation-states should employ compulsory national ID cards, equipped with a citizen's photo and thumbprint digitally embedded in the card. Such cards are to be used in conjunction with databases, alongside biometrical technology—including fingerprint matching, iris or retinal scanning, and face recognition—the existence of which was first brought to public attention in 2001, when it was used, unbeknownst to those in attendance, to scan the sea of assembled faces at the Super Bowl. These technologies are now used to scan the fingerprints and irises of all foreign visitors to the United States, and while such techniques are capable of identifying people at airport security checks, thereby increasing safety, it seems quite obvious that they could just as easily be used illegitimately to track people's movements.

Yorke's previous claim that the Bible provides him no spiritual enlightenment or inspiration must be considered suspect when one considers the last verse of "Living in a Glass House," which even employs direct allusion to the words of Christ. Conjuring the Racak incident in Kosovo, the CIA's red swimming pools, and the crowded traffic conditions with people about to "spark off," the verse points out that "we are hungry for a lynching" but acknowledges that this is "a strange mistake to make." Drawing on the old adage that "those who live in glass houses shouldn't throw stones," the song makes reference to the spirit of self-criticism that the Judeo-Christian perspective introduced into Western history. And since we have assimilated the substance of the Bible far beyond what we can comprehend, this spirit is frequently mistaken as the inheritance not of culture but of some type of natural dispensation.

As an aspect of apocalypse, I've noted that violence is prevalent in Radiohead's work. For instance, among the phrases on the special liner notes found beneath the CD jewel case of *Kid A*, one can find "this is the sound of boots crushing hands"; "in the bunker sitting ducks, do we look like the enemy to you"; and "responsibilities of power, the terrible terrible strain it must make on your every waking hour, on your playstation trigger finger." In this regard, we might also refer to the "we got heads on sticks" in the lyrics of "Kid A," in addition to the command to "cut the kids in half" found in "Morning Bell/Amnesiac." We should also recall the flash animation feature on the Radiohead website for *Amnesiac*, where we were invited to torture the weeping minotaur with our mouse by moving a pitchfork over him, an action that made him cry and moan, as the line plotted between the anger and revenge axes of the accompanying graph increased.

Of course, in this relation, and in response to the 9/11 attacks in 2001, the United States and its allies were to invade Afghanistan. Two months after the initial invasion and six months after the release of *Amnesiac*, in a Christmas message to fans posted on the website of Radiohead's official subsidiary W.A.S.T.E., and reprinted in *NME*'s "Thom for Peace, Love, and Understanding," Yorke very effectively illustrated the nature of conflict and the need for the International Criminal Court, whose adoption the United States had just rejected under George W. Bush:

> Violence breeds violence. We need a world court not a Republican with his hands covered in oil and military hardware lecturing us on world security. We need love and understanding and tolerance and good laws that apply to everyone, upheld by those who are in a position to judge. . . . Praying for world peace is not such an embarrassing thing to do anymore I think, especially not this Christmas. . . . Thank you everybody on w.a.s.t.e. for still listening and sticking with us and understanding the records we make, I hope your Christmas is peaceful and loving and spiritual. Does that sound silly? Don't care.

7

CREEPING TOTALITARIANISM (2002–2003)

In a 2002 interview with the *New Yorker* noted in Mac Randall's *Exit Music*, Nigel Godrich was to say of the band's conflicts surrounding the *Kid A* and *Amnesiac* sessions that they were redundant "because the band ultimately kept doing what it has always done—zigzagging between extremes. . . . All the drama was just a form of procrastination. Next time . . . three weeks, and we're out." With this in mind, Radiohead remained out of the public eye for the first half of 2002, though early in the year, Thom Yorke sent around demo recordings of new material for the rest of the group. They then spent about three months rehearsing the songs before taking them out for a test run on a two-week tour of Spain and Portugal that July, performing multiple shows in five different cities. Immediately following this, the band flew to Los Angeles for two weeks, again at Godrich's insistence, where they were to begin recording their final album for EMI at Hollywood's Ocean Way Studio, where the Beach Boys had, too, once recorded. The band succeeded in more or less recording one song per day, after which they returned to their own Oxfordshire studio for a few further weeks of recording that was to take them into the fall. That October, Yorke performed two solo sets for Neil Young's annual Bridge School Benefit for children with disabilities, at which a personal highlight was being able to perform Young's "After the Gold Rush" on the very piano used on the original recording.

Though leaked on the internet in advance again, Radiohead's sixth album *Hail to the Thief* was released in June 2003, where it debuted at number one in the UK and a number of other countries, and at number three in the United States. Its appearance coincided with that of *True Love Waits*, classical pianist Christopher O'Reilly's arrangement and rendition of Radiohead songs for solo piano. A month prior, the band released the first of three UK singles, "There There (Boney King of Nowhere)," which reached number four, matching their previous best showing with "No Surprises." Their next single, "Go to Sleep (Little Man Being Erased)," was released in August and reached a high of number twelve, while the band's last single, "2 + 2 = 5 (The Lukewarm)," was to emerge in November, spending only one week on the chart, where it peaked at number fifteen. Among new B sides were the songs "Gagging Order," "I Am a Wicked Child," "Paperbag Writer," "Where Bluebirds Fly," "I Am Citizen Insane," and a reworking of "Fog." During California's Coachella Valley Music and Arts Festival in May, planes flew overhead, trailing *Hail to the Thief* banners. Meanwhile, in June, the album was officially launched in North America with a concert performance at the Beacon Theatre in Manhattan that was simulcast across Canada and the United States at IMAX movie theaters.

That month, the band also debuted Radiohead Television, which was accessed through their website, a particularly impressive move, given that YouTube wasn't to see its launch for another two years. For promoting the new album, the band and their creative partners created four half-hour episodes of a series called *The Most Gigantic Lying Mouth of All Time*. From the German artist John Heartfield's anti-Nazi photo collage, the title conjures previous instances of being fed on "little white lies." Prior to its release as a DVD at the end of 2004, the episodes ran on continuous loop throughout 2003 and much of the following year, featuring content solicited from fans and studio performances by the band. Among other amusing highlights are the series' shadowy, twitching, computer-generated host Chieftain Mews; some mock band interviews regarding their celebrity (for which the sound of their voices is humorously manipulated); and the opening credits and theme song. Accompanying their smiling faces, the music resembles "Spanish Flea" by Herb Alpert and the Tijuana Brass, which provided the "Bachelor's theme" for the long-running television show *The Dating Game*. Over the latter six months of 2003, the band was to perform in fifteen countries, including their October performance at the Brooklyn Academy of Music for the premiere of *Split Sides*, a new work by celebrated choreographer Merce Cunningham. The lifelong partner of composer John Cage, Cunningham had asked the group to provide the soundtrack for his work while they were in the midst of recording *Hail to the Thief.*

Radiohead also ramped up its activism in 2003. In April, for instance, Phil Selway ran in the London Marathon to raise money for the Samaritans. June, meanwhile, saw the band back the Trade Justice Movement's "Scale Up for Trade Justice." This was a national action campaign to lobby all UK MPs in their local constituencies, and Ed O'Brien observed prior to the event, as reported by Mark Davies of the BBC, "Our politicians have failed to grasp what harm this government is doing by pushing for more and more free trade—without taking into consideration its effect on poor people and the environment. We want to make sure every MP gets a clear message that British voters want the rules on international trade rewritten to make world trade work for the whole world." Meanwhile, in a *Guardian* op-ed piece titled "Losing the Faith," published in September, Yorke was to consider a number of related issues. With regard to the West, he wrote, "It has reneged on its agreement to cut subsidies to its own farmers, and rules on intellectual property rights mean drugs are too expensive and 30,000 people die every day as a direct consequence. When developing countries export to the west they have to pay tariffs four times that between western countries themselves, costing £63bn per year," he added. "Western governments, as they increasingly lose their grip on the reality of the situation, see the key to fixing these problems (that they have helped to create) to be . . . more liberalisation." As he was effectively and succinctly to summarize the situation, "The west is creating an extremely dangerous economic, environmental and humanitarian timebomb."

That November, Yorke also did a combined interview with Howard Zinn on the topic of politics and art, which was published in *Resonance Magazine.* And recalling Yorke's suggestion that the election of George W. Bush would "radicalize" people, activists in the global movement who'd flocked in 2001 to Genoa to participate in the demonstrations began to question, in their aftermath, whether peaceful protests had become a thing of the past. And then, of course, two months later, the September 11 attacks in the United States were to occur—events that radicalized many Americans in a much more powerful way but rather in terms of supporting the Bush administration in a jingoistic type of groupthink, which it was then to harness in its launching of the war in Afghanistan. During its subsequent preparation for the 2003 invasion of Iraq, Yorke participated in antiwar demonstrations in Los Angeles and San Francisco, and he told *Rolling Stone* magazine's David Fricke how much more dangerous a place Bush and Blair had made the world. "In choosing to subvert the United Nations, to go around it, to treat it with complete contempt, we're entering a state of anarchy," Yorke remarked. "When two of the most powerful nations on Earth choose to go above international law, that's saying, 'Whoever has the most weapons is in charge now.' We've entered that phase, and that should have been taken into account. . . . In flouting international law, you set the most dangerous precedent. It's insane." Observing the dangerously unbalanced state of Iraq and the concurrent clandestine activities of Al Qaeda, Fricke asked Yorke what the opposing vocal minority ought to do now—a question to which Yorke replied,

> It's not a minority. And I don't have the answers. But the thing that keeps me awake at night is that my particular government is not answerable to the population. A majority of British people were not into this war, yet it still occurred, and it didn't matter what we said. . . . It is the theater of the absurd. It's certainly not democracy. And in your country, fear of speaking out, of using your constitutional right to speak out—that is not democratic. If one is supposed to be fighting for one's freedom, how come people are more scared now than they've ever been?

With regard to democracy in the United States meanwhile, O'Brien agreed with American film producer Saul Zaentz's remark that America is now a country governed by the few for the few. "And the trouble is," as O'Brien added in conversation with Jane Stevenson of the *Toronto Sun*, "that those few have, at present, such a strong influence upon what goes on in the rest of the world, vis-a-vis money. It's very frightening." Yorke was next to lead a protest in November, in opposition to the UK visit of George W. Bush. Regarding the coalition's failure to find any weapons of mass destruction in Iraq—the pretense for the assault— Yorke said of Bush and Tony Blair in *NME*'s "Thom Yorke Leads Protest Over Bush Visit" in November 2003 that both men were liars: "We have the right to call them such, they are putting our children's future in jeopardy. They are not controlling the terrorist threat, they are escalating it," as was to be evidenced over a decade later with the rise to prominence of the Islamic State of Iraq and Syria (ISIS).

HAIL TO THE THIEF

Of course *Hail to the Thief* is not only Radiohead's first post-9/11 album but also the first work to be composed following the controversial election of George W. Bush in late 2000. When asked by David Fricke in "Bitter Prophet: Thom Yorke on 'Hail to the Thief'" when he'd first heard the phrase that was to give the album its title, Yorke said, "It was a formative moment—one evening on the radio, way before we were doing the record. The BBC was running stories about how the Florida vote had been rigged and how Bush was being called a thief. That line threw a switch in my head." Continuing, he said, "I couldn't get away from it. And the light—I was driving that evening with the radio on—was particularly weird. I had this tremendous feeling of foreboding, quite indescribable, really. To me, all the feelings on the record stem from that moment." In Washington, Bush was greeted on the day of his inauguration by thousands of protesters with placards, many of whom were shouting, "Hail to the thief, our commander in chief." In another instance, Yorke suggested that "religious maniac bigots" had stolen the election, and he was further to add, as Trevor Baker in *Thom Yorke: Radiohead and Trading Solo* records, "The most powerful country in the world is run by someone who stole an election. Now that's bad. That's bad for everybody. Especially as he was bought the election by extremely powerful companies with lots of money." On the other hand, as we saw earlier, when asked about the title a few weeks later by interviewer Chuck Klosterman, Yorke was to say, demonstrating the emerging post-911 zeitgeist, "The trouble with your question—and we both know this—is that if I discuss the details of what I'm referring to in *Spin* magazine, I will get death threats. And I'm frankly not willing to get death threats. And that sort of sucks, I realize, but I know what is going on out there."

Remembering Yorke's comment about the fires on the covers of *Kid A* and *Amnesiac*, by the time we get to *Hail to the Thief*, the fires have been and gone, as evidenced by the charred and smoking ruins of the forests it portrays on its own cover. The artwork was largely inspired by

Los Angeles, where Stanley Donwood had accompanied the group during the recording of the album. Of the "city of angels"—"scaled for private motor vehicles"—he was to write, unflatteringly, in *Dead Children Playing*, "Part of the massive scale of this particular version of hell on Earth involves the many advertising materials employed along the multilane highways that dissect this place." Being driven around the city, and taking pages of notes regarding the similarly massive advertising messages, Donwood began to observe that 90 percent of them were made up of only seven colors, "all made from plastic, all made from pigments derived from the petrochemical industry," the industry that defined the city in some ways and that Donwood was to support in employing solely those colors in painting the album's artwork. "[A] sort of homage to The War on Terror," and treating the canvas like real estate, Donwood painted maps of city districts within Grozny, Kabul, London, and Baghdad, in addition to Los Angeles. Yorke told *Q* magazine that the world media's coverage of the Middle East conflict also influenced the album, with the band calling the limited-edition fold-out poster "the roadmap," referring to the Bush administration's 2003 plan for peace between the Israelis and Palestinians.

The recording begins following the sounds of Jonny Greenwood plugging in his guitar, and Yorke is heard to comment, "That's a nice way to start, Jonny." Presumably a deliberate reference to the foregrounding of electric guitar, his comments suggest that the gesture communicates even more, namely, a return to a different type of aesthetic approach. "The last two studio records [*Kid A* and *Amnesiac*] were a real headache," Yorke exclaimed in an interview with MTV's Jon Wiederhorn, just after *Hail to the Thief*'s aforementioned simulcast performance. "We had spent so much time looking at computers and grids, we were like, 'That's enough. We can't do that anymore.' This time, we used computers," he continued, "but they had to actually be in the room with all the gear. So everything was about performance, like staging a play."

Hail to the Thief is the first recording since *OK Computer* for which the lyrics are included, though Yorke employed a similar Dadaist technique in their composition to that used for the group's previous two albums. "I was cutting these things out, and deliberately taking them out of context, so they're like wallpaper," the singer suggested to John Robinson of *NME*, adding, "when I needed words for songs I'd be taking them out of this wallpaper, and they were out of any political context at all." To David Fricke in "Bitter Prophet: Thom Yorke on 'Hail to the Thief,'" he was to put it differently, suggesting that this involved "writing down little nonsense phrases, those Orwellian euphemisms that our government and yours are so fond of. They became the background of the record. The emotional context of those words had been taken away. What I was doing was stealing it back." While many lyrical snippets can also be found on the album's cover art, Yorke was also to point out that several of the songs make reference to children's fables and stories, including *Chicken Licken* and *Bagpuss*, both iconic figures from Yorke's own childhood. The latter he attempted to interest his newborn son in, to no avail, but ended up rewatching all thirteen episodes himself. Unsurprisingly, thus again the theme of childhood runs through the album's lyrics and titles.

Every track on *Hail to the Thief* features a bracketed subtitle, as does the album itself, which is subtitled "The Gloaming." From the Middle English meaning "twilight," this formulation is likewise the primary name of the recording's eighth song and was at one time intended to be the album's main title, only to be jettisoned for sounding too "prog rock." As Yorke was to explain on the Capitol records web page,

> It refers to a general all-enveloping darkness that's slowly taking over mankind: like some plague from the middle ages that seems to be on the horizon again. In the middle ages, everyone was obsessed by people who were "possessed." The same thing is happening now. The same sense of a malignant force ripping apart civilisation. Then toward the end of the record I read a Murakami book called *Wind-Up Bird Chronicles* and it all fell into place in my head. That's what I was trying to say about the darkness that envelops people. They don't know it's happening to them and they think they're doing the right thing but the rise of fascism and ignorance are what they're really calling into play. And that to me is the real "thief." The thief is someone who takes possession of one's soul in order to inhabit their body. And with the few politicians I've encountered personally, I've always got the sense that there's fuck-all going on behind their exteriors. If I met Blair, I wouldn't say anything. I'd just sit and watch him. I'd sit and watch his mouth move and see the air flying around.

The above image of "soul thieves" Yorke derived from Dante, and he was further to explain of this imagery, "Certain people have done things that are so bad that they're still here but their souls have gone. I don't know about you but I've met people like that." Clearly no longer feeling quite so charitable toward either "Tony and his cronies" or the other politicians he'd confronted to that point, Yorke said with regard to reservations about experiencing potential backlash in the United States, "If we got into a situation where people start burning our records, then bring it on. That's the whole point. The gloaming has begun. We're in the darkness." And he then added, directly connecting *Hail to the Thief* to the primary concerns of *Amnesiac*, "This has happened before. Go read some history."

In addition to drawing upon George Orwell's *1984* for the title "2 + 2 = 5," with its allusions to totalitarian thought control, Yorke explains the origin of its bracketed alternate title (The Lukewarm), which has an indirect connection to the vision of the Christian afterlife, as per its culmination in the worldview of the European Middle Ages: "The lukewarm, is something from Dante . . . it's the least nasty bit of hell, just as you walk through the door there're the 'Lukewarm.' And the lukewarm hang around and they were never really bothered about, they didn't believe in anything particularly," Yorke suggests to John Kennedy of XFM Uploaded. "They were like, 'Oh, you know, whatever, there's nothing I can do about it. No, no, no.' And it's quite a curious thing that Dante presents you with. All of a sudden you have these people and you think, 'Well, they haven't really done anything wrong, they just didn't do anything,'" he continues. "And so he judges them and puts them there which, I think, is actually a really good way of explaining '2 + 2 = 5.'" Yorke's comment is reminiscent of the aforementioned quote attributed to Dante, which circulates within activist circles and posits, "The hottest seats in Hell are reserved for those who in times of great moral crisis choose to do nothing." This is clearly not the first time that the band has satirized people's general political ignorance, apathy, or passivity, recalling "No Surprises" and the lines I earlier noted from the *Kid A* concealed booklet—"responsibilities of power, the terrible terrible strain it must make on your every waking hour, on your playstation trigger finger." "One of the things Thom's singing about is whether or not you choose to deal with what's happening," Jonny Greenwood remarked on Capitol's website; on an even more basic level, he said, "There are a lot of lines about escaping and avoiding issues, about keeping your head down and waiting. Everybody feels like that from time to time as much as they feel frustration about things they can't change."

A sense of the gloaming is established immediately with the song's minor key, melodic and harmonic dissonances, and imbalanced 7/4 meter. The initial voice appears to be that of the lukewarm, opting to remain comfortably in the realm of "2 + 2 = 5." Of the person who seeks "to put the world to rights," the lukewarm suggest that the individual is but "a dreamer." The second verse, with its "January has April showers," seems to portray the lukewarm protecting themselves from natural events like flooding, without an understanding of the circumstances surrounding global climate change. At the end of the second verse, there appears a shift in perspective, however, signaled by the transition to a different musical section in 4/4 time and by the use of block capitalized lyrics. These announce in reply to the lukewarm that they will be lost to hell, because "IT'S THE DEVIL'S WAY NOW" and "YOU HAVE NOT BEEN PAYING ATTENTION." The last section of the song again introduces new musical material, and the lyrics appear to belong to the king himself, specifically to Bush, whose line "I swat em like flies but like flies the buggers keep coming back" alludes to the president's words, as reported by national security advisor Condoleezza Rice in the London *Times* of London in April 2004: "He made clear to us that he did not want to respond to al-Qaeda one attack at a time. He told me he was 'tired of swatting flies.'" The character denies being a thief and resists being put on trial, singing, "Don't question my authority or put me in the dock." The last line, however, would appear to revert to the voice that earlier lambasted the lukewarm, and now sings, in reference to the children's fable known in North America as *Chicken Little* and, variously, elsewhere as *Chicken Licken* or *Henny Penny*, "Go and tell the king that the sky is falling in when it's not, maybe not." Following these words in the lyric sheet is "ahh diddums," something that people say to indicate they feel no sympathy for someone who behaves like a child.

In relation to versions of the fable that have the fox devouring the other animals before they can speak with the king, Yorke was to say, as Mark Paytress records in *Radiohead: The Complete Guide to Their Music,* "I love that idea of there being no intention of a happy ending." At other times, though, such fables feature different endings that make light of paranoid, hysterical, or mistaken beliefs that catastrophe is imminent. Orwell's *1984* addresses this phenomenon in relation to its main protagonist Winston: "He wondered, as he had many times wondered before, whether he himself was a lunatic. Perhaps a lunatic was simply a minority of one. At one time it had been a sign of madness to believe that the earth goes round the sun; today, to believe that the past is inalterable. He might be *alone* in holding that belief, and if alone, then a lunatic." As Orwell adds, however, "The thought of being a lunatic did not greatly trouble him: the horror was that he might also be wrong."

In this light, *Hail to the Thief's* second track, "Sit Down. Stand Up (Snakes and Ladders)," is among the oldest on the album, and its bracketed subtitle was another that was early on also bandied about for the name of the album. Purportedly written while Yorke was attending to news reports of the 1994 Rwandan genocide, the song even quotes the Anglican Church's *Book of Common Prayer*, instructing the listener to "walk into the jaws of hell." To the accompaniment of its gloomy xylophone, piano, and drum machine, the authoritarian character orders his addressees to "sit down" and "stand up," and demonstrates a remarkable type of totalitarian power: "I always think of the 'we can wipe you out any time' line," Yorke was to remark in James Doheny's *Radiohead: Karma Police*, explaining how people were now able to be targeted by armed drones on the strength of their mobile signal. "Then they wipe someone out on the basis of that, that's what I always think of," also adding "be careful what you say." After its gradual thickening of texture through the addition of instruments, a kind of mass attack takes place toward the end of the song, when the tempo of the drum machine is significantly increased and "THE RAINDROPS" is repeated forty-six times in the vocals, invoking an environment where targeted missiles are soon to be heard, dropping down like "raindrops" on the unsuspecting target.

Following this intense sonic assault, we're transferred to the gentle musical scene of "Sail to the Moon (Brush the Cobwebs Out of the Sky)," whose subtitle derives from episode twelve of *Bagpuss*, and its theme song about the woman who brushes the cobwebs out of the sky. Written as he was awaiting the birth of his son Noah, Yorke was to refer to it as "a hopeful song" and was later to articulate, as Doheny notes, "Having a son has made me very concerned about the future, and about how things in the world are being steered supposedly in my name." With the acoustic piano prominently laying down its basis, the song acquires an air of intimacy. And alongside its numerous time changes, exotic harmonic directions, and lyrical imagery, the song presents an unraveling journey of discovery that will soon become that of Noah. As Yorke sings, "Maybe you'll be president but know right from wrong," or alternatively, like his biblical namesake, "in the flood you'll build an ark and sail us to the moon." With the piano's increasing upper range, and the song's receding and dreamy harmonic content at the end, the listener is transported off into space, an experience that the electronic sound effect also helps to achieve.

But we are soon brought back within the earth's orbit, and the electronic sound effect connects it to the next track, the almost exclusively electronic "Backdrifters (Honeymoon Is Over)." The basis of the song was established as a sampled loop of sound on a QY70 machine during a situation in Japan, in which the band members were traveling to a performance on a bullet train and eventually got stuck in an automobile-deep drift of snow that obstructed their way. Throughout, the song moves from "backdrifters" to "backsliding" and "backtracking," and appropriately, along with the descriptive phrases "rotten fruit" and "damaged goods," the song's subtitle was routinely directed at the Blair government, for proving to be a disappointment to so many, so soon in its mandate. This is reflected throughout the piece, with its narrow, claustrophobic harmonic range and in the song's chorus, where Yorke sings, "You fell into our arms, we tried, but there was nothing we could do." Accordingly, the narrator makes the suggestion that "one gust and we will probably crumble." Equally, however, as Yorke was to maintain, "all the way through the record, there is this sense of trying to understand how one human being can make a decision and affect thousands of other people's lives." The narrative perspective within the song thus shifts and observes that "all evidence has been buried" and "all tapes have been erased," in order to protect an administration perceived as "backtracking"; its "footsteps" ultimately, however, give it away. As Yorke was to summarize effectively to John Kennedy in 2003, the song makes reference to the "slide backwards that's happening everywhere you look. There was a time when everybody sort of felt like maybe the world was progressing, and maybe we were getting better at understanding other people and ignorance; there was a higher level of tolerance and compassion and so on." But then, "suddenly, someone literally flicked the switch, and the light went on, and everyone just scurried for the dark."

The prominent place given the acoustic guitar at the beginning of the next track, "Go to Sleep (Little Man Being Erased)," along with the song's general "West Coast feel," represents a shift in subject position. This shift is toward the little men "being erased," "the rag and bone man" and his advocates, and more close to home perhaps, "someone's son and someone's daughter." "Something big is gonna happen," we hear, in conjunction with the refrain, "over my dead body," which, by being separated by quotation marks in the sleeve, appears to indicate a contrasting perspective. The second verse alludes to *Gulliver's Travels*, with Yorke singing, "We don't want to wake the monster" and "we don't want the loonies taking over," the solution being to "tiptoe round" and "tie them down." In the previous song, the character Tony and his cronies were "so full of sleep," and the little men here are trying to encourage the same of both "the monster" and "the loonies."

The special effects in the guitar solo at the end were processed through a digital patch for musical software called Max/MSP, commonly used among experimental and electronica artists. "We're starting to play with computers and write stuff for them, that does things like that," as Jonny Greenwood was to say at the *Hail to the Thief* release party regarding the special effects in the second verse. "So it's like, we're still using computers, but we're getting rid of other people's programs, in a way, and building really wonky kind of broken pieces of software like that one, that makes that noise and then crashes a computer." "Little Man Being Erased" was apparently also the name of an animation that Stanley Donwood created, which Yorke had suggested would find its way to Radiohead's website, though it's unclear whether it ever did so.

With "Where I End and You Begin (The Sky Is Falling In)," we are again reminded of *Chicken Little* and "2 + 2 = 5 (The Lukewarm)." The song's opening lyrics likewise connect us to *Kid A* and its liner notes, which refer to "the gap between you and me," as does its reference to "the dinosaurs roam the earth," which recalls the song "Optimistic." The protagonist evidently feels "sorry for us" and, after a barely audible and fragmentary "count-up," finds himself "up in the clouds." In this relation, Yorke suggests to John Kennedy that he seems to have experienced a kind of temporary schizoid breakdown, which is outlined in the song's third verse. "I went through a phase where I couldn't actually, where I couldn't get back into my head," he explained. "I'd walk around and I'd be, I could sort of see myself from above. It's not much fun, I tell you." Invoking again the cannibal imagery from *Amnesiac* and the "little white lies" of the songs "Kid A" and "Motion Picture Sound-track," the protagonist sings toward the end, "I will eat you alive" and "there'll be no more lies."

This ethic is sustained in "We Suck Young Blood (Your Time Is Up)." While the song is meant to be "funny" and an example of "vaude-ville," the shift from the previous song's tonic major to the present context's tonic minor reveals also its "sick and perverse" quality, to highlight Yorke's own words. Appropriately, given the location at which they recorded the album as the singer said to John Kennedy, "it's all very tied up with Hollywood . . . and . . . you know the constant desire to stay young . . . fleece people, suck their energy, corporations, corporate 'media groups' love to do that, blah blah blah." Noting how sex is a form of Hollywood currency, Yorke pointed out that there is also "a sex thing" about the song. "We did this thing where we're putting up these ads that go 'Hungry? Sick? Begging for a break? Ring this number,'" York remarked, speaking about the album's promotion. "Someone I heard on the radio completely missed the point. Or maybe they didn't. They kind of thought we were running some kind of Radiohead talent show." As he was further to note, jokingly, "It's called 'Your Time Is Up,' simply to take the piss out of the fact that we're basically old gits now, and that we need to suck young blood to keep young!"

The minor tonal coloring of the piece, combined with its very slow tempo and collective clapping, gives it the character of what Yorke refers to as a "slave-ship tune" and conjures, overall, a kind of demonic-sounding ritual environment. As Yorke was to observe to Kennedy again, accordingly, "There's a malignant quality to it, a dark force de-vouring everything in its path. It's an expression of that desperate urge to be somebody at any cost, even if it means being preyed on and sucked dry by every scheming parasite in the world." Continuing, he maintained, "You find examples of this in the music industry and the porn industry, but it could just as easily relate to the way the extreme right seduce young people to enlist in their ranks," pointing out as well that "fascism starts with the embittered 50 year old sadomasochist who finds dysfunctional teenagers who he then works on for a couple of years until they become transformed into homicidal little skinhead mo-therfuckers."

With the arrival of the laptop sonic environment of the album's eighth track, "The Gloaming (Softly Open Our Mouths in the Cold)," we experience the dread and unease of our cultural twilight. Its unsettling sounds and rhythms were apparently assembled not with a computer but with pieces of tape or "tape loops." With the entry of his plaintive melody we experience what Yorke identifies as "the tension between what's human and what's coming from the machines," his voice exemplifying the former here. With the Afghan invasion in 2001, he sings that the genie is now "let out of the bottle" and that "the witching hour" has arrived. Singing, "we are not the same as you," the protagonist differentiates himself and his associates from his addressees, who are "murderers." Some years later in 2013, Yorke was to refer when speaking with Phil Fisk of the *Guardian* to the Blair years in relation to these lines: "We are still the generation who went into an illegal war. And the guy who took us there is giving lectures around the world and sitting in his lovely house with an armed guard. Every time I sing those words, I think of him sitting there. Thinking, what the fuck, how did we let him get away with that?"

In relation to individuals who experience "no alarms and no surprises," the song chillingly ends with "your alarm bells should be ringing," followed by the declaration that this is the gloaming. "It's about the rise of Fascism, intolerance, bigotry, and fear, and all the things that keep a population down, keep a population in their place," Yorke was to say to Kennedy, adding, "When things get sticky the economy starts to go pear-shaped, what do we do? 'Ooh, need some scapegoats, I know, let's do this.' So they open the bottle," he continues, "they find some scapegoats, they let the genie out of the bottle and the next thing they know, they have . . . a state of terror, fear, and the rise of the right, and they all need to be put back in the bottle as far as I'm concerned. They're very, very dangerous people."

The album next finds its way to "There There (The Boney King of Nowhere)," which Yorke was to describe as paying homage to Cans' album *Tago Mago*. Its subtitle references a song from another episode of *Bagpuss*, and the band was to enquire with the series' creator Oliver Postgate about making the song's video, an invitation that was to be declined. The song, with its dark minor tonality, chronicles a treacherous journey through forests and rock-laden oceans, complete with the notorious mythical siren, "singing you to shipwreck." Like Orwell's main character Winston, having to entertain the prospect that you "might be wrong," with regard to some apparently calamitous state of affairs, the protagonist, set to the bright major flavor of the song's chorus, reassuringly affirms, "Just 'cause you feel it, doesn't mean it's there." With this nevertheless horrifying announcement, the protagonist, singing "There there," continues attempting to comfort his addressee.

In the final section of the song, acknowledging that "heaven sent you to me," the protagonist asks of his listener, "Why so green and lonely?" But it's not necessary to hear the addressee's response since moments later he adds, reminding us of our emerging global state of affairs, "We are accidents waiting to happen." This, of course, includes the implications of a stolen presidency and brings us back to George W. Bush, "the boney king of nowhere." According to Yorke, Bush's namesake is "a pipecleaner king with a boney arse who moans about the hardness and coldness of his throne" and who is unable comfortably to sit down. "He's the king, but he's very boney," Yorke again suggested to Kennedy. "And he keeps sitting down on his stone throne, and it's too cold, and he just doesn't feel comfortable. And he's this new king but he just can't get comfortable in his throne. And so eventually they find him a little cushion for him to sit on, and I thought that was very appropriate."

The next hymn-like piece, "I Will (No Man's Land)," creates a much different effect, consisting of guitar accompaniment, with lead and background vocals. Suggesting that "the whole record is about thinly veiled anger," Yorke also said at the time that this may be the angriest song he's ever written. Originally the source of *Amnesiac*'s innovative "Like Spinning Plates," the minor key sets the tone for the protagonist, who sings, "I will lay me down in a bunker underground." The song was written in response to what was to become known as the Amiriyah shelter massacre, which occurred during the first Gulf War on February 13, 1991. "I had an extremely unhealthy obsession that ran through the *Kid A* thing, about the first Gulf War," Yorke was to tell Kennedy. "They did that lovely thing of putting the camera at the end of the missile and you got to see the wonders of modern military technology, blow up this bunker. And then sometime afterwards in the back pages it was announced that that bunker was not full of weapons at all, but women and children." He went on to say, "It was actually a bomb shelter. And so we all got to witness the wonders of modern technology.

And it ran through so much stuff for so long for me. I just could not get it out of my head. It was so sick. That's where the anger comes from."

As the protagonist sings, "I won't let this happen to my children," and with the end of the song, he expresses hope and resolve with the lines "I will rise up, little babies' eyes." Jonny Greenwood was to say in this respect, as Randall's *Exit Music* notes, "The parts of the record that I really respond to are the sound of Thom shrugging his shoulders and saying, 'I'm gonna go home and look after my family and make sure I've got enough food for my family when it all kicks off.'" No doubt this is one of those moments, but as Yorke was to elaborate in Doheny's *Radiohead: Karma Police*, "Someone fucks with my family. I'm gonna kill them." Prior to the album's release there was the buildup to the 2003 invasion of Iraq, and as noted, Yorke participated in antiwar demonstrations in San Francisco and Los Angeles, and spoke at an antiwar rally in England. When asked by David Fricke in 2003 how much of the Iraq War he'd seen on television, Yorke responded by rebuking the medium. "I didn't watch any of it," he pointed out. "I'm not into cowboys and Indians. I find it deeply offensive. I listened to the radio. Watching those reporters get so terribly excited instead of having something useful to do with themselves—I found it the most sickening fucking thing I'd seen on TV."

The next song, "A Punchup at a Wedding (No No No No No No No No)," has a rather different flavor, and much of its lyrics came out of Yorke's listening religiously to BBC Radio 4 every day for a period of six months. He likened most news reporting to "a punchup at a wedding," where no one typically knows what's happening, even in the midst of some kind of riot, though people's lives can easily be utterly ruined by how it's reported. According to the song's protagonist, "I was there and it wasn't like that," but for people such as these, "nothing's ever good enough," and they "had to piss on our parade." Yorke had a particular incident in mind, in fact, explaining it as the reason he no longer reads anything written about the band.

The specific instance was a review of Radiohead's 2001 homecoming Oxford gig, which Yorke was to describe as the biggest day of all the band members' lives. The review, however, tore the event to shreds, with the reviewer focusing not on the band but on the audience, falsely suggesting that they were a bunch of white, middle-class students. Finding that the reviewer had forever ruined that day for him, regrettably, he suggested that the incident had taught him a lesson. Neverthe-less, he still didn't understand why someone would want to write off an event that had so much meaning for most of the people who attended, and who saw something completely different.

Quiet, repeated synthesizer figures enter toward the four-minutes mark and are the last things heard before listeners are startled by the loud, overpowering, and even "scary"-sounding synthesizer keyboards that dominate the scene of "Myxomatosis (Judge, Jury, and Execution-er)." Also the name of a poem by Philip Larkin, and even mentioned in Douglas Adams's *Hitchhiker's Guide to the Galaxy*, myxomatosis is a viral disease that affects rabbits and was introduced into the UK in 1953. It was used as a method of population control, apparently initially decimating almost 90 percent of the population. In continuity with ref-erences to the feline character Bagpuss throughout *Hail to the Thief*, the song's narrator sings, "The mongrel cat came home, holding half a head." However, after having his way with some romantic interest, the "mongrel cat" apparently contracts myxomatosis (notwithstanding that the condition doesn't in reality affect other species).

As evidenced in the lines "But it got edited, fucked up" and "used as a photo in *Time* magazine," Yorke likewise powerfully employs the dis-ease metaphor to represent a kind of paranoid illness that haunts the narrator due to the disparities between media-reported reality and that of his personal experience. "The song is actually about mind control," Yorke was to tell Chuck Klosterman. "I'm sure you've experienced situ-ations where you've had your ideas edited or rewritten when they didn't conveniently fit into somebody else's agenda. And then, when someone asks you about those ideas later—you can't even argue with them, be-cause now your idea exists in that edited form." Yorke points out that the Jubilee 2000 experience in Cologne and London was just such an experience. "And 'Myxomatosis' was really sort of born out of . . . this idea . . . 'I was there, and no, it wasn't like that.' But yet . . . I must be ill, because what I saw and what was reported was a totally different thing." Part of the event's being written up so poorly was that the media gener-ally ignored the fact that protestors were presenting the signatures of millions of people. "It just stuck with me how utterly powerless people are to really represent what goes on, if other people elsewhere see fit." Recalling once again being fed on "little white lies," Yorke was further to explain, "If they see a nicer and more convenient story to be written another way, they can write off the wishes of millions of people in a split second at editorial decision, which I feel is immoral." It's also the reason that the protagonist of "Myxomatosis" feels "tongue tied" and "so skinned alive" (words that had previously appeared in the song "Cuttooth").

Regarding the line "My thoughts are misguided and a little naive," Yorke was to offer Klosterman the following: "That's the snarly look you get from an expert when they accuse you of being a conspiracy theorist. In America, they still use the 'conspiracy theorist' accusation as the ultimate condemnation." In this respect, Yorke reported that he'd been reading Gore Vidal's book *Dreaming War* and noted how Vidal was routinely thus accused. "But the evidence he uses is very similar to the evidence used by a lot of well-respected British historians. Yet they still call him crazy," he said. "To me, that's part of what 'Myxomatosis' is about—it's about wishing that all the people who tell you that you're crazy were actually right. That would make life so much easier."

That they may have a point, however, appears to be the case, as we find ourselves submerged in the soft and reassuring sounds of "Scatterbrain (Dead Leaves)." For all intents and purposes, and despite its musical accompaniment, the song begins with a description of storm conditions, apparently Yorke's undisputed favorite type of weather. The song is meant, in part, he suggests, to be a celebration of that kind of storm. Yet, as he adds, it's also a very lonely song. And as all the album cover artwork demonstrates, one of the negative effects of the metaphorical storm in which we find ourselves is that of information overload, where "yesterday's headlines, blown by the wind" make it impossible to remain aware of what is happening in the public sphere, whether it's reported accurately or not. Perhaps more in relation to advertising specifically, the protagonist also sings of being "a moving target in a firing range" and, ultimately, that "yesterday's people end up SCATTER-BRAIN." In this regard, the closing lines of the song appear either to express a desire to be "somewhere I'm not Scatterbrain" or to address the problem with a "lightning fuse, power cut" by having the rug pulled out from behind our electronic communications. As Jonny Greenwood was keenly to point out, the song offers no sense of resolution, cadencing in a different key from that in which it began.

The album's fairy-tale aspect continues into its final track, "Wolf at the Door (It Girl. Rag Doll.)," a fearful image drawn from the *Three*

Little Pigs and invoked for "waking you up at the end to something not pleasant." As Yorke was to say of the album to the *Toronto Star*, in June 2003, "I desperately tried not to write anything political, anything expressing the deep, profound terror I'm living with day to day. But it's just fucking there, and eventually you have to give it up and let it happen." Among the foremost disturbing things, of course, is climate change, and reinforcing his emphasis on considering what we're leaving for the coming generation of youth, the singer was to point out, as Baker records, "My son really loves wildlife and draws polar bears, and every time he draws a polar bear, I want to tell him they probably won't be there by the time he's my age." Likewise, clearly the creeping totalitarianism that the album documents is of profound concern, and Yorke was disturbingly to summarize, as Paytress records in *Radiohead: The Complete Guide to Their Music*, "I see politics, in terms of controlling one's own life, being removed permanently."

Accordingly, with its rap-style verses, "Wolf at the Door (It Girl. Rag Doll.)" is partly an expression of anger, which also contains considerable violent imagery directed toward politicians. The "flan in the face" specifically refers to an incident where Clare Short, a Labour Party MP and the secretary of state for international development under the Blair administration, received a custard pie in the face, during an antiglobalization protest, an act apparently perpetrated by one of Yorke's friends. When the protagonist sings "dance you fucker," one envisages a gangster humiliating his victim before dispatching her, while tauntingly asking, "Are you on the list?" Most of the anger, however, is directed at male politicians, with their "cold wives and mistresses," and the phrase "Stepford wives" makes reference to Ira Levin's 1972 satirical thriller novel of the same name that also provided the basis for a couple of film versions of the work, in which gorgeous housewives are portrayed as submissively fawning after their husbands. This also relates to the song's subtitle "It Girl," an early twentieth-century formulation that was used to describe a beautiful and stylish young upper-class woman who possesses sex appeal without flaunting her sexuality. The reference to "investments and dealers," meanwhile, relates to the "city boys in first class" who "don't know we're born." And of the mess they made, illustrating their sense of privilege, they "just know someone else is gonna come and clean it up" as someone "always does"—someone "born and raised for the job."

The chorus indicates the protagonist's attempt to "keep the wolf from the door." But the wolf, instead, calls him by phone to alert him to the variety of ways he can be harmed, including by the threat of stealing his children if he doesn't pay the ransom, and whom he'll never see again "if he squeals to the cops." Yorke apparently had a specific incident in mind: "It's kind of blackmail. . . . I had a gagging order served on me, indirectly, at one point, over something, which I obviously can't tell you about," he remarked to Kennedy. "But I have to say, gagging orders are the most unpleasant legal inventions known to man. They are sick, they are bad news . . . it amazes me that if one lives under democracy . . . you can basically be gagged, and when you're gagged, you're gagged, that's it."

Hail to the Thief was an album that, because recorded over such a short duration of time, left the band not entirely satisfied with its work. In this relation, Yorke was later to say, "I wish [I'd] had another go at that one." And some years later, in 2013, Nigel Godrich was also retrospectively to articulate to Lucy Jones at *NME*, "I think there's some great moments on there—but too many songs. I think that's kind of agreed amongst the camp these days but at the time it was just what happened." Godrich spoke of the charm the recording nevertheless has for him because of its lack of editing: "But personally it's probably my least favourite of all the albums. . . . It didn't really have its own direction. It was almost like a homogeny of previous work." As he was to conclude, however, "maybe that's its strength."

8

GOING SOLO

Goodbye EMI, Hello "Pay What You Want"
(2004–2008)

Among initial performances in support of *Hail to the Thief* was a concert at the first ever Field Day music festival held at New York Giants' stadium, which Radiohead coheadlined with the Beastie Boys and which also featured the bands Blur and Underground. Following this, they launched a tour that visited fifteen countries overall, with performances concluding in Japan and Australia in April 2004, followed by a final concert the next month at the Coachella Festival. The band did no further work together for the rest of that year, however, and their activity declined even more so into 2005, in part because Nigel Godrich's services had become ever more in demand after the reception of his 2004 Grammy for *Hail to the Thief* in the category of Producer of the Year.

In 2003, Jonny Greenwood had become the first band member to put out solo work in the form of his almost guitar-free soundtrack for the Simon Pummell documentary film *Bodysong*, which Parlophone released that October. The next year he was selected as composer in residence for the BBC Concert Orchestra, a post he would hold until 2012. Miscellaneous instrumental compositions followed up this appointment, and his second film project was released at the end of 2007, the orchestral soundtrack for Paul Thomas Anderson's dramatic film *There Will Be Blood*. In April 2004, meanwhile, the band released *Com*

Lag (*2plus2isfive*), a compilation of *Hail to the Thief* B sides and remixes featuring a live version of "2 + 2 = 5." Toward the end of the year, Greenwood and Thom Yorke joined others, including Paul McCartney, Dido, Chris Martin, and Bono, in rerecording the 1984 charity song "Do They Know It's Christmas?" on behalf of the Darfur region of Sudan.

In March 2005, backed by the Nazareth Orchestra and the London Sinfonietta, Yorke joined Greenwood as part of the Ether Festival at London's Royal Festival Hall. The focus of the program was Greenwood's own material, though Yorke took the stage to sing a couple of Radiohead tracks. September saw the release of *Help! A Day in the Life*, the follow-up to the War Child benefit album for which the band had provided "Lucky" ten years earlier, and to which they now contributed the song "I Want None of This." A few months later saw the release of Jonny Greenwood and Phil Selway's collaboration with Pulp's Jarvis Cocker for three songs in the movie *Harry Potter and the Goblet of Fire*. Interspersed with all this activity, from late 2004 through pockets of 2005, Yorke was working on what was the next year to become his first solo album.

In late February 2005 the band itself had reconvened at Canned Applause to begin rehearsals for their next album, and these ended up dragging on for months. Part of their paralysis involved the fact that they now had no external obligation to a record company to fulfill, though it also demonstrated a long familiar pattern: "One of the biggest things not just for me but for everybody," according to Yorke, as Trevor Baker records, "was that at the end of the *Hail to the Thief* thing, we completely lost our confidence. . . . We couldn't work out whether we should be carrying on or not." Yorke described in further detail what this involved: "One of the things I find hardest is being part of the whole Radiohead thing. . . . I'm not really interested in that anymore. . . . None of us really want to be part of that band, like that anymore, just because it's a particular monster. And you don't want to be in this situation where you're just feeding the monster."

Their initial attempts to produce the album by themselves zigzagged from August until October, when Yorke posted on their website's new blog *Dead Air Space*, "We're splitting up. It's all shit. We're washed up, finished." Another of the reasons for their difficulties in making progress was that life had become much more complicated, as each of the band members was now more or less married, with at least two kids each. Nor, again, did they have the steady mediation that Nigel Godrich had typically provided. Having also wanted to try working with another producer, the band recorded with Mark "Spike" Stent from January to April 2006 at their Oxfordshire studios but found the relationship ultimately unproductive, thus interrupting the sessions with a tour that included festival dates, the essential purpose of which was to force them to come up with basic arrangements of the new songs and to test them out on audiences. The tour saw them on the road from May to August through parts of North America and Europe, playing a total of thirteen new songs.

In the midst of all this activity, July saw the release of Yorke's *The Eraser*, recorded with Nigel Godrich over a period of only three weeks, its cover artwork courtesy of Stanley Donwood. Its appearance was preceded by one of its songs, "Black Swan," being used over the credits in Richard Linklater's animated film *A Scanner Darkly*. Portending what was to come, the album was released as a one-album deal on the mainly electronic dance record indy label XL. Entering the *Billboard* chart at number two and the British charts at number three, its nine tightly structured songs with recognizable verses and choruses featured many keyboards, programmed beats, and few guitars.

Meanwhile, of the further work toward what would become the *In Rainbows* release, Phil Selway was to report that the key thing in actually propelling it forward was producer Nigel Godrich coming back into the process, which he did that October, working with the band at a mansion called Tottenham Court House in Marlborough, Wiltshire. Having no running water, the property was quite run down, and everyone stayed in trailers on the grounds. Recording continued at another such property called Halswell House in Somerset, before heading to Godrich's studios in Covent Garden, and then returning in January 2007 to the band's own studios in Oxfordshire, where work would finally be completed that July.

Three months later, on October 1, Jonny Greenwood posted a message to *Dead Air Space*, reading, "Hello everyone. Well, the new album is finished, and it's coming out in 10 days. We've called it *In Rainbows*. Love from us all." Recalling that the band was now out of contract, readers were then directed to the link inrainbows.com, where it was indicated that the album would be released as a digital download. Alternatively, fans could get the download *and* buy the limited Discbox edition, which contained six other tracks from the sessions, two vinyl discs, song lyrics, and an attractive art booklet—all contained within a sturdy case for the price of £40 or roughly $80. This would be delivered in December through the band's mail-order merchandizing company W.A.S.T.E.

Those who opted only for the download were directed to a page reading "Price?"—and if they clicked on the question mark, they were taken to a new page that read, "It's up to you." Another question mark yielded an additional page saying, "No really, it's up to you." It soon became clear to users that they could name any price from £0–99, but no matter what they paid, they were asked to provide an email address to which would be delivered a unique code used to activate the download (at the same time, of course, providing a direct means for potential ongoing communication with their audience). The "pay what you want" idea was actually that of their management, but it garnered Radiohead sufficient notoriety to make *Time* magazine's Top 100 most influential people of 2008—recognition that was further amplified when the *New Musical Express* named them the most influential of contemporary musical artists.

The download idea was in part a response to the band's refusal to renew its contract with record label EMI but also to the fact that every Radiohead album since 2000's *Kid A* had been leaked to the internet in some form or another prior to its release (including *The Eraser*). What this meant, of course, was that, no matter who or where they were, everyone was able to hear the album for the first time simultaneously. As Yorke suggested, moreover, over a year prior to the *In Rainbows* release, another motivating factor was that "it would be really nice to just let off this enormous stink bomb in the industry." Radiohead had been particularly irked about EMI's refusal to relinquish ownership of the band's back catalog and decided that in the future it was going to own its recordings and license them for distribution, instead of signing a standard recording contract, an arrangement that would have enabled Radiohead to block EMI's 2008 release of the "Greatest Hits" package, which was put out against the band's wishes.[1] The group was also miffed about the label neglecting to pay bands anything for online sales. "All the contracts signed in a certain era have none of that stuff," Yorke relayed to David Byrne in *Wired* magazine, and as Radiohead manager

Bryce Edge told the *New Musical Express*, even in the case of bands who did sign contracts that included such rights, record companies were still deducting "packaging costs" from royalty payments on digital downloads, despite the fact that they require no packaging.

Radiohead and their management were at first tight-lipped about the success of their "pay what you want" scheme, leading to much speculation as to the success of the download experiment, the facilities for which were left up for three months before the indie labels XL and TBD Records physically released the album on January 1, 2008. But as Yorke told Byrne, "In terms of digital income, we've made more money out of this record than out of all the other Radiohead albums put together, forever—in terms of anything on the Net. And that's nuts." Radiohead was likewise closemouthed about the publishing company Warner Chappell's involvement in overseeing the release of the album, and though its head of business affairs, Jane Dyball, refused to reveal the average price for which people downloaded the recording, on the first anniversary of the release at a music industry conference in Iceland called "You Are in Control," for which she gave the keynote address, she pointed out that while most fans downloaded the album for free, the company and Radiohead's management daily monitored the average price and were mobilized to dismantle the download facility should the average price become too low. "We knew that if we put it out for nothing at all," Yorke explained to Mark Binelli of *Rolling Stone*, "it would end up costing us an absolute fortune. Simply because you end up having to pay every time someone downloads it." Evidently not an unexpected outcome, free BitTorrent downloads greatly outnumbered those from Radiohead's official site. Nevertheless, in its first year, according to Dyball, a total of three million units of *In Rainbows* were purchased, including the box sets, CDs, and downloads from both iTunes and the band's own site. That Radiohead purportedly made more money from the album before it was physically released than in total from *Hail to the Thief* (2003) would appear to demonstrate the experiment's commercial success.

It also reflects the fact that new technologies always create winners and losers, as suggested when Music Ally, an outfit billing itself as "the digital music experts," reported how, though this was all good news for the publishing company and the band, it was bad news for rights collection societies like the MCPS-PRS Alliance (which in 2009 was rebranded as "PRS for Music"). Initially, even having to bend its rules for the project to go ahead, the Alliance did so only to allow an initiative that would illustrate, ultimately, how much more money can be made without its involvement. "For Warner it served to prove a point that by licensing directly (i.e., outside the collecting society network) and by offering a genuine one-stop shop for licensing," to combine all the digital rights into one offer from just one entity in other words, "the publisher was able to generate far more money for both themselves and the band than would have been possible under the traditional system." Also reflecting the fact that winners always seek to reassure the losers with regard to the positive effects of the new technology, Dyball clarified that such results were "not about to lead to the publisher withdrawing rights en masse from the society network."

Pointing out to Byrne that what Radiohead had done was not intended as a model for emulation, Yorke suggested also to the *New Musical Express* in 2000 that neither was it meant "to be a big announcement about 'Everything's over except the internet. . . . The internet's the future.' Utter rubbish. It's really important to have an artefact," recognizing that not all audiences' relationship to music is dominated by MP3 files and the internet. Instead, as Jonny Greenwood put it to John Del Signore in Gothamist, the "pay what you want" download was meant to be a type of art happening and thus would not be repeated. "It's just interesting to make people pause for even a few seconds and think about what music is worth now," Greenwood posited. "I thought it was an interesting thing to ask people to do and compare it to whatever else in their lives they value or don't value." Ed O'Brien, on the other hand, spoke of the exciting "spirit of the thing," which was about not being greedy in the midst of an industry devoted to maximizing profit. Another aspect of the experiment highlighted by Colin Greenwood was the interesting observation that music is the only commodified art form that has generally been sold at a uniform price, notwithstanding the identity of the artist, and that it might be time to rethink this one-size-fits-all price for albums. But as Yorke had commented to Brian Draper a couple of years earlier,

> Music has always been a commodity but now it's a commodity that's almost free—you can download it for a quid and you can do it through McDonald's, you can do it through Metro magazine or anything. I always felt that it was more valuable than that, and somehow

at the moment it feels cheap. It's just so disposable. It's like, "I'll download another 50 tracks and listen to them once and then throw them away," that sort of thing. I find it sort of depressing.

Noting the mixed blessings that always accompany new technologies, when he was asked in the wake of the "pay what you want" download whether he had ever downloaded a song from the internet for free, Yorke replied—"No, I always pay."

The EMI Radiohead box set was released in December, containing all seven of the band's Parlophone albums, including MP3 versions on a USB stick, while the previous month the band hosted a pair of webcasts known as *Entangled* and *Thumbs Down*, during which they debuted the video for "Jigsaw Falling into Place" and played most of the new tracks live. The webcasts were just a warm-up for the New Year's Eve presentation *Scotch Mist*, an hour-long program, not unlike *The Most Gigantic Lying Mouth of All Time*, which was broadcast on the internet and on cable channel Current TV, and which included short films, live performances of songs from *In Rainbows*, and the video for "Nude." In the new year on January 16, the band performed a secret concert at 93 Feet East, a club adjoining the Rough Trade record shop in London that was also webcast live, while another performance program was assembled for Nigel Godrich's podcast and television show *From the Basement*, then broadcast on VH1 in May 2008 and later sold as a video album through iTunes.

Alongside Yorke's *Eraser Rmxs*, a collection of remixes of songs from his solo album, the other singles and videos from *In Rainbows* were released throughout 2008 and into 2009 and included "House of Cards/ Bodysnatchers," "Reckoner," and "All I Need." The most meaningful chart activity saw the first single, "Jigsaw," reach only number thirty in the UK, while "Nude" achieved number twenty-one (UK) and number thirty-seven in the United States, the band's second-ever American Top 40 hit ("Creep" being the first). The first few videos were more or less produced in a DIY style, and just as Radiohead had made available component stems of "Reckoner" for people to remix, for the song's video the band announced a competition and chose a number of winners for the best representations. For the production of the "All I Need" video, they teamed up with MTV, which then premiered it on their stations around the world. This collaboration was part of the broadcaster's EXIT campaign to end exploitation and trafficking. Using various split-screen techniques, the video paralleled the life of two young boys, one a typical middle-class kid from a developed nation and the other working in a sweatshop in a developing country. It is implied that the former boy's footwear is made by the latter, who works all day while the first is in school. Fittingly, the video ends with the caption "some things cost more than you realise."

Radiohead's activism had continued in other ways throughout this time frame as well, beginning with Yorke's penning of an op-ed published in the *Guardian* January 31, 2004, in response to the Hutton Inquiry, which was intended to study the circumstances of the death of UK government biological weapons expert and former Iraq weapons inspector Dr. David Kelly. Kelly was identified to the BBC as the source of leaks that had maintained the UK sexed-up 2003 intelligence reports that Iraq possessed weapons of mass destruction. Yorke and many others were critical of the report for clearing the government of any wrongdoing and for strongly criticizing the BBC and specific journalists. With its line "did I fall or was I pushed?" Yorke's *Eraser* song, "Harrowdown Hill," addresses the mysterious and suspicious circumstances surrounding Kelly's death, officially deemed a case of suicide. But regarding his solo album's title, Yorke said to Jay Sweet in *Paste*, "I was reading this book about the death of Aldo Moro, the head of the Christian Democrat party in Italy who was murdered by the Red Brigade in the '70s," making reference to merely one of his meanings of "erasure." "Before he died he'd written all these letters and was disowned and 'erased' from Italian Politics," Yorke continued, referring to another of the title's meanings. "Even before he died everyone was saying, 'Well, he's obviously lost his mind; the person writing these letters to newspapers in desperation is obviously not the real thing.' It got me thinking. For me, a lot of the record is about living in a world where things like Iraq happen." Though to some extent also indicating our propensity to "erase" things like global warming from our minds, Yorke asserted in *Paste* that the record was "much more a response to the political environment and general psyche." To this he was to add, "It's a response to the ability to [snaps his fingers] and these issues can just go away." This was more or less what the Radiohead front man thought of the Hutton Inquiry, suggesting it concluded that "the Ministry of Defense was probably at fault with the way they handled his outing, so obviously the prime minister can't be held responsible, which everyone thought was a crock of shit, but—poof—it went away; it was whitewashed." Referring again to Kelly he remarked, "It was erased, and the culprits are all still there, and this poor man died for whatever reason. It seems like this very, very small thing, but it's an expression of something much wider and much more frightening."

In September 2004, meanwhile, Yorke had led a group of about four hundred demonstrators, organized by the Campaign for Nuclear Disarmament in Yorkshire, against the establishment of the American Missile Defense system on UK soil. "How dare Tony Blair sign us up to 'Star Wars' without even giving it a really serious thought . . . without even consulting us?" Yorke asked the crowd, according to *NME* in "Thom Yorke Leads 'Star Wars' Protest." "It's important that people like us can get off our backsides and come to these events. We need to make it clear that we will not let America govern the world we live in." A couple of years hence, Yorke inadvertently pointed out in the *Observer* one of his country's direct connections to the American military-industrial complex, referring to the British Ministry of Defence as "a profound cancer at the centre of this society."

In spring 2005, Yorke performed solo at a London Trade Justice rally, and following the 2003 UN report on climate change, he became involved with the Big Ask campaign of Friends of the Earth, with which he became heavily involved from 2003 until 2006, when he and Jonny Greenwood performed an acoustic set at a benefit to raise funds for the ongoing collective effort. In September 2005 he sloppily wrote the following to fans on the Radiohead website:

> Friends of the earth have asked me whether i would meet Tony Blair at downing street to discuss what our government is not doing about climate change. . . . i dont know if this will ever happen for certain. . . . it is rattling around in the back of my mind and concerns me a lot. i have no intention of being used by spider spin doctors to make it look like we make progress when it is just words. id love to know what you think but i cant ask. youd say oh there he goes again interfering and meddling in politics why doesnt he get on with the music and shut u perhaps because i feel like a hypocrit if dont do anything, and equally feel like a hypocrit if i try getting involved. nobody wants to know. none of us do, me included id love to forget about it like your average Times reader. wed all like it to go away. turn to the

rising sea and say come back later im busy right now. Blair has been uttering nonsense lately about kyoto and such, real la la stuff . . . looks like the american right have finally eaten his mind . . . blah blah why on earth would i meet this man? or perhaps that is exactly why i should. but i dont have powers of persuasion, i just have temper and an acid tongue. trust me i find this as dull as you do . . . politics is poison. . . . what do you think i should do?

Yorke was ultimately to decline the invitation, later explaining in "All Messed Up" to Craig McLean of the *Observer* that he did so because there were all sorts of conditions being put up in relation to the proposed meeting. "[Blair's advisers] wanted pre-meetings. They wanted to know that I was onside," explained Yorke. "Also, I was being manoeuvred into a position where if I said the wrong thing post-the meeting, Friends of the Earth would lose their access. Which normally would be called blackmail."

Climate change is likely the central and most visible social issue in the developed world today, and this concern was to provide a backdrop to both *The Eraser* and *In Rainbows*. The cover art of the former depicts the legendary English monarch King Canute, who demonstrated the limits of kingly power by trying and failing to command the ocean. The allusion was originally made by the environmentalist Jonathan Porritt, who suggested that the British government's gestures toward addressing global warming were "like King Canute trying to stop the tide." As Yorke was to add in *Paste*, "It's not political, really, but that's exactly what I feel is happening. We're all King Canutes, holding our hands out, saying, 'It'll go away. I can make it stop.' No, you can't."

In this relation, when Jonny Greenwood was asked by John Del Signore if he was going to be in New York at the beginning of 2008 for performances of some of the music he'd written while he was BBC composer in residence, he reported, "I'd love to but I can't really justify the flight just to come to that. I'd feel a bit weird about it. If I was in America already for touring or something I'd love to go but I can't really justify it. It's a shame." The band members had also begun collectively to undertake efforts to reduce their environmental impact. But as Yorke recounted to Andrew Harrison in regard to his reaction when Friends of the Earth asked him to front its campaign, "You must be fucking joking. Me? The last person in the world. It's a bit like saying, 'Everybody stop flying, except us.' . . . But FoE wanted me involved because I wasn't holier than thou. None of us is, we live in a carbon society."

Nevertheless, hiring carbon footprint analysts Best Foot Forwards in 2007 to audit the carbon impacts of their 2003 and 2006 performance schedules, the band confirmed that the greatest environmental damage resulting from their tours was the travel of audiences to and from the shows. The band, therefore, began to encourage its fans either to carpool or to leave the car at home, recommending instead that they take public transportation to the *In Rainbows* performances, which the band ensured would be presented at venues accessible to good transport links. The band's website also offered travel information to all the venues and directed fans to an online calculator showing the CO_2 that different methods of transport would generate. Radiohead, moreover, banned the use of air travel both for freight and for themselves and crew, and in Yorke's words to *NME* in January 2008, "At this stage the normal protocol would be to fly in/fly out every night, so to choose to bumble about on a bus is going to be interesting." All the buses and trucks used on the tour ran on biofuel (now seen as controversial), while the band converted its light show to one that relied on less energy intensive LED technology and had an ecocoordinator develop rechargeable batteries for their light and sound gear. They also used two sets of gear on the tour, one based in Europe and the other in North America, and they negotiated deals with trucking companies to ensure they cut their emissions as well. The second leg of Radiohead's 2008 American tour would be the first for which the band would be able to completely obtain, in guitarist Ed O'Brien's words to Craig McLean in "Rainbow Warriors," "all the information about where fans go to and from so we can do a proper environmental audit and a breakdown. Friends of the Earth are using it as their template," he pointed out, adding that "any bands who come to them and say, 'What can we do?' they can tell them, 'Well, Radiohead did this. . . .' It's sort of becoming an industry standard."

IN RAINBOWS

When approaching *In Rainbows* we should note Yorke's comment that the album's content amounted to a kind of "psychic dumping" for which he thought little about what sense could be made of it, explaining that "of all the records we've done, this is the one I feel I can least explain." With this in mind, then, we could start by observing that the most common rainbow imagery known to the majority of Radiohead's audience is probably that of the story of Noah and the flood from the Hebrew Bible. Of course, we've already seen Yorke allude to this story on *Hail to the Thief* in the song "Sail to the Moon," what he called "a song of hope," sung to his soon-to-be firstborn child Noah. There he sang, "In the flood you'll build an ark and sail us to the moon," and in this perhaps can be found some initial significance for the album's rainbow symbolism. In the story of Noah, the rainbow is said to be a perpetual sign of God's renunciation of violence and destruction, a universal compact made with the earth and its inhabitants:

> This is the sign of the covenant I am making between me and you and every living creature with you, a covenant for all generations to come: I have set my rainbow in the clouds, and it will be the sign of the covenant between me and the earth. Whenever I bring clouds over the earth and the rainbow appears in the clouds, I will remember my covenant between me and you and all living creatures of every kind. Never again will the waters become a flood to destroy all life. Whenever the rainbow appears in the clouds, I will see it and remember the everlasting covenant between God and all living creatures of every kind on the earth. (Genesis 9:12, NIV)

Given its evident religious imagery then, and particularly its allusions to the story of Faust, this seems a reasonable association to make, especially with the album's reference to the "Reckoner," a song that Yorke describes as "the heart of the record" and the only one in which the words "in rainbows" actually appear. What the hopeful Hebrew reference suggests is that there should be no reason to build another ark, unless of course it's humanity that should rival God by obtaining the scale of violent destruction alluded to in the biblical story. This of course is the very possibility said to exist if we are unable to prevent catastrophic global warming.

The rainbow, thus, is a positive image that symbolizes beauty, enlightenment, and the promise of fulfillment of our purposes and desires. In this sense, Yorke describes the title as a reference to "thinking beyond where you are at the time," or "the desire to get somewhere that you're not." But the album clearly also provides a backdrop for which much negative imagery is likewise present. In this regard, Yorke has said that *In Rainbows* "explores the ideas of transience," that it's about the "panic of realising you're going to die," and that it pertains to "that anonymous fear thing, sitting in traffic, thinking, 'I'm sure I'm supposed to be doing something else . . . it's similar to *Ok Computer* in a way. It's much more terrifying," as he told *NME* in April 2006.

In this regard, when Brian Draper asked him in 2004 whether there was any hope of redemption from the brokenness that permeates his lyrics, Yorke replied,

> I don't think about redemption. I focus on the most imminent eco-
> logical things. You know, there are so many scenarios on the horizon
> at the moment that will result in mass suffering, and that to me is
> what everybody should be thinking about. That's what I spend most
> of my time thinking about. It wouldn't take that much for people to
> turn their heads and see that we have just been looking the wrong
> way, our priorities are wrong.

Once again emphasizing our need to awaken to the potential dangers that the future holds in store, a theme that's reiterated throughout *In Rainbows*, Yorke was also to recommend to Chris Mincher following the release of the album: "There is a certain way of life, a certain way of being, that is, one way or another, going to come to an end. Hopefully something good to come to fruition, or maybe nothing will."

This apocalyptic tension is evident in the Radiohead front man's mythic use of light/dark imagery throughout the album's songs. Recalling how Yorke referred to "The Gloaming" on *Hail to the Thief* as "being in the darkness," Ed O'Brien was tellingly to make the following statement in 2012 to FM Reactor:

> With *OK Computer* we entered this quite dark space, this quite dark
> era. It was like being in a tunnel. We were in that tunnel for *OK
> Computer, Kid A, Amnesiac*. . . . [With] *Hail to the Thief* we thought
> we were out but we weren't. And with *In Rainbows*, part of the
> struggle was getting out of the tunnel. When we released the album
> it felt like we were out of that tunnel—and it was dark, it was a dark
> place. We realized that we didn't want to go back there, because
> we'd been there a long time. It can be very, very creative, but it kills
> you as a person. . . . We're now in a much lighter place. . . . This is

like a new era of Radiohead, and it has been for the last two years or so.

In this relation, rainbows are of course the products of a perfect harmonic amalgamation of light, and thus an extension of the hope that light typically represents, in contrast to the gloom inherent in the imagery of darkness. In this it's also interesting that the album's final song, "Videotape," makes reference to "Mephistophelis," whose name, as a combination of three Greek words, means "not light loving." The name first appears in late sixteenth-century German folk literature, possibly as a parody of the Latin "Lucifer," which translates as "light-bearer." In the Faust legend, the demon is trapped in his own hell as Lucifer's agent, but in contrast to his name, when first appearing to Faust, "Mephistophelis" advises him not to forgo the promise of heaven in pursuit of his goals, which, not unlike those of Yorke and Radiohead, are to tame the forces of war and nature. The latter of course predominantly involves the profundity of humanity's contemporary influence on the remainder of the natural world and the planet's ecosystems.

It's worthwhile noting for a moment that the light/dark imagery is evident as well in the lyrics of *The Eraser*. Among other songs to which I'll refer, these include "Analyse," where Yorke laments, "There's no spark, no light in the dark," and the more optimistic "Atoms for Peace," where he sings to his addressee, "No more going to the dark side with your flying saucer eyes." This is also true of some of the extra tracks of the *In Rainbows* release—"Down Is the New Up," for example, with its lyrics "Get yourself together, let the light pour in," or the warning within the song "Bangers + Mash": "If you stare into the dark, the dark will stare back, back into your soul." The remaining songs on the extra disc, "Go Slowly," "Up on the Ladder," and "4 Minute Warning" eschew the light/dark imagery, with the exception of "Last Flowers," whose conclusion in contrast says of the naked light itself, "It's too much, too bright, too powerful," something, perhaps, like what we experience during the middle part of "Reckoner" as we will address below.

This imagery isn't present in the lyrics of the album's opening track, "15 Step," however. Nor do we find the rainbow's hopeful promise of human purposes fulfilled. Instead, the song's narrator, and the individual that he addresses, are both stuck, as Yorke remarks above, in an apparently permanent state of aspiring "to get somewhere that they're not." Clearly making repeated mistakes and little to no progress, the song's protagonist questions why he always ends up where he started and where he'd gone wrong. That the situation arises in part from his misdirected attention is evident in his not taking his "eyes off the ball again." And the person he addresses appears to have severed their connection by first "reeling him out" and then "cutting the string." He notes that the person "used to be alright" and questions why they no longer are so. Enquiring whether this is because the cat had got their tongue, or because their own "string"—like that of the protagonist—had come "undone," this image reappears in a more positive light at the conclusion of the album in "Videotape." In particular, as the narrator of that song sings, "you are my center when I spin away, out of control," it suggests that the individual addressed in that context functions much more like an anchoring force. Here, however, these individuals are speechless and similarly disconnected, and the narrator suggests in the song's central, unrepeated section that this is something that gradually "comes to us all," doing so quietly, "as soft as your pillow."

Presumably this applies also to the children, who, following Yorke's singing of the phrase "fads for whatever" in the next verse, make their first and only appearance on the album, emerging out of nowhere and three times enthusiastically shouting "yeah!" Perhaps "fads" are among the primary means by which we, along with our children, continue to take our "eyes off the ball." In any event, the phrase is followed by the line "15 steps, then a sheer drop." What this precarious image represents isn't clear,[2] but it certainly doesn't appear positive in the context of the song's general sense of unease, partly achieved through its unusual and driving 5/4 meter and also through some of its effects, as with the echo that's applied to instrumental sounds toward the conclusion of the piece as well as when Yorke sings "15 steps." The echo appears to signal something like a change of dimension and then a musical interlude with a decidedly more menacing, dissonant, and minor-sounding flavor begins. A sense of unresolve is further conveyed through the song's lack of harmonic resolution at the end and in its gradually decaying electronic timbre, again connoting some kind of interdimensional shift or the like. Along these lines, the original version of "15 Step" had come out of "bits assembled in the computer," and Yorke remarked in December 2007 to *NME* in this regard, "We deliberately did this thing to get a sense of disembodiment when we were assembling tracks. So the vocal may be from one version or the drums may be from another. If there was something that you were particularly fond of," he added, "you kept it from that take and forced it on to the other version."

Clearly, a kind of disembodiment is likewise evident in the next song, "Bodysnatchers," apparently inspired by a Victorian ghost story of the same name that involved people digging up corpses, selling them on, and the animated bodies eventually coming back to get them. Also an inspiration was the original 1975 *Stepford Wives* film, with which Yorke says he became obsessed, especially by the ending, where you learn that all the wives have been turned into robots. Yorke also described as an influence on the song a personal feeling he'd possessed for some time, explaining it as being like "your physical consciousness trapped without being able to connect fully with anything else."

Whereas in "15 Step" the narrator asked why he ends up where he went wrong, at the beginning of "Bodysnatchers" he admits, robotically, "I do not—understand—what it is—I've done wrong." As indicated by the suggestion to "check for pulse," it's unclear whether the person that he addresses is actually alive; that the individual is "full of holes" may refer to "leaky holes" in his brain, as in the song "Atoms for Peace" from *The Eraser*. And just as in the previous track the cat had got their tongue, here the person must blink his or her eyes to communicate, not unlike the protagonist, who's "trapped in this body and can't get out." In the process of refashioning his exterior, all sound has been killed, and his "backbone" removed, leaving merely a "pale imitation" of himself. Reflecting the general lack of connection, the narrator confesses he has no idea what either himself or the other individual is talking about. Of the latter he says, "Your mouth moves only with someone's hand up your ass," suggesting that they're no longer responsible for their own thoughts and statements. Like the narrator of the later song, "Faust Arp," they appear "stuffed" and "dead from the neck up."

Likewise, the musical setting of "Bodysnatchers" is telling. With Greenwood's eerie ondes martenot parts, and its distorted electric guitars, in the vein of *OK Computer*'s "Electioneering," the first half of the song is characterized by its punctuated or interrupted rhythmic movement, its minimal harmonic variation, and its repeated and sustained pedal point in the bass, from which the section doesn't break away, reflective of the characters' entrapment in bodies from which they're similarly unable to escape. This section of the song is predominantly set in a major tonality, until the end of each verse, where there's a sinister-sounding shift to the minor. Significant musical contrast is achieved during the second half of the piece, when the wall of distortion gives way to a much sparser texture, featuring a more driving rhythm with acoustic guitar, accompanied finally by a break from the insistent pedal point, with the song's first significant harmonic shift. A sense of poignancy is signaled through its minor tonality, combined with the E-bow guitar part's high, dissonant first note, which, representing a significant gesture of striving, similarly breaks away from the previous bass-heavy texture.

As the character appears to regain consciousness, this transition represents a similar shift or escape. Returning to the light/dark imagery, and noting that though we're now in the twenty-first century, the character asks, "has the light gone out for you, 'cause the light's gone out for me," indicating an absence of hope that, as he points out, can "follow you like a dog" and, as with him, bring you "to your knees." As he recounts regarding his apparent abduction, it was at that point that "they got a skin and they put me in." Again, "dead from the neck up," part of this skin entails lines wrapped around his face that indicate to everyone else "he's a lie." And as the song returns to the original confines of the pedal point and its associated texture of distortion, Yorke sings, "I seen it coming."

The next track, "Nude," which dates back to the *OK Computer* days, is a slow and gentle song, which Yorke sings in a high falsetto. "Ten years ago, when we first had the song, I didn't enjoy singing it because it was too feminine, too high. It made me feel uncomfortable," remarked Yorke to Mark Paytress in *Mojo*. "Now I enjoy it exactly for that reason—because it is a bit uncomfortable, a bit out of my range, and it's really difficult to do. And it brings something out in me." In the previous song, the individuals appeared no longer responsible for their own thoughts and statements, while here, against a surrealistic background of vocals looped both backward and forward, the song's narrator counsels not to get any "big ideas" as "they're not going to happen." Though "nude," the song's addressees apparently paint themselves white and fill themselves up with distracting noise, only to find something is missing. As soon as they sense what this element is, however, it disappears, and the narrator accuses the individual of having "gone off the rails" by somehow indulging in bad or wrong behavior. In this relation, the character sings with a snarling tone, "You'll go to hell for what your dirty mind is thinking." Originally containing mildly erotic lyrical imagery about an unobtainable stewardess, the song, with its association of sex and hell, appears to be in conflict with pursuing "the promise of heaven," at least according to this authority, about whom we should probably be suspect, anyway, given his discouragement of "big ideas."

In the next song, "Weird Fishes/Arpeggi," we encounter the first of three references to water throughout the album and enter a more hopeful environment that inheres in its bright major chords, its driving rhythm, and in the unrelenting arpeggiation from which it gets its title. Despite being at the "bottom of the sea," a location typically in complete darkness, the character says of the apparently shining eyes of the other whom he addresses, "They turn me." This other, evidently not "dead from the neck up," and reinforced by O'Brien's triumphant backing vocal gestures, turns him into "phantoms" and provides him with the fortitude to leave the darkness of the "deepest ocean." Having no physical reality, or perhaps being a dream or illusion of the mind, the protagonist follows this other "to the edge of the earth," where he "falls off." Shortly after, suddenly and unexpectedly, the band, except for guitar and keyboard, drops out, suggesting a new scenario, and one in which he's being "eaten by the worms and weird fishes." This interlude transitions into the song's final section, which returns to the original driving rhythm. At its sudden and dramatic conclusion, though characterized by its minor tonality, the character "hits the bottom" and apparently escapes.

Although the next track, "All I Need," begins by outlining a major-sounding tonality, it's not clear that it represents any kind of proper "escape." With its protagonist no longer at the bottom of the sea but now disturbingly "lying in the reeds," the portrait seems a menacing one, its concealment curiously contrasting the more conspicuous image of being "in the middle of your picture." For the most part the song is dark, primarily the result of its very low, droning bass synthesizer, particularly when combined in the second verse with the much higher glockenspiel that enters to add, in this context, a spooky effect, as does Jonny Greenwood's highly dissonant string arrangement, heard toward the end of the song. The second verse sees the light/dark imagery return, with the singer likening himself to a moth that "wants to share

your light" and an insect "trying to get out of the night."[3] When he
sings, "I'll stick with you cause there are no others," there are intimations that some kind of catastrophe has occurred with few survivors.
The first verse, again, paints the picture of a lack of attention to the
things that require it. This appears accompanied by a sense of potential
guilt, as with "all the days you choose to ignore," the "animal trapped in
your hot car," or for that matter, the child laborer in Asia who makes
your shoes in squalid living conditions, as in the song's video. Of the
band's collaboration with MTV's campaign to end exploitation and trafficking, Yorke said to the music channel,

> If MTV Exit does one good thing, it would be to make this concept of
> slavery—which is what it is—less taboo. If they can make it some-
> thing that is OK for us to talk about, and for politicians in the West to
> actually accept that actually this is an issue, well, then we're doing a
> good thing. . . . If you are in the West, it's a luxury to be able to talk
> about the importance of human rights for everybody, but yet in the
> East, or the poorer countries where slave labor is going on, if you talk
> to certain companies, it seems that it's much more important that
> they're on some sort of economic ladder, and somehow the rights of
> the workers are secondary to economic growth. . . . So it would be
> useful when the West talks about human rights, they actually consid-
> er countries where, for a lot of workers, it's not really on the agenda
> yet.

With the intensely dissonant conclusion of the song, Yorke repeatedly
sings, "It's all wrong—it's alright," and as mentioned, against this backdrop, the video ends with the powerful caption "Some things cost more
than you realise."

Given our previous discussion about Faust and "Mephistophelis,"
this would seem an appropriate message likewise to consider as we
transition from the extraordinary dissonance of the strings at the end of
"All I Need" to the next song. Called "Faust Arp," "arp" is likely intended as the short form for "arpeggi," as in the subtitle of "Weird
Fishes." With its playful metrical shifts, and its light, gentle nylon-
stringed guitars and string arrangement, the piece seems appropriately
arranged for a song that alludes to a folk tale, but its disturbing content
is also indicated in Yorke's bizarre, double-tracked voice, its consistent
shift back and forth between the tonic major and minor, and its inclu-

sion of unusual harmonic content. Its folksiness is a characteristic that's reinforced by its nursery-rhyme-type reference to "blackbird pie" and, though undocumented in the official lyrics, by its concluding lines: "You've got a head full of feathers, you're gonna melt into butter." These latter lines of course relate to the fact that, like his addressee, he's "stuffed" and "dead from the neck up"; therefore, it's not "what you ought to," or what's "reasonable and sensible," but "what you feel." Again, the singer of the song urges his listener to awake, singing "wakey wakey, rise and shine," and saying of the individual's attention, "it's on again, off again, on again." Foreshadowing the sense of catastrophe in "House of Cards," he talks of himself falling "like dominos," while "the elephant that's in the room" appears to be the environment, conjured by the image of "tubes and empty bottles," and "plastic bags in duplicate and triplicate." Though toward the end we also get the line "enough of that stuff," the tubes and empty bottles may also bring to mind the album's cover art, heavily influenced by online photos from NASA, for which the combination of molten wax and hypodermic needles squirting ink are the dominant motif.

The cosmic quality of the album's artwork nicely fits the character of the next song, "Reckoner," which conjures a vast sense of space through its generous use of reverb. A piece that Yorke refers to as the "heart of the record" and the "center of the album," its spiritual or religious character is evident in lines such as "can't take it with yer" and "take me with yer," and even the idea of the "reckoner" itself. The image conjures an arbiter of justice, typically portrayed symbolically as a woman with scales who measures the strength of support and opposition for a case, but as suggested by the image of dancing for another's pleasure, sometimes such arbiters take the form of monarchs or divinities. The latter is certainly suggested here, with the universality of its dedication "to all human beings" and its emphasis on implied forgiveness and innocence. Once again focusing on the misdirection of our attention, the protagonist sings in falsetto, "You are not to blame for bittersweet distractor," and it's not clear who or what this is. Though it's sometimes common among Jews to avoid speaking the name of God, one wonders if it's not "Mephistophelis" who is here the "bittersweet distractor" whose name we "dare not speak." It's in the middle part of the song, in the richly harmonized background vocals, that we hear the hopeful, peaceful, and universal image of "in rainbows" and learn that the song is dedicated to all human beings, "because we separate like ripples on a blank shore." Here, in contrast to the setting of "All I Need," there are no "reeds" along the shore that menacingly obscure or conceal what might lurk, and the ripples are like the colors of the rainbow, indirectly a symbol of the light and of the compact to which we're all said to be attached. Singing to the reckoner, "take me with yer," the protagonist foreshadows his arrival at the pearly gates in the song "Videotape" at the album's conclusion.

But before he arrives, and immediately following the fade-out of the song, we hear the introduction of "House of Cards," a tune that sounds, according to Yorke, "satisfying, really mellow and summery." The track is performed in the style of 1960s West Coast music and therefore also connotes sexual liberation, particularly in the context of the first line, which expresses interest in another, in being not their friend but their lover, without any regard to how the relationship either begins or ends. And though it could simply be a reference to responsible driving at a gathering where alcohol is being consumed, it's not clear whether there's an intended reference to what were called key parties, a sort of swinger sex event, where keys are randomly chosen from a bowl and people go home with someone other than their partner. In any case, there are certainly grounds for considering that, in relation to an earlier admonishment, the character might go to hell for his "dirty mind." From falling off the edge of the earth in "Weird Fishes" to watching him fall like dominos in "Faust Arp," here people "fall off the table and get swept under," forgetting about their "house of cards." The musical style connotes a carefree attitude that the song then identifies as "denial," and the associated "voltage spike" and infrastructure collapse would tend to entail an encounter with darkness, though in the song "Analyse," from *The Eraser*, we get the lines "the candles in the city, they never looked so pretty, by power carts and blackouts," suggesting there are remedies to such situations. During an April 2008 performance of the song, transmitted from a London studio for the American television show *Late Night with Conan O' Brien*, Yorke dedicated the chorus of the song ("Denial, denial") to George W. Bush—"that man who walked away from the Kyoto." But addressing all listeners, regarding their complicity in the situation, is the sweet-sounding repeated line that their "ears should be burning."

This theme of denial, or trying to forget, continues into "Jigsaw Falling into Place," the next to last song on the album, in which the setting is a typical Friday night at the pub after just getting paid. Where bad days disappear, and the protagonist's addressee is "no longer wound up like a spring," nor prone perhaps to spinning away "out of control," the individual is advised, before they've "had too much," to regain focus. "'Jigsaw Falling Into Place' says much about the fact I used to live in the centre of Oxford and used to go out occasionally and witness the fucking chaos of a weekend around here. But it's also about a lot of different experiences," Yorke told *NME* in December 2007. "The lyrics are quite caustic—the idea of 'before you're comatose' or whatever, drinking yourself into oblivion and getting fucked-up to forget. When you're part of a group of people who are all trying to forget en masse it is partly this elation. But there's a much darker side." And this darker side, as he says elsewhere, is seen when it "all goes wrong." This is apparently during the climactic last verse of the song in which Yorke frantically sings in his highest vocal range following the line "dance dance dance," whose added electronic effect once again connotes a kind of interdimensional shift.

The theme of "falling" continues with the reference to "jigsaw falling into place," an image that denotes a situation that's in the process of becoming clearer or more obvious. We learn that the situation amounts to a nightmare, and a dramatic interaction takes place between the addressee and a woman, who, as they pass, "eye each other," looking back multiple times and reminding us of the eyes at the bottom of the sea that earlier "turned" the protagonist of "Weird Fishes/Arpeggi." While the image here would appear to portray some kind of conflict, it's also reminiscent of the story in Genesis 19 of Lot's wife, who, in fleeing the city of Sodom with her family, disobeyed God's warning not to "look back" at its destruction and thereby turned into a pillar of salt. In this scenario, however, the individual has indeed "got the light" and can feel it on his or her back. Nevertheless, the image of the "jigsaw falling into place" implies an inevitable end.

This conclusion comes in the album's last song "Videotape," a piece that Yorke referred to as "pretty dark." The recording process was also considerably dark, with the singer being semibanished from the studio for being a "negative" influence. The process had become bogged down while trying to get the right arrangement, and when he returned from his exile with Stanley Donwood, "a bit worse for wear at about 11 in the evening," Godrich and Jonny Greenwood, in Yorke's own words, had "done this stuff to it that reduced us both to tears." The song's sobriety is achieved by its slow tempo, its solo acoustic piano, its predominantly minor key, its sparse, somber drums, and its chant-like background vocals that give the song a religious flavor.

With memories of Faust and earlier threats of going to hell, it's thus appropriate that here we encounter the non-light-loving "Mephistophelis," reaching up and trying to grab the protagonist, who finds himself at the pearly gates of heaven, capturing the moment for posterity on videotape. According to the dying individual, "This is my way of saying goodbye, because I can't do it face to face," though he addresses another, who, not "cutting the string," functions as his anchor or center when, "wound up like a spring," he "spins away" out of control. Faust had agreed to give the demon his soul, in exchange for taming the forces of war and nature, and for the corresponding experience of a perfect moment that he would wish to last forever. After this moment of happiness, "Mephistophelis" tries to seize Faust's soul when he dies but suffers frustration and rage as angels intervene, due to the grace of God. Hence the protagonist's admonition not to be afraid because, as he says, "today has been the most perfect day I've ever seen." One for the good old days, the protagonist has captured the moment in "red blue green" with his RGB Component Analog Video. Of course, you need light to see any color, and these are three of the seven that comprise rainbows, which are created when water droplets break white sunlight into the component colors of the spectrum, again not unlike the image of separating "like ripples on a blank shore."

When asked by John Del Signore in late 2007 whether the band had considered purchasing carbon offsets as part of its solution to reducing its ecological footprint, Jonny Greenwood responded, "We've heard bad things about that. I'm not sure that that's enough; to buy off our guilt with money. That might not be the best way to do it." That the intended virtue of the band's actions was rubbing off on others was illustrated by the band Liars, which opened for Radiohead on the first leg of the 2008 U.S. tour and, as reported in *NME* in May, wrote on their blog shortly after the experience, "In a world full of fear and ripe with insincerity it's such a relief to have met Radiohead. They are purveyors of truth, beauty and a moral responsibility to the planet." To this, Liars then added,

"We've been welcomed with literal open arms and thoroughly schooled on how to function as a band—not just musically, but ethically, too." But as Yorke had previously suggested to McLean in June 2006, "No one's going to come out of this dirt-free; I don't come out of it dirt-free. It's basically [about] having to make a decision whether to do nothing or try to engage with it in some way, knowing that it's flawed." To this he was to add, "It's convenient to project that back on to someone personally and say they're a hypocrite. It's a lot easier to do that than actually do anything else. And yeah, that stresses me out, because I am a hypocrite. As we all are." Nevertheless, as Yorke wrote in the *Observer*, with regard to changes the band was putting into place, just prior to his editing a special climate change edition of its weekend magazine in early 2008, "These changes might be small, but they are in the right direction. Unlike pessimists such as James Lovelock," Yorke suggested, "I don't believe we are all doomed. It was good to hear Sir David King recently saying he was an optimist and human behaviour is changing." Yorke also referred to George Monbiot's observation about how odd it was that in the course of a year, "we went from listening to sceptics who denied this was happening to suddenly saying we're all doomed—how interesting that both scenarios demand that we do nothing," Yorke suggested, to which he was to add, "That can't be right," concluding his article with the suggestion that "you should never give up hope."

9

POSTAPOCALYPSE? (2009–2012)

Ed O'Brien and Phil Selway returned to New Zealand again at the end of 2008 into the beginning of 2009 to participate in recording and performing on behalf of Neil Finn's 7 Worlds Collide project. Meanwhile, Thom Yorke and Jonny Greenwood began the new year with a February performance at the Grammy Awards with the University of Southern California Trojan Marching Band, where they performed "15 Step," and Radiohead received the award for Best Alternative Album for *In Rainbows*. The next month, the band made their first trip south of the U.S. border since 1994, with two shows in Mexico City, followed by five shows in Chile, Argentina, and Brazil, countries in which they were performing for the very first time. That August the band returned to the UK and Europe, where they also played their first show in Poland since 1994, along with their first-ever appearances in Austria and the Czech Republic. Yorke had also made a solo appearance at a UK festival in July and then performed three October shows in Los Angeles that featured mainly repertoire from *The Eraser*. The musicians with whom he was playing were soon to become known as Atoms for Peace and included Nigel Godrich, drummer Joey Waronker from REM and Beck, Forro in the Dark's percussionist Mauro Refosco, and bassist Flea from the Red Hot Chili Peppers.

That June the audio content for the second album disc of *In Rainbows* was added to the band's website for download at a set price, but over that spring and summer, and with no input from the band, EMI also released deluxe editions of their Parlophone/Capitol albums. Following just months after the previously mentioned boxed set had been released, this collection included things like extra audio CDs comprised of B sides and radio sessions, along with DVDs that featured special TV appearances. In August, the band released for download, at the price of one pound, the song "Harry Patch (In Memory Of)," the proceeds of which were donated to the British Legion. A tribute to the last British veteran of World War I, Yorke wrote the song after hearing an interview with Patch, who, at the age of 111, was the oldest person in England at the time. A couple of weeks later another new song, "These Are My Twisted Words," was made available for free download, leading people to wonder if this was to become characteristic of future music releases, and to question whether an emphasis on individual songs was subverting the central place of the album form. O'Brien pointed out how this was really nothing new, however, since even the Beatles had frequently released songs only as singles. Illustrating that there'd been ample studio time taking place that summer as well, the next month saw two new Yorke solo songs appear as a limited-edition vinyl single and then as a digital download: "The Hollow Earth" and "Feeling Pulled Apart by Horses" (an early version of "Reckoner" from 2001). At the end of the year, O'Brien announced on the blog *Dead Air Space* that the band would return to the studio to continue recording in January 2010. But additional solo activities had been taking place in the background as well and would continue to do so.

First, Jonny Greenwood debuted a new multimovement work called "Doghouse" in February at the BBC's Maida Vale Studios, composed in large part while he was on the road with Radiohead. Later the piece was expanded into his score for the Japanese film released later that year called *Norwegian Wood*, based on Haruki Murakami's novel of the same name. In April, Yorke did a number of shows with Atoms for Peace, a name taken from one of *The Eraser* songs, itself an allusion to the title of Dwight Eisenhower's 1953 speech to the UN. Yorke, along with Philip Glass and Damien Rice, also contributed to the soundtrack of a documentary about Tibetan exile called *When the Dragon Swallowed the Sun*. Having written two of the songs on the last 7 Worlds Collide project, it was no surprise when, that August, Phil Selway released his first solo album *Familial*. What was surprising, however, was the extent to which he yielded the drumming chair, instead primarily playing guitar and singing, with the record featuring backup from fellow

7 Worlds Collide contributors Lisa Germano and Sebastian Steinberg, along with Glenn Kotche and Pat Sansone of Wilco fame. Selway also did a number of live shows in 2010 with the backup of other musicians.

Radiohead returned to work in September and by January were putting the finishing touches on *The King of Limbs*, which was self-released as a download on February 18, 2011. Other formats emerged the following month by way of Ticker Tape Limited, the band's newly established record distribution label through which they intended to license their future work from the album. In the manner of the *In Rainbows* release, the group also offered a special edition of the recording, which was to arrive at purchasers' homes in May. Aside from releasing the video of "Lotus Flowers" and distributing a different version of the newspaper that was to accompany the special edition at sixty-one independent music stores worldwide, the band did not in the usual sense promote the album: they released no singles, performed only three shows over the entire year, and did no interviews, in Yorke's words, because "we didn't want to explain it." Nevertheless, he and Stanley Donwood gave copies of the newspaper out on a London street at the end of March.

The album—their first to clock in at under forty minutes—nevertheless peaked at number three on the Billboard 200 and at number seven on the UK Albums Chart, and although it was to do so in the UK and Canada, it was the first Radiohead album not to achieve gold in the United States, suggesting that its lack of promotion was to affect its commercial success. According to co-manager Chris Hufford's comments to David Fricke in "Radiohead Reconnect," notwithstanding "financially, it was probably the most successful record they've ever made, or pretty close," adding, "In a traditional deal, the record company takes the majority of the money."

Members of the group were also quite involved with their own activist and other projects during this period. Through his campaign work for Friends of the Earth, Yorke had attended the Copenhagen Climate Summit in December 2009. He posted commentary on the Radiohead website concerning his frustration not only with the positions being presented by the United States but also with the closed-door meetings from which nongovernmental organizations were being excluded, as well as with the summit's ultimate outcome. According to a letter from Ben Stewart of Greenpeace that Yorke likewise uploaded, the summit was a "historic failure that will live in infamy." Earlier in the year, O'Brien had become the founding director of the Featured Artists Coalition, an organization dedicated to making change in the music industry that was to lobby on behalf of young musicians and fans, an effort for which he predicted aggressive backlash from the entertainment establishment. In addition to making a special appearance toward the middle of 2011 DJing on Domino Radio, Colin Greenwood was the following year to become the global ambassador for the Children's Radio Foundation, in his own words, promoting "young people's voices in Africa through radio," focusing on their "stories and lives," and the training of young journalists and broadcasters. In this regard, Greenwood spoke about how African music had inspired him a lot, particularly music of the mid-1970s from Nigeria and Ghana. Greenwood and O'Brien were interviewed in April 2011 for a film called *Anyone Can Play Guitar* about the history of the Oxford music scene, with the latter also interviewed the previous month for a short promotional documentary called *It Cuts Both Ways . . . The Alternatives*, which encouraged public demonstrations against the 2011 UK budget cuts that resulted in eliminating important remedial programs, in an environment of record youth unemployment. Selway, meanwhile, had become a patron of the Pegasus Theatre in Oxford, helping it launch its fiftieth birthday celebrations in November with two special solo gigs that raised funds for the youth development programs that the theater runs. Through his ongoing involvement with the Samaritans, Selway was to say to Jamie Hill, "I managed to get both organisations to start working together and they've come up with this fantastic production called 'The Listener' which will be touring schools around the country next year." To this he added, "For me it is great to see two organisations that are very close to my heart helping each other out." The following month, shortly after its most high-profile action to date—the Occupy Wall Street demonstrations in New York—Yorke spoke in support of what was to become an international force called the Occupy Movement, which had arisen shortly after the demonstrations associated with the Arab Spring. A reaction to the 2008 financial meltdown, Yorke called the movement "inspiring," and in regard to banks being "too big to fail" suggested that they "can't have it both ways." He was also to DJ at Occupy London alongside 3D from Massive Attack (now thought to be mysterious graffiti artist Banksy).

Some of the intervening time before the band was to reassemble in late 2011 was spent with Yorke performing a couple of U.S. dates with Atoms for Peace. Selway meanwhile was preparing to play more solo dates in Europe and Japan over August and September following his second release, the four-song EP *Running Blind*. Meanwhile, in addition to scoring the film *We Need to Talk About Kevin* (a film based on Lionel Shriver's novel of the same name), Jonny Greenwood was collaborating on September performances in Poland with the renowned composers Steve Reich and Krzysztof Penderecki, the latter with whom, just over six months later, he was to release an album that combined their work. These included Penderecki's celebrated compositions "Polymorphia" and "Threnody for the Victims of Hiroshima," alongside Greenwood's "Popcorn Superhet Receiver" and "48 Responses to Polymorphia."

Though they played a surprise set at Britain's Glastonbury Festival in June, the band left their major promotional work until toward the end of 2011, when they played two September shows at New York's Roseland Ballroom. This was accompanied by TV appearances on *Saturday Night Live*, *Late Night with Jimmy Fallon*, and a special one-hour edition of *The Colbert Report*. For these performances they recruited Clive Deamer of Portishead to supplement Selway's drums, in an effort to reproduce the overdubbed drum loops used in songs from the new album. October saw the band release a double-CD remix of *The King of Limbs*, called *TKOL RMX 1234567*, which features remixes from Caribou, Jamie xx, and Four Tet, among others, many of whom participated as DJs for a celebration of its release at London's Corsica Studios, at which Yorke also indulged in some DJing. In this regard, he was to say of this whole effort, "It was kind of my baby." Concurrently released was the song "Retarded Fren," which Yorke and Jonny Greenwood collaborated on with Doom for a compilation celebrating the tenth anniversary of Lex Records.

Just as, in the months following the emergence of *The King of Limbs*, the band had released a single and downloads for the songs "Supercollider" and "The Butcher," December had them release "The Daily Mail" and "Staircase," song performances taken from the video *The King of Limbs: Live from the Basement*, also released that month. From this time up until January 2012, the band was working on new material at their Oxfordshire studio, rehearsing also for their upcoming tour. In addition to preparing his score of Paul Thomas Anderson's film *The Master*, released later that year in September, Greenwood hosted another joint concert with Penderecki in London, which coincided with the March release of their aforementioned recording. The band's tour had begun in February, meanwhile, and extended to November—the most extensive the group had undertaken since 2008, and which included fifty-eight shows over ten months in Europe, North America, Asia, and Australia. For the tour Radiohead had worked up more than seventy-five songs, including some new material written during their rehearsals, and it was common practice that Yorke, Selway, and O'Brien would sit around on the days of shows to compile that night's set list. O'Brien emphasized that they were concentrating on inside performances rather than outside ones, to enjoy better light and sound and not to be at the mercy of the elements. In relation to the DJing ethos and rhythmic emphasis that Yorke and Godrich had brought into the work, O'Brien said, "We've been calling this show 'the big rave.'" Suggesting that their performance had become "like a rave with guitars," he also indicated that he thought they were "the best shows we've ever done" because, typical of rave culture, they possessed a spirit of "love and light," which contrasted some of the dark energy characterizing the band in its earlier days. Of the Beatles' song "All You Need Is Love," one of the songs that had been released in the form of a single, O'Brien was to say, "It's true! . . . we've found that . . . and bring it to our shows."

But, sadly, as I was leaving home to see Radiohead's June 16 performance in the city of Toronto, tragedy struck the band, and they announced that the show was cancelled. Part of the stage had collapsed during its setup, killing Selway's drum technician Scott Johnson and injuring three others. Radiohead's European tour dates were likewise postponed, and the band was not to return to Toronto again for six years.

THE KING OF LIMBS

"None of us want to get into that creative hoo-ha of a long-play record again. . . . It's just become a real drag," Yorke remarked to *Pitchfork* in February 2011. "It worked with *In Rainbows* because we had a real fixed idea about where we were going. But we've all said that we can't possibly dive into that again. It'll kill us." Such comments of course, again, fed the ruminations about whether albums were becoming a thing of the past, and while *In Rainbows* foregrounds guitars, *The King of Limbs* emphasizes electronic experimentation, a characteristic that was once again to alienate some listeners, much in the way *Kid A/ Amnesiac* had done in the wake of *OK Computer.* During their time in Los Angeles as suggested, Yorke and Godrich had become more interested in DJing. Thus, although Yorke reported that he didn't think anything would come of it, Godrich proposed a two-week experiment involving each band member creating loops, using turntables and vinyl emulation software rather than their usual instruments, an experiment that the producer later reported had in fact consumed six months. "We didn't want to pick up guitars and write chord sequences. We didn't want to sit in front of a computer either. We wanted a third thing, which involved playing and programming," said Jonny Greenwood, who'd written sampling software that he described as a "wonky, rubbish version of Ableton Live." In this way the album was what O'Brien referred to as "studio-conceived," and Yorke once again likened its creation to editing a film. "I can see why it's alienated people," the singer later said to *Rolling Stone*'s David Fricke in "Radiohead Reconnect." "I didn't realize it was its own planet." That it *was*, however, something of its own planet was evident in the fact that the band had to learn how to play the songs once they were finished. But as Yorke was to add, "There is no way in hell we could have come up with what we're doing now, live, if we hadn't been sitting in front of turntables and samplers, piecing the record together in this method. There is no way it would have turned into this dynamic thing."

In this relation, when the band finally did turn to granting interviews in late 2011 and were asked what the new album was about, Yorke suggested that it was about "wildness" and "mutating" and again, in large part, a response to the environmental question. He also recommended that it related to "breaking out of things" or "breaking free," and Stanley Donwood, in *Pitchfork*, pointed out to Jon Severs that the digital music format had in a way freed the band up. "Before, the way the music was produced determined the packaging, be it vinyl, tape, or CD," said Donwood. "But, with digital, that's irrelevant," explaining that "now you could just make a whole load of art and sell it with the digital files."

In this way, the band and he were to make the packaging in its entirety part of the special edition artwork. In addition to the digital download, consisting of two ten-inch vinyl records, a CD, and an accompanying newspaper, the latter tells us that the full-color piece of plastic film holding the package all together is made of oxo-biodegradable or OBD plastic. Reporting that while conventional plastics will typically take hundreds of years to degrade, the newspaper says the process is shortened with OBD ones to a period of years and months. Similarly, the curious sheet of LSD or "acid" blotting paper, though not of "archival quality," is said to be "FSC certified"—FSC being the Forest Stewardship Council, which certifies that a wooden product is made with or contains wood from FSC-certified forests or from postconsumer waste. It notes also that the board used for the records and CD sleeves are similarly certified as coming from responsibly sourced material that should last a little longer than the newspaper, which is printed on paper comprised of approximately 30 percent recycled material. The newspaper similarly informs us that the chemical processes used to produce newsprint paper result in its becoming brittle and yellowed through its exposure to air and sunlight, "mirroring the inexorable decay of all things." Nevertheless, we're also informed that, if such items are retained with care, all "the materials used will outlast the owner."

The album had its own official website called "Universal Sigh," also the name used for the newspaper, and likewise a formulation found in the first lyrics of the album's opening track "Bloom." Again exhibiting an awareness of environmental concerns, the website promised that the band would "measure the carbon footprint of this project, and to offset the potential ecological impact, we will retire the carbon credits used," adding that carbon retirement "is the most effective method of offsetting, because it is the only way you can be 100% sure that the emission reduction you pay for will take place." Interestingly, the site also referred to Radiohead's latest offering as "the world's first newspaper album." In this regard, when further asked by NPR's *All Things Considered* about meaning in *The King of Limbs*, Yorke explained, "It's sort of a visual thing rather than anything else. That's why all the images we used when we did . . . the special edition thing with the newspaper, that was a very important part of the music, this time, where I didn't really feel lyrics were . . . there weren't conscious thematics going on at all. It was like, physical movements."

The website, as well as Yorke's comments, recommend that the newspaper, then, is a good place to start thinking about the album's significance, and in this it's interesting to consider the further comments of Stanley Donwood to *Pitchfork*: "The whole idea of this album was to have something that was almost not existing, so we chose clear vinyl and the newspaper format." He also noted that the *In Rainbows* special edition had been a very heavy and substantial thing: "It was very much a definitive statement, and that isn't where the band are at the moment," suggesting where they were as being, instead, more transitory. "When a newspaper comes out, that doesn't mean news stops, what you have is just a snapshot of how things were at the moment that newspaper was printed." As he also emphasized, "The music is a continuing thing. And we wanted to make the album representative of that."

Reinforcing many commentators' view that the album probes the theme of technology in conflict with the natural world, Donwood continued, also in relation to his enthusiasm for newspapers, "They are disposable. They are recyclable. They fall apart so easily. They are not like iPads or Kindles that can't be disposed of and end up on some third-world shore." He also talked about a large pile of old late 1960s magazines that someone had left at Colin Greenwood's country place. "They were really cheaply printed and produced in a hurry and were decaying and had lost their corners, but they had become this archive that didn't exist on the internet," in addition, thereby, suggesting the theme of technology in conflict with *culture*: "And since they're not posh enough to be in the British Museum or elsewhere, they acquired a value because of their disposability." Along these lines Donwood also pointed out, "If you turned the electricity off, digital records would all disappear, but newspapers have the physical reality, the longevity." Additionally, he mused, regarding the Gutenberg printing press and the history of the newspaper industry, in its relation to the cultural evolution of modernity, "I love the history of Fleet Street (which featured in The Eraser's art), the revolution that was moving type." As he explained, newspapers "changed the world from being a really class based, feudal system to people being able to cheaply get information that informed them."

From print to paper to trees, near Tottenham House in Wiltshire, where Radiohead had recorded parts of *In Rainbows*, is Savernake Forest, and there can be found an ancient tree, referred to as "The King of

Limbs." Between 1,000 and 1,100 years of age, the tree is older than the English nation itself, thus establishing a tension in the contrast between transience and longevity or continuity. This sense of deep time is evoked, moreover, through the inclusion of a number of words appearing on the paper's front page. These include "Pangaea," which, aside from being the title of a Miles Davis album and the alias of electronic dance artist Kevin McAuly, is a supercontinent that broke apart roughly 175 million years ago in the Southern Hemisphere. Surrounding this supercontinent also was a superocean, known as "Panthalassa" (or "Proto-Pacific"), another word found on the front page, and these existed during the late Paleozoic and early Mesozoic eras. The Permian period, conjured by the inclusion of a painting featured in the newspaper called *Permian Beast*, marked the distinction between the two eras and is understood to be the largest mass extinction recorded in the history of life on earth. Yorke also spoke, in this regard, of the "mutating of creatures" and of the little we know about the world from our understanding of fossils and the like. In line with the forest imagery are the inclusion of words like "fauna" and "game," along with "sprite" and "hob." A sprite is an ethereal entity or supernatural, fairylike creature, often used in reference to elves in European folklore, while a hob is a small mythological household spirit, found especially on the Anglo-Scottish border, as per the traditional folklore of the region. Donwood pointed out that much of his inspiration for the album's artwork had derived from "the northern European imagination," in the sense that "all our fairy stories and mythical creatures, they all come from the woods—Little Red Riding Hood, Sleeping Beauty, Hansel & Gretel."

Among other things featured in the newspaper, there's a piece about climbing trees by landscape writer and academic Robert Macfarlane, along with a story called "Forests of the Mind" by Jay Griffiths, who has frequently written about nature's transformative power. Items like these are seen alongside images of trees, ghosts, and other strange creatures, and toward the center of the newspaper are found a number of illustrations accompanied by the following words and phrases: "root of roots," "Ragnarok," "Urpflanze," "The King of Limbs," "codex," "axis mundi," "Yggdrasil," and "Arbor Philosophica."

Trees have often been seen as powerful symbols of growth, death, and rebirth, due to the annual death and revival of their foliage. In Norse cosmology, Yggdrasil is an enormous mythical ash tree, the axis mundi or pillar that connects the nine worlds, and similar mythical power and meaning is clearly associated here with the "King of Limbs." The center of the cosmos and the root of roots, Yggdrasil is considered very holy and the location at which the gods daily assemble. The ancient concept of mankind originating from the trunks of trees is common in Germanic regions, and this creation of humans from trees is repeated, following what's called the Ragnarok. In Norse mythology, the Ragnarok is the apocalyptic battle that the gods will fight against the giants, prior to the world's consumption in flames and its creation anew. Of course, we've seen such imagery used in the previous two albums, through the story of Noah and the flood, but here it is, again, evidently implicated in ongoing concerns about global warming and technological apocalypse.

The title of one of the album's songs, "codex" is originally a Latin word, meaning "trunk of a tree" or "block of wood," but it's also the name given to the medieval book that, at first, tended to be mostly holy scriptures and commentaries upon them. We've seen how the importance of literacy has been a theme across Radiohead's earlier work, and especially when combined with paper and printing, the codex, as Donwood observed, was a technology, alongside the newspaper, that greatly enhanced the creation and transmission of knowledge and information. A fine example of this would be Goethe's famous 1791 booklet "The Metamorphosis of Plants," prior to which he was developing his hypothesis of the Urpflanze, or primal plant from which he thought all others may have derived. The Arbor Philosophica or "philosophical tree," meanwhile, was a representation frequently used by medieval alchemists and also the title for the last of five essays in Carl Jung's volume "Alchemical Studies," found in his *Collected Works*. Sustaining the motif of transformation, alchemists are of course best known for their attempts to transform other metals into gold, and Jung was specifically interested in alchemy's psychological and religious implications, given it was first introduced more as a religion than a science, that is, until eventually shunned out of existence.

It's no accident, therefore, in the aftermath of the 2008 global financial crisis, that following the first pages of paintings and illustrations in the *King of Limbs* newspaper is a full-page item called "Sell Your House and Buy Gold," suggesting perhaps a connection between alchemists and those responsible for the financial crisis. Also, in this regard, it's no accident that Donwood uses fonts from 1930s-era American newspapers, pointing out how they're all from the Great Depression. Apparently written by Donwood, the narrative presents another Radiohead antihero and begins, "I had disregarded a thousand different types and variations of warning for years." The character tells us he had "believed implicitly in the power of the Authorities to deal with any situation that may have worried me," and noted too that his bookshelves were full of books loaded with "scientific explanations." Representative of us all in relation to global warming and climate change, he says, "I did not think that my life, or more precisely, the manner in which I lived it was effectively an inexorably lengthy suicide, although, of course, it was." Hopefully in contrast to us, however, he adds that he didn't miss the butterflies, or the birdsong, which he reports reminded him, in any event, of car alarms or mobile phones. "There seemed to be no particular urgency regarding the disaster," he suggests, "only a dull sort of inevitability." Employing Yorke's light/dark imagery, the character reports, "We built a house with too many shadows in it," referring to massive technological and economic failure, as telephones became unreliable, bank machines frequently empty of money, and petrol also no more. This, as he says, "led to some very unpleasant scenes." Next, one could no longer buy newspapers or other commodities, such as lightbulbs, razors, and soap. As he mentions in regard to when electricity disappeared, however, "That was where our real problems started."

Recounting how our challenges had compounded, encouraged by "our sneers," "casual indifference," and "the ignorant manner in which we chose to live," these problems represented "the dark, inevitable spectre that accompanied us to the cashpoint, into work, to the supermarket." After there was no more electricity, "the shadows conspired against us," he writes. The writer tells of killing a dissenter, and though no one witnessed him do it he was not ashamed, conveying, "Mine was a necessary act, an act which intended to prove that we had to be strong and united against the looming disaster." As with any ritual scapegoat situation, he reports how they carried the individual's dead body "beyond the perimeter wire and left it in a ditch." To this he added, "Inevitably, there were people who objected, and they were next." He observes that the shadows appeared to increase in density and number as the people in the house decreased, and concludes, "When I was at last alone, when the people were all gone, I waited for the disaster on my own."

It's interesting that this overwhelming sense of darkness does not so much color the album's music and lyrics, at least during its second half. Perhaps this is related to its rootedness in rave culture, raves often being uplifting and quasi-religious events, but there's much religious imagery evident in the album as well. Recalling how he works alongside the band when they're writing and recording, Donwood was to say to the *Independent*'s John Severs of the early stages of the project, "As I listened, I had this vision of these old churches where you had these huge ceilings of overarching, intertwined colors, and this led me to painting all these colored trees." Referring to the ceiling tracery and fluted columns of churches, Donwood suggests that they owe their form to the interlocked tree trunks and branches of the forest, adding, "I wanted to free that imagery from religion and give it back to nature." In addition to inspiring this overarching "canopy of detail," Donwood reports becoming fascinated with the idea of "a cathedral of sound." In this relation, among the various musical influences that permeate the album are dubstep (no doubt influenced by the time Yorke spent with Flying Lotus), tribal, Afrobeat, and jazz artists such as Alice Coltrane and John Martyn, who'd largely worked outside genre and commercial considerations. As one reviewer keenly observed of the aging Gen Xers, it perhaps made sense that they were increasingly to align themselves with jazz and the experimental tradition, rather than with rock 'n' roll's youth and "virility-obsessed" conventions.

Tellingly employing a visual metaphor, Yorke said of *The King of Limbs*, "Almost every tune is like a collage." In this way the album's first song "Bloom" was inspired by the BBC nature documentary series *The Blue Planet* and emerges from a repeated piano motif, very much in the style of composer Philip Glass, and this is followed by a relentless sequence of electronic and actual drum loops, reflective of the "somersaulting" found in the second verse. The opening lyrics conjure the image of both terrestrial and aquatic plant life as the lungs of the earth, beckoning the listener to "open your mouth wide" and to participate in "the universal sigh." Returning to the use of water imagery, which is sustained in the second verse through references to a giant turtle and jellyfish floating by, the divine-sounding voice acknowledges that what keeps him alive is the blooming ocean. As indicated by the use of quotation marks on the newspaper's front page, it's our protagonist who asks, "So why does this still hurt?" to which the voice advises not to blow his mind with "whys." The horns and trumpet calls bring the middle instrumental section to a climax and launch the divine voice's somer-saulting out of orbit through space and time, perhaps back to Panthalas-sa.

As the song scales down toward the end and forcefully concludes with Colin Greenwood's inventive bass motif, we're transferred to "Morning Mr. Magpie," a song thought, in this context, to be about the global financial crisis, even though its composition actually preceded it by some years. An old live acoustic ballad, here the song is recast in a more anxious Afrobeat light, with its unrelenting, muted, two-note funk, dueling guitars, adding a sense of agitation and amplified by the song's crackling hi-hats and crisp polyrhythmic percussion. Originally also referred to as "Morning M'Lord," a solo version of which Yorke was seen performing on Radiohead Television back in the *Hail to the Thief* days, the combined titles conjure our thieving magpie financial "Au-thorities" being rebuked by our protagonist. Tense and threatening after the immersive opening number, he accuses them of stealing everything, and of having the nerve to even show their faces. Demand-ing of them that they "give it back," he notes in the second verse that they don't, despite knowing they should. Not only stealing all life's magic, the protagonist asserts in the song's chorus, hearkening back to *Amnesiac* and its association with the codex, that Mr. Magpie has like-wise indirectly deprived him of his memory. The spooky bridge por-tends the protagonist's developing shadows, evident in the next song, and he's portrayed in the second iteration of the chorus as a fellow bird from whom the magpie has deprived of his "melody." The song con-cludes with sound effects of birdsong, heard in conflict with the elec-tronic sounds of white noise, representing the antagonism between technology and the natural environment.

At the bottom of a subsequent page of the album's newspaper, the following is printed: "I will tape myself up, build myself a raft from whatever is hanging around, and push off from our imaginary desert island that I forgot to tell you existed, at least to me. Wish you well like a brave tin soldier. With all the strength I have left in me, let the currents and forces of nature do what they will, having no interest in their wholesome fucking worthy fluorescent reality." Sustaining the water imagery, on yet another page we get the phrase, "I claw and I grasp, cling onto a raft," and the protagonist's sense of darkness visible is evident in the next song, "Little by Little," where things have turned very nasty and he acknowledges his soul's dark "pillar." Describing himself as "the last one out of the box," presumably a reference to being the last to leave the house of encroaching shadows, we know that he's also the self-appointed one who "broke the spell" of dissent. Yorke's bizarrely articulated singing of the chorus reveals the character's possessed state, where he achieves his ends "little by little" and "by hook or by crook," the latter a phrase first recorded in the fourteenth century, meaning "by whatever means necessary." The character describes a life of never being judged and of not living earnestly, and remarks, "I don't know where I should look," reflective of a lingering inquisitiveness like that he expressed in the album's opening song. The second verse sees the dissenter's clue "on hold," while the teasing protagonist and his flirtatious love curl up together. The flag and pole, representing unity and unanimity, are still strongly in the background, however, despite the character's presumed previous rejection of such collectivism (inherent in another line from the "Universal Sigh" newspaper, "spare me all your waving flags"). Having broken the dissenter's spell, he's also the one who, little by little, breaks "the seal" of the community's bonds. Recalling "No Surprises" from *OK Computer*, the song's unsettling bridge suggests that the character's disintegration is also the product of obligations, complications, routines, schedules, and "a job that killed you."

For a period Yorke continued to plug singles by the likes of Zomby, Untold, and Ramadanman on the Radiohead website, and the next track, "Feral," is the clearest example of the influence of such conduits of the UK-bred dance subgenre dubstep. But the piece also bears signs of influence from trip hop and Afro bounce. The song features a sharp-as-glass and mulched-up drum pattern, occasional synth sounds, overloaded bass, and scattered vocal samples. Though they're practically inaudible, the lyrics associated with the track appear to be, "You are not mine, and I am not yours. And that's okay. Please don't judge me— judge." "Feral," of course, means wild, and we should recall Yorke's comment concerning the album being about "wildness." It's likely, in this regard, that Yorke took the title from the journalist George Monbiot's 2013 book *Feral*, a book about revitalizing and reconnecting with the natural world, published with separate subtitles (first as *Searching for Enchantment on the Frontiers of Rewilding* and then as *Rewilding the Land, Sea and Human Life*). The expectation of not being judged and the casual sense of the love attraction suggest continuity with the previous song. Alternatively, the lyrics may refer to the disintegrating relationships with those around him in "the house" or "box."

Yorke first performed the trip-hop-influenced "Lotus Flower" with Atoms for Peace, and Radiohead's video for the song was to go viral on social media through the hashtag #thomdance. According to Yorke, with the song being about "having it off" or having sex, it has an erotic tinge both musically and lyrically, with mention of shaping oneself into another's pocket and the repetition of invitations such as "do what you want," or "while the cat is away, do what we want." But the song creates unease, too, as when he sings about the empty space within his heart "where the weeds take root." Also it's unclear what he means by "now I'll set you free," which could either mean that this individual's about to be taken to the heights of erotic bliss or refer to the one who's next to have his or her carcass carried out to the ditch. The chorus has the protagonist singing, "Slowly we unfurl as lotus flowers," which conjures the lotus-eaters of Greek mythology, whose island was dominated by lotus plants, the fruits and flowers of which were a narcotic that caused those who ate them to sleep in peaceful apathy. Like some kind of sorcerer, all the protagonist wants is "the moon upon a stick, just to see what if, just to see what is," and toward the end of the piece, he's portrayed dancing around a pit with darkness beneath. The character's unable to help his addressee kick their lotus habit and associated apathy, presumably as doing so is likely to balloon their head and turn them into a dissenter. The line "listen to your heart" adds to the song's ambivalence, as does another that appears prior to the final iteration of the chorus: "Bird that's flown into my room." This phrase is also prominently displayed as a headline in the newspaper, and as we find out in the recording's final song, the creature appears to be some kind of savior for the protagonist, as the album begins its turn toward the light.

This turn begins with the rapid fade-in of "Codex," comprised partly of a peculiar vocal fragment that seems to emphasize the sudden shift of context. Recalling that the word "codex" derives from the Latin for "trunk of a tree," the song, particularly with the reappearance of birdsong at the end, returns us to an emphasis on nature and to the setting of a lake. The milieu reminds us of our protagonist and his raft, and though he's alone and the song is somber sounding and in a minor key, it does not portray the kind of distress associated with the newspaper references. Accompanying the change of context is a shift of instrumentation that signals authenticity, the song's basis being a murkily flanged acoustic piano with brass and string accompaniment. The opening phrase, "sleight of hand," suggests that a kind of dramatic deception has been involved in his being saved from the darkness, and the "fantasized" dragonflies suggest that the scene is, at least in part, a fantasy. That the previous dark aspects of the recording may also have been fantasy is reinforced in the album's closing number, where the protagonist feels he's awakened from a long dream. Perhaps the most important part of "Codex" is the lines "no one gets hurt" and "you've done nothing wrong," and the song's imagery of immersing oneself in the "clear and innocent," cleansing water is indicative of a kind of spiritual purity and renewal. Since it very early adopted the format for use with the Bible, the spread of the codex is often specifically associated with the rise and spread of Christianity.

And despite the frequent disavowals of his childhood religious background, the next song, "Give Up the Ghost," is likewise a phrase that conjures Christianity, occurring as it does frequently throughout the Bible, including its use to describe the death of Christ himself. The sense of authenticity and rebirth is reinforced and sustained, as birdsong accompanies the listener into a sonic environment featuring a gently plucked acoustic guitar, which has Yorke's hand rhythmically and gently tapping the wood of its body. Singing, "don't hurt me" and "don't haunt me," a mystical-sounding refrain in a sort of call-and-response with the lead vocal of the protagonist establishes continuity with the previous song. The imagery evoked in the lyrics also seems very Christian, with what appear to be the voices of "the lost," "the pitiful," and "their souls" singing this refrain. Before confessing to having had his fill, the protagonist pleads for them to be gathered up, remarking in a sigh of submission, "I think I should give up the ghost" and enter into "what seems impossible"—the arms of the divine.

The song "Separator" concludes the album on a sweet and easy note, characterized by its major key, its highlife guitar, its trebly and upbeat drums, and Yorke's relaxed-sounding voice. It's here we find the protagonist reporting that it's as if he's "fallen out of bed from a long and vivid dream," most recently one in which "sweetest flowered fruits were hanging from the trees" and where, at least part of the time, he's been carried around by a "giant bird." In this way, it's as though we return to "Lotus Flower" and the woman dissenter who "blows her cover," but here the protagonist unambiguously speaks of having lost her number and of wanting to "slip over and get back under." Among the lines continually repeated toward the conclusion of the song are "wake me up," which suggests that aspects of the song's title, "Separator," include a pulling back or separation from death, the afterlife, and sleep toward nature, the divinity of life, and wakefulness. Armed with his renewed spirit and vision, the protagonist awakes from fantasy, hopelessness, and complacency, singing, "If you think this is over then you're wrong." By "this," he could mean a number of things, including his own life, his relationship with the woman, or the apocalypse itself, which is of course not predetermined. In this regard, he could likewise mean the fight associated with resistance to the apocalypse.

In any case, free from all the weight he's been carrying, he says, "I've my heart in my mouth," recalling Ed O'Brien's comments about the band bringing love to their *King of Limbs* performances. As we also note the prominent full-page "love?" that appears toward the end of the album's newspaper, it's clear that love is meant again to be the most prominent theme. This is perhaps best expressed by Yorke to Brian Raftery in *Spin* magazine, some years earlier in acknowledgment of how bad things were and still are: "I have to be positive," he says, in the context of having two kids and a family, "because when it comes down to it—how do I say this without sounding really revolting?—you have to get up every day with love in your heart."

10

FORGING FORWARD (2013–2016)

The 2012 tour in support of *The King of Limbs* was to end in Australia that November. And as Colin Greenwood reported to Kyle McGovern of *Spin* magazine early in the new year, "We're taking some time out whilst people are doing some other stuff, doing their own things, and the plan is to get back together again [at the] end of the summer." However, Thom Yorke was suggesting by July that the band would be taking an entire year off, because "Ed wanted to go live somewhere else and switch off," moving to Brazil to devote his full time and attention toward being a father. As it turned out, Radiohead was not in fact to reconvene properly until the fall of 2014.

In the meantime, Yorke's supergroup, Atoms for Peace, had released their first and second singles as downloads—"Default" in September 2012 and "Judge, Jury and Executioner" in January 2013. February saw the band upload a video for "Ingenue" to YouTube, and their new album, *Amok*, released on XL Recordings, had been temporarily made available for streaming on the band's official website prior to its release. A third single called "Before Your Very Eyes" was then released in July, followed up by the song's video in October. Yorke talked about the strangeness of opting for the relative obscurity of starting afresh with a new band and name, and was surprised when one interviewer pointed out that, in addition to reusing the title of a track on *The Eraser* for the band name, Yorke had unintentionally reused the title "Judge, Jury and Executioner," the subtitle of *Hail to the Thief*'s "Myxomatosis." Some of the *Amok* material, including "Stuck Together Pieces," likewise came from music that Yorke composed in late 2011 for the following spring's New York Fashion Week, in particular for the show of the Rag and Bone clothing label of the New York designers David Neville and Marcus Wainright. Yorke was regularly to provide the annual soundtrack for this event in the coming years, combining forces with Jonny Greenwood in 2013 and with Nigel Godrich in 2014.

Accompanied by sporadic performances in Europe, the United States, and Japan throughout much of 2013, *Amok* was the product of three days of jamming and recording in a Los Angeles studio that immediately followed the conclusion of the band's 2010 tour dates. The ensemble bonded over their shared love of Afrobeat and Fela Kuti, and in this regard, Yorke tellingly remarked to Tim Adams of the *Observer*, "When I'm DJing I always put an afrobeat tune in between dance tracks of the same speed because it suddenly loosens everything up. Because it's more human." Having his fellow band members re-create electronic music he'd composed on his laptop, he suggested to Michael Roffman of *Time* in regard to the music's angularity, "When you get people to play like that, it's so peculiar. . . . One of the things we were most excited about was ending up with a record where you weren't quite sure where the human starts and the machine ends."

In one sense, this was likewise manifested by the fact that Yorke and Godrich took the results of these brief three days of sessions and, over the next couple of years, edited and arranged them, in conjunction with further augmentations of Yorke's electronic music. But this theme was likewise evident in Stanley Donwood's album cover artwork, which had apparently been widely viewed prior to the recording's release, including at his solo 2012 exhibition called "Lost Angeles," held the previous April at Subliminal Projects on Sunset Boulevard. The *Amok* cover images portray the Hollywood Hills underwater, a stretch Hummer tilting toward the sky, and landmarks such as Grauman's Chinese Theatre and the Walt Disney Concert Hall are also seen, while meteorites are pictured raining down on Griffith Observatory. The following message from Donwood greeted visitors to the exhibition: "There is no future. We have evicted ourselves from our own cities, rendered our agriculture poisonous, criminalized the poor, aggrandized the rich, honored the stupid and ridiculed the intelligent. . . . I have no solutions, no wisdom to offer. . . . Whilst Rome burns, I take up my little chisel and I carve a panoramic apocalypse of my own . . . and if you want to see it, you're more than welcome." In this relation, Yorke wasn't able to put into words the strange detachment he observed at the time in himself and those around him, suggesting that there's "a lot of fear and panic out there and not much sense of a future, and these are things not easily expressed in lyrics."

Jonny Greenwood, meanwhile, had accepted a three-month residency in Sydney with the Australian Chamber Orchestra in 2012, during which time he composed a new orchestral piece called "Water." The celebrated American composer Steve Reich also debuted his Radiohead-inspired piece "Radio Rewrite" in March 2013, following his encounter the previous year with Greenwood in Poland. Almost a year later, at the Wapping Hydraulic Power Station, Greenwood performed a concert of his own compositions, alongside the London Contemporary Orchestra, which also presented works by Baroque composers. The Australian premiere of "Water" occurred toward the end of 2014, which likewise saw the release of Greenwood's soundtrack for the Paul Thomas Anderson film *Inherent Vice*. Greenwood was to articulate his increasing appreciativeness of live classical performance and noted that Radiohead had reconvened that fall to begin work on the follow-up to *The King of Limbs*. In early 2015, he and Nigel Godrich spent three weeks recording at Mehrangarah Fort in Rajasthan, India, with the Israeli composer Shye Ben Tzur and twelve Indian musicians, an effort that also culminated in a festival performance. The project blends Arabic, Indian, and Western music and is associated with Paul Thomas Anderson's documentary *Junun*, also the title of the accompanying album released that November. That fall, too, he was to perform again with the London Contemporary Orchestra, first as part of David Byrne's Meltdown at the Southbank Centre in August, followed by a fall performance at Yotaspace in Moscow. His brother Colin, on the other hand, in September 2013 had surfaced to play a solo bass guitar soundtrack for a Parisian Runway event known as Nowfashion, and early in 2014, the elder Greenwood acted as the UK's live music ambassador for Independent Venue Week. This involved him sharing stories regarding Radiohead's experience of the UK circuit and promoting the importance of independent music venues for new and developing bands. He was to do this also at the University of Gloucestershire, where he fielded questions about the music industry posed by young music students.

In late 2014, Phil Selway began a stint that was to last years, filling in on occasion for Elbow singer and DJ Guy Garvey's BBC 6 radio program, *This Finest Hour*. And though it was completed back in February, the Radiohead drummer released his second solo album *Weatherhouse* only at the beginning of October, following the appearance of music videos for his first and second singles, "Coming Up for Air" (July) and "It Will End in Tears" (September). Appearing on *The Tonight Show*, Selway was to play more drums with this project, recording with the musicians who'd previously toured with him and who were to do so again across Europe, Japan, and the United States over much of the following year, when Selway also played a role in the donation and dedication of a drum set to the Manchester Central Library in memory of his former drum technician Scott Johnson, who had tragically died in the 2012 Toronto stage accident.

During this period, the band also maintained its reputation for technological savvy. Speaking of their previous tour, Yorke noted to Alex Baldwin of WNYC that it was the "scariest" one that Radiohead had ever undertaken, because it consisted mostly of "big gigs" from which they had typically tried to shy away. In this regard, however, he maintains that the band spent "a lot of time and effort coming up with . . . a stage design which used screens in a certain way which made it intimate even though . . . some nights it was like thirty or forty thousand people." Making reference to items like Jaron Lanier's 2010 book *You Are Not a Gadget* and Adam Curtis's 2011 BBC television series *All Watched Over by Machines of Loving Grace*, Yorke reminisced to Adams of the *Guardian* about the band's initial reception of the internet: "We were so into the net around the time of Kid A. . . . Really thought it might be an amazing way of connecting and communicating," he said. "And then very quickly we started having meetings where people started talking about what we did as 'content.' They would show us letters from big media companies offering us millions in some mobile phone deal or whatever it was, and they would say all they need is some content." Yorke, accordingly, referred to the new and emerging social media environment in terms of the "commodification of human relationships through social networks."

With the help of Godrich, Donwood, and a digital arts studio called Universal Everything, Radiohead was to curate their own content, with the February 2014 release of their Polyfauna app for Android and iOS.

The app featured experimental, interactive digital game worlds that employed ambient music and abstract visual landscapes from *The King of Limbs*, and these altered depending on how users tilted their devices. As Yorke suggested, this project had come "from an interest in early computer life-experiments and the imagined creatures of our subconscious." Atoms for Peace had teamed up the previous year with a British startup called Soundhalo, in order to sell audio and video of two performances at London's Roundhouse venue. Each song was made available shortly after its performance, through Soundhalo's website and its apps for iPhone, iPad, and Android devices.

Yorke pioneeringly released his second solo album, *Tomorrow's Modern Boxes*, in September 2014 via the website BitTorrent, a platform ordinarily associated with "illegal" downloading but taking the form here of its first "pay-gated bundle," an arrangement from which the site kept 10 percent of the $6 price for each download. "If it works well, it could be an effective way of handing some control of internet commerce back to people who are creating the work," Yorke and Godrich explained to Denver Nicks of *Time*, in their attempt to enable people who make digital content to sell it themselves and bypass the self-elected gatekeepers. "If it works, anyone can do this exactly as we have done." As it was to turn out, however, the experiment wasn't so successful. Characterizing it as a reaction against everything that was happening at the time, and everyone always talking solely about Spotify as the future of music consumption, Yorke later said to Larry Bartleet of *NME*, "I wanted to show that in theory today someone can follow the whole chain of music production, from start to end, on their own terms. In theory." But as the singer was to note, in practice it's very different. "You can't take on all the responsibility," he pointed out. "But I'm happy I did it, to have tried it."

Back in Sydney, Australia, from May 21 to June 6, 2015, Donwood held a twenty-five-year retrospective exhibition of his work that included thousands of original pieces, with many, of course, for sale. Known as *The Panic Office*, Yorke provided a soundtrack for the event with his ever-evolving piece "Subterranea," no minute of which was the same throughout the exhibition's eighteen-day duration. In addition to his solo performance at Suffolk's Latitude Festival in July (the live debut for many songs from *Tomorrow's Modern Boxes*), he sat in for a song with Portishead earlier the same day. And surprisingly, that August saw Yorke and his partner Rachel Owen announce that they had amicably separated, "after 23 highly creative and happy years."

Having been working on and off over 2015, the members of Radiohead reconvened from September to December to work on their anticipated follow-up to *The King of Limbs*. They were also busy during this time working on a theme for the new James Bond film, something that, according to Godrich, had thrown the band a massive curveball. "We stopped doing what we were doing and had to concentrate on that for awhile since we were told it was something that was going to come to fruition. I haven't seen the movie and I think they ended up with something more suitable for it," he maintained to Andy Greene of *Rolling Stone* on June 8, 2017, "but in terms of making *A Moon Shaped Pool* it caused a stop right when we were in the middle of it." On Christmas Day the band released the completed song for free on SoundCloud, with the following accompanying tweet from Yorke: "Last year we were asked to write a tune for Bond movie *Spectre*. . . . It didn't work out . . . but became something of our own which we love very much. . . . As the year closes we thought you might like to hear it. Merry Christmas. May the force be with you."

Yorke, Godrich, and others throughout this period were also vocal about the emerging online music platforms, insisting that the business models being employed don't give musicians a fair shake. When asked toward the end of 2015 how he listened to music, the Radiohead singer said that he primarily used the online electronica specialist retailer Boomkat, in the process slagging YouTube and its owner Google. "They've seized control of [art]—it's like what the Nazis did during the Second World War. Actually, it's like what everyone was doing during that war, even the English—stealing the art of other countries." Yorke noted to Tim Ingham of *Music Business Worldwide* that such services make huge amounts of money, "trawling like in the ocean, taking everything there is. 'Oh sorry, was that yours? Now it's ours. No, no just kidding—it's still yours.'" Prior to this the Radiohead singer had famously referred to Spotify as being "the last desperate fart" of the industry's "dying corpse," and Yorke and Godrich followed Radiohead in pulling their music from the platform in protest. However, after XL purchased the band's back catalog from EMI in the first half of 2016, Radiohead added the remainder of their work to the streaming service, and this was soon to be followed by the addition of Yorke's solo albums and *Amok*. This didn't change Yorke's view regarding the "corrosive effect" he perceived that digital was having on music, however: "I pulled out all my vinyl collection recently," he pointed out to Ingham. "With every single vinyl there's some relationship. . . . [That] doesn't exist with USB and digital."

This period also saw further activism from the band. Colin Greenwood, for instance, went to South Africa in January 2013 in his role as ambassador for the Children's Broadcasting Service, and continued to promote the cause, telling the BBC, "It's a democratic campaign for me, that's what I love about it." The following year he also participated as part of a team of twenty-two dads in Oxfordshire's largest triathalon, in order to raise money for a blood cancer charity. Yorke, Jonny Greenwood, and other artists, meanwhile, contributed music to a 2013 documentary about UK corporate tax avoidance called *The UK Gold* (the soundtrack of which was released for free on SoundCloud in February 2015). "Now is the time to reveal the revolving doors between government and the City that has bred lies and corruption for so long," Yorke was quoted on the UK Uncut campaign website. "Siphoning money through our tax havens for the global super-rich, while now preaching that we the people must pay our taxes and suffer austerity. Just who does our government work for?"

Yorke also discussed with Baldwin of WNYC his efforts to oppose any rush toward arctic oil drilling: "I was helping Greenpeace do this thing, which was trying to stop drilling in the Arctic," suggesting, "the challenge now is to turn the Arctic into a reserve so it can't happen." Yorke admitted that his political involvement had been highly stressful, and with regard to his work with Friends of the Earth, in particular, he remarked, "It burnt me out, getting that close to politics." Of his attendance at the 2009 Copenhagen summit on climate change he was to say to *Dazed and Confused* in 2013, "That permanently flipped my lid, because the whole thing was so wrong. Obama stormed straight past me after the meeting he had with China, and it was just horrible. It sort of spun me out permanently to be honest." Nevertheless, Radiohead signed their names to an open letter calling for an "ambitious" climate deal, ahead of the December 2015 United Nations Climate Change Conference in Paris, in conjunction with which Yorke also performed two solo numbers from the band's upcoming album. The singer likewise noted to Bartleet of *NME*, at the time, the assistance he gave to the UK

Green Party, but he clarified, "I couldn't ever run. . . . The problem of politics is that you have to make everyone happy. And I'm terrible at that."

Work on the band's ninth studio album *A Moon Shaped Pool* occupied the last third of 2014, along with smaller patches of time throughout 2015, including three weeks at La Fabrique studios in southern France. According to Jonny Greenwood, 80 percent of the album was actually recorded within a two-week period, while string and choral parts were recorded that November at London's RAK studios with musicians from the London Contemporary Orchestra. "We've certainly changed our method again," said Greenwood to Akhil Sood of the *Guardian* after the first group of sessions. "We're kind of limiting ourselves; working in limits. So we'll see what happens. It's like we're trying to use very old and very new technology together to see what happens." What this fundamentally amounted to was that Godrich had insisted that the band forgo the unlimited potentialities of modern digital recording in order to focus on the project and instead to commit the album to magnetic tape with analogue multitrack recorders. When the sessions were concluded, Godrich apparently took over the rest of the project and put it together by himself.

As with *In Rainbows* and *The King of Limbs*, a primary signal of the imminent release of *A Moon Shaped Pool* was the creation of two new companies, Dawn Chorus LLP and Dawnnchoruss.[1] Again, in contrast to what would be standard industry practice, the band conducted no interviews and did not tour in the months preceding the album's release. Rather, eight days beforehand, they sent to people who'd previously made direct orders from the band embossed cards that included the threatening line "We Know Where You Live," a lyric taken of course from their introductory single "Burn the Witch." The following day the group deleted their entire website and social media content, replacing it with blank images. And after having already uploaded excerpts to Instagram, Radiohead released "Burn the Witch" as a download two days later, along with the song's video. Four days following this, the band released the album's second single, "Daydreaming," with its Paul Thomas Anderson–directed video, which was to be projected in 35 mm across select movie theaters. Anderson was also to direct videos of Yorke and Greenwood performing "Present Tense" and "The Numbers," which emerged that autumn.

Five years following Radiohead's previous studio effort, *A Moon Shaped Pool* was itself finally released as a download on May 8, 2016, debuting at number one on the UK Albums Chart (their sixth UK number one), with CD and LP versions emerging the following month, again, through XL Recordings. The special edition, meanwhile, with its additional artwork and two additional tracks, "Ill Wind" and the afore-mentioned "Spectre," shipped in September. As well as seeing the band begin their tour in support of the album, the month of May saw them release the first in its series of video vignettes, set to short clips of music from a number of the album's songs, and the products of several well-known directors, such as P. T. Anderson, Ben Wheatley, Yorgos Lanthi-mos, and Richard Ayoade. For "Daydreaming," the last of these that appeared in the fall, the band held a "short-film" contest, releasing alternate audios of the song ahead of time for contestants to work with. On the day of the album's release, to mixed reviews, the band held a daylong audio stream called "Live from a Moon Shaped Pool," which included participating record stores around the world and featured oth-er competitions and activities, along with "instructional artworks."

From May to October the band performed dates in Europe, North America, and Japan, including festival dates, for which they were joined again by drummer Clive Deamer. Within mere minutes of being re-leased, tickets for every headline show were sold out, an especially interesting occurrence given the band's management had been involved the previous year in efforts to obtain tougher controls on secondary ticket sites. At a concert in Iceland, meanwhile, the band advertised the venue's Wi-Fi codes and encouraged fans to stream the show, using their phones and the Periscope live video-streaming app. Shortly into their tour, the band made headlines by playing "Creep" for the first time in seven years, and the live album *Pathways to Paris* was released in July; in addition to featuring Patti Smith, Flea, and others, it included Yorke's performances from the previous December's concert. Along with Eddie Vedder, Trent Reznor, and others, Yorke signed an open letter to the U.S. Congress in the hopes of stopping American gun violence and urged his Twitter followers that June to call for a second EU referendum, following the successful, though flawed, "Brexit" vote. At a performance in Los Angeles two months later he remarked, in reference to the new U.S. Republican presidential candidate Donald Trump, "I've got a great idea. Let's put an unhinged, paranoid megalomaniac in charge!" Most profound on a personal level, however, was that Rachel Owen—Yorke's ex-wife and mother to his two young children—passed away that December following a long battle with cancer, of which only a tight circle of confidants had been aware.

A MOON SHAPED POOL

As I write, two years after its release, in contrast to their previous work, the band has barely discussed the conceptual content of their most recent studio album *A Moon Shaped Pool*. "There was a lot of difficult stuff going on at the time, and it was a tough time for us as people," Yorke told *Rolling Stone* in 2017. "It was a miracle that that record got made at all." Jonny Greenwood elsewhere referred to the experience as "traumatic." The album was dedicated to the memories of drum technician Scott Johnson, as well as to Nigel Godrich's father, who was to pass away during the sessions that produced the album. As Godrich was to tweet upon the album's release, "Making this album was a very intense experience for me. I lost my dad in the process. . . . Hence a large piece of my soul lives here." The suggestion of many observers that Yorke's breakup with Rachel Owen significantly likewise colors the album appears highly likely, moreover, and her death seven months after the recording's release simply amplifies its overall poignancy. "We weren't in a position to really talk about it when it came out," Ed O'Brien told Greene of *Rolling Stone* in "Radiohead's Rhapsody in Gloom," a year following its release, explaining why the band did few interviews. "We didn't want to talk about it being quite hard to make. We were quite fragile, and we needed to find our feet." Immediately following this, he told the interviewer, "I don't want to talk about it anymore, if that's all right. I feel like the dust hasn't settled. It was a hard time."

In this regard, though the album still features the band's typical outward-looking expressions of cultural concern, much of its content is more inward looking and personal, involving a kind of looking back or midlife appraisal. Godrich, Donwood, the rest of Radiohead, and Generation X—the new adults in the room—were suddenly approaching their fifties. And given the universal themes of absence and loss that permeate much of *A Moon Shaped Pool*, it's therefore appropriate that "In Search of an Author" is the title of one of the thirteen paintings

Donwood completed for the album, specifically the one that depicts a crowd. The masking of authorship is suggested also in the techniques Donwood employed in order to reflect more "chance and happenstance" and "to do away with human agency." Another of the album's paintings, in this relation, bears the title "Anselm Keifer Can," and Donwood recounts how Yorke brought the contemporary German artist and sculptor to his attention after seeing a documentary on the subject of Keifer's life and work. According to Donwood, Keifer used "unstretched canvasses and massive pots of paint, and basically just chucked them around, like a nutter." As Donwood explains, this suited their effort to get away from narrative and figurative art, and thus the Radiohead artist employed similar huge canvasses to experiment with what he could do in conjunction with weather, therefore allowing the elements like high winds and thunderstorms to affect the paint. Noting that the album was recorded on tape—another manifestation of "looking back," Donwood decided "to go totally analogue" as well. But the analogue/digital blend, likewise inherent in the rest of the work, is reflected in the remainder of his artistic process, which involved photographing the finished projects and, with Yorke's assistance, then editing them in Photoshop. This is apparent, too, in the album's alphabetic track listing, a sequence that connotes the automatic ordering technique of computers. The hypothesis that "The Numbers" replaced the song's original title "Silent Spring" to achieve the desired sequencing is convincing and supports the idea that the order was nonetheless deliberate.

A song that in some form has existed since *Kid A*, the album opens with the leadoff single "Burn the Witch." It's therefore appropriate that another of Donwood's paintings is called "Witches Brew Too"—an apparent parody of the Miles Davis album cover for *Bitches Brew*. In addition to working on the song during the *Kid A/Amnesiac* period, it was further developed during the *Hail to the Thief* and *In Rainbows* sessions. Fragments of its lyrics had also made appearances on the Radiohead website and in the art booklet of *Hail to the Thief*, which included, among other lines, "avoid all eye contact," "cheer at the gallows," and "burn the witch." Scapegoating, as we've seen, has been a central abiding theme of every Radiohead work since *OK Computer*. But the song gained resonance for the band, particularly in response to the UK tabloid witch-hunts of pedophiles that came to a climax in 2012.

The trend even involved naming where such individuals lived, their perceived evil evident in the title of another Donwood painting, "Scelerate." Of course, the song relates also to Yorke's fear of the increasing rise of far-Right ideology among anti-immigration politicians in response to the recent European refugee crisis, and its manifestation as an escalating sense of paranoia, anger, and Islamophobia.

These themes are portrayed in the video, specifically through its reference to the 1973 horror film *The Wicker Man* and its employment of the stop-motion animation of the late 1960s English children's television series *Trumpton*. The series' name is also the name of the town that provides the setting for the video, and Donald Trump's formal entry into politics connects the song to what was to become, before the end of the year, the new global context of "Trump Town." In the video, the community's demonstration of collective violence is reflected in the song's "popular" refrain, heard "on the jukebox." Such persecution typically occurs when any kind of serious crisis develops within a human community. And other titles of Donwood's paintings, *Zelotypia*, *Omphalos*, and *Skull 2*, point toward this phenomenon's role in the founding of primitive communities through the form of archaic religion and sacrificial ritual, as per the theory of René Girard—the so-called Darwin of the human sciences. During the sixteenth century in England, "red crosses on wooden doors" signified that a dwelling's residents were or had been afflicted by the plague, while the song's refrain is a "song of sixpence," the title of a children's nursery rhyme, the initial verse of which was first published in 1744. Instead of singing of "black birds," however, the original spoke of "Four and twenty Naughty Boys Baked in a Pye."

When Yorke sings "abandon all reason," it reminds us that the Age of Reason, or eighteenth-century Enlightenment, is typically viewed as having properly begun only following the conclusion of the last major trials and executions of witches during the 1690s in both Europe and North America. Like much of the album, the song foregrounds Jonny Greenwood's strings, and present from the beginning, they help conjure the seventeenth century, which encounters the present with the bass synthesizers heard in the chorus. The song's imagery portrays the actions of a society driven by superstition and paranoia, and its "low-flying panic attack" was anticipated in the embossed pamphlets sent to fans ahead of the album's release, as well as in the startling erasure of the band's internet presence. This panic is also conveyed through the irregular rhythm of the chorus music and the detached, rhythmic chords of violins being "strummed" with guitar plectrums. As it approaches its conclusion, the song expresses increasing hysteria, as the strings climb toward their highest register, attaining a disturbing, screeching effect.

The next song, "Daydreaming," was finished early in the recording sessions, and Yorke soon revealed the song to be his favorite. The track opens with a wavering pitch that sounds like tape slipping off-speed—that most analogue of effects. It's also an audio cue that signifies looking back, as does the use of a slowly and gently arpeggiating acoustic piano. The backward-recorded vocals resemble the sounds of struggling for breath, as both the painful and redeeming elements of this internal examination are encountered. Much discussion has been devoted to the idea that the song's about a potential tension, perhaps between Yorke's musical career and his relationship with Rachel Owen. "Rachel and I have separated," announced Yorke as *NME* noted in the summer of 2015. "After 23 highly creative and happy years, for various reasons we have gone our separate ways. It's perfectly amicable and has been common knowledge for some time." Amicable or not, of course, the separation doubtless involved a great deal of pain, as "Identikit" later suggests, with its repeated line "broken hearts make it rain." From the second verse, we learn that the situation "goes beyond me" and "beyond you," bringing to mind not only Radiohead but also the separation's entanglement of the couple's young teenage children. The manipulated vocals at the end of the song, when reversed, reveal the simultaneously sung lines "half of my life / half of my love," whose effect, when heard forward, is like the sound of some menacing beast that we later encounter in the song "Tinker Tailor Soldier Sailor Rich Man Poor Man Beggar Man Thief." The couple's marriage—and they *were* secretly married in 2003—ended when Yorke was forty-seven, their relationship having begun when he was twenty-three. Fittingly, that point was also the beginning of the band's and his musical career. In conjunction with the initial backdrop of the "daydreamy," electronic sound effects, we find in the first verse that dreamers "never learn" and that it's too late to return to a time prior to which some serious damage occurred.

The video for "Daydreaming" shows a somewhat haggard, white-bearded Yorke, walking through twenty-three doors, and prevalent throughout the different spaces into which he enters are images of caring mothers. It seems no accident, then, that the video was released on Mother's Day weekend, nor that it also features scattered images of "mother nature." Yorke is portrayed throughout as moving in an upward direction, apparently trying to transcend his situation, until he reaches a firelit cave, high on a snow-capped mountain, a scene reminiscent of the *Kid A* album cover. A sort of solemn, religious sense is maintained in the lyrical image of a white room, with a window through which "the sun comes," demonstrating Yorke's continued use of light/dark imagery. First appearing in the previous song's directive to "stay in the shadows," Yorke is seen as the video begins, emerging, along with others in the crowd, from some kind of mystical light. The song, in this regard, features a notable shift from the singular to the plural first person, with its concluding line "We are just happy to serve you."

In this, it's interesting that Jonny Greenwood posted to Facebook a compilation of parallels between the music video and various older Radiohead-related images (among which one could include, in addition to the *Kid A* album cover, Yorke's appearance in a grocery store, recalling the video for "Fake Plastic Trees"). It may be, then, that some kind of stress between the singer's career and his relationship with Owen is conveyed in the rhythmic tension that exists between the hands of the song's piano parts, the left playing a duple rhythm against the right hand's triplets throughout both sections, a technique not particularly easy to perform, as many piano players and drummers know. The key of the song's first and main part is in a minor key, and a lightness and liveliness, both times, characterizes its shift to the parallel major in the song's second section. But the effect is different in each instance. Whereas the transition is first heard after Yorke sings "the damage is done," where it connotes a lighter side to present circumstances, the second time it seems to suggest insincerity of the kind that attaches to the phrase's identity as a commercial slogan.

Conveying a lighter side or partial sense of acceptance of present circumstances is a common theme throughout the album, as in the following track, "Decks Dark." Notwithstanding its lyrical account of a coming darkness in the lives of those the singer addresses due to a spaceship's blocking the sky's light, the first section of the song is set in a bright major key. Like that of the album itself, the song's title gives cause for confusion, there being no apostrophe in the word "decks," much as there's no hyphen separating the words "moon shaped." The former is likely meant to have a double meaning: first pertaining to the deck of a moon-shaped swimming pool, and second, to the flight deck of spaceship earth, itself potentially becoming, with further climate change, a giant moon-shaped pool of water, as the planet's glaciers melt and raise sea levels.

With no hiding from this darkness, bringing to mind the title of another of Donwood's paintings for the album, "Wanhope," the space-craft creates an unpleasantly loud sound that forces people to cover their ears. Portraying us as a "trapped rag doll cloth people" for whom resistance appears helpless, Yorke conjures the popular image of voo-doo dolls and their implications for social control. This image relates to the "spells and chimeras" that the listener later encounters in "The Numbers," a song that clearly provides an update on the goals of the global environmental movement finally to address climate change seri-ously. Some years earlier, in the wake of the 2009 Copenhagen climate summit, Yorke perceived it had been decided on humanity's behalf that the global economy was more important than anything else, and he suggested therefore that we'd been "bewitched by an old-fashioned spell that no one's found a way of breaking out of." The absence of agency here contrasts his later suggestion of at least its partial existence in "Identikit," where he sings of "the pieces of a rag doll mankind that we can create."

Despite the lighter musical background, we head "into our darkest hour," and it's only with the singing of this line that we're ushered into the dark setting of the parallel minor. The second section's harmony is circular and constrictive, and its accompanying female choral back-ground voices add to the overall sense of sobriety, the sole use of female background voices throughout the album no doubt serving to evoke the lunar imagery's connections to femininity. A less accepting sense of the situation is now conveyed, with the character saying it was "just a laugh" and "you've gotta be kidding me," and reporting how "we crumble." Though a rag doll with "a ten ton head made of wet sand," he still envisages his death, singing about the grass growing over him.

The shift from the first to the second sections likewise appears to signal a change of perspective, with the protagonist now addressing someone with whom it's impossible to reason, since "it's whatever you say it is, in split infinities." This line appropriately conjures Piers Anthony's 1980 science-fiction book *Split Infinity*, whose world features many human-inhabited planets. The one that the book's politically motivated protagonist lives on is, familiarly, technologically decadent, most of its atmosphere destroyed from the mining of a valuable energy source. Thus, its inhabitants live in domed cities endowed with artificial life support. Perhaps adding further meaning to the previous song's concluding line, "we are just happy to serve you," the socioeconomic scheme of the protagonist's planet is a type of industrial feudalism, the bulk of its inhabitants "serfs," employed by wealthy "citizens," who have complete authority over them. Insofar as this resembles the present global plutocracy, it appears that the similar-sounding outro music and lyrics also address the plutocrats, with Yorke singing, in his activist role, "when you've had enough of me . . ." Anticipating the repetition of a similar line in "Ful Stop," here, as well, he sings of "sweet times."

The electronic sound effects that conclude "Decks Dark" merge into "Desert Island Disk." Not only is the song rare for offering a powerful glimpse of hope in the context of the album, but also it's unique in the band's entire career for the same reason and thus no doubt a fortifying disc to have on hand if stranded on a desert island. Highlighting a solo acoustic guitar and a bright-sounding major mode, its melody and minimal harmony connote Indian music and thus Indian spiritualism. This is suggested by the open-hearted and light-spirited character of the singer, who, in stark contrast to the previous song, feels "totally alive," "totally released," and "born of a light." The latter phrase, returning us to the light/dark imagery, parallels the opening scene of the video for "Daydreaming," as do lines that describe the protagonist upon his way, "through an open doorway," and across the street, "to another life." A greater confidence of attained self-awareness characterizes this song, however, as he catches his reflection in a window, "switching on a light" of which he'd been formerly unaware and thereby waking up from what seems like "a thousand years of sleep."

Another theme that Radiohead has explored throughout their career, this image of awakening into a higher awareness is heightened by the brief, sudden, and exotic-sounding shift to the parallel minor. Following this, his repeated buoyant refrain, "You know what I mean," returns us to the major, and in the midst of it, Yorke, with his inclusion of the line "standing on the edge," appears to allude to the song "Lucky" from *OK Computer*. Aside from recognizing the encroaching dangers of

potential civilizational collapse, Yorke emphasizes, again, the importance of love in helping us prevent such a calamity. Additionally, when
he sings "different types of love are possible," we're offered the impression that the self-awareness he's achieved helps him attain reconciliation also with his personal circumstances. Similarly enhanced with the
reappearance of the minor flavorings, extra emphasis is achieved as well
when, following the first appearance of the word "possible," the song
briefly shifts away from the primary drone of the key. But a sense of
satisfying resolution is immediately achieved as the song returns to it for
the remainder of the track.

Through its title and foregrounding of acoustic guitar, "Desert Island Disk" connotes nature, especially in contrast to the cold-sounding
synthesizers and electronic drums employed in the next Kraut-rock-
influenced track, "Ful Stop," on which Portishead's Clive Deamer was
to add additional drums. The initially muffled sound, as well as the
distant, agitated melodic figures on the synthesizer, create a certain
unease when heard closer, as we return to the relationship "damage"
first encountered in "Daydreaming." As tends to be the case, this suggests that the state of awareness and spiritual satisfaction achieved in
the previous song was merely a kind of fleeting glimpse. The protagonist here seems to address himself as the one who "messed up everything," and who thinks about the possibilities of taking it all back, so
that, when "striking up the tinderbox," he's not left to tend his fire
alone, as in the "Daydreaming" video. One imagines that the line "Why
should I be good if you're not?" might have been a comment directed
by the other toward the protagonist, who finds being "trapped" in her
"full stop" of the relationship a "foul tasting medicine." The song's middle section sees an increase in intensity, with the entry of drums, its
haunting repetition of the line "truth will mess you up," and its harmonic escape from the persistent bass drone, heard repeatedly since the
song's opening fade-in. The intensity continues to build, reinforced by
the echo-laden synthesizer melodies, and he passionately remembers
"all the good times," until the drums all of a sudden drop out. This
occurs with the singing of "when you take me back," which becomes the
plea "take me back," and then the question "will you take me back?"
The bass again breaks from the drone during this section, but this time
ascends by a tone, an indication of his aspiration to transcend these

issues and reconcile, an unlikely prospect given the unresolved ending of the song—a "ful stop" rather than a "full stop."

The confident acceptance of "Desert Island Disk" is also notably absent from the next song, "Glass Eyes," which features strings, Yorke's solitary vocal, and acoustic piano, with the latter receiving treatment from one of Jonny Greenwood's software programs. The lyric is very personal and has the character of an imaginary phone call to his significant other, completed after arriving at a train station in "a frightening place." When, upon his arrival, he encounters the "concrete grey" of people's faces, the caller wonders if he shouldn't turn around and return. Panicked and cold, the light of day is "oh so smug" and "glassy-eyed," an expression that often refers to the state of daydreaming. It's appropriate, therefore, that the twice-repeated second section of the song again conjures imagery from the "Daydreaming video," including a path trailing off and heading down the mountain and through a dry bush. The protagonist neither knows nor cares where it leads, and the acoustic piano and strings encode his sober and authentic demeanor when he sings, "I feel this love to the core."

When performing the next song, "Identikit," in early 2012, Yorke amusingly introduced it by name, saying, "I have no idea what it means or what it's about or anything like that." This notwithstanding, throughout almost the entire verse sections, his background vocals repeatedly sing, "a moon shaped pool / dancing clothes / won't let me in / and now I know / it's never gonna be / oh me." Most of these lines appear to pertain to acceptance of the protagonist's unrenewable family relationship, and hence the song's repeated refrain, "broken hearts make it rain." But the phrase also recalls the idea of a moon-shaped spaceship earth, while "dancing clothes" look ahead to the centrality of the "dance as self-defense" imagery, employed in the upcoming track "Present Tense."

Despite the upbeat quality of the song, the opening lyric appears to refer to our abandonment of the children, "the sweet-faced ones with nothing left inside that we all can love." Pairing this line with the refrain, however, where "broken hearts" lead to tears, indicates recognition that we still in fact possess a humanity that, in its mutual vulnerability, "we all can love." The refrain's musical setting is uplifting, on account of its powerful shift to the relative major, and this sentiment is reinforced through the extended female background vocalists' empathetic and soothing repetition of the line. The opening lyric, likewise, suggests that the children have no identities and no will or agency, but this is countered at the end with the previously noted reference to "a rag doll mankind that we can create." In this regard, through its title, the song reiterates the analogue/digital theme of the album, since "Identikit" is the name of a software program that police use to build a suspect's likeness, as reconstructed from strips that display facial features selected to match witness descriptions. Of course, it's the plutocrat technocrats who are perceived as "messing him around" with their "spells and chimeras," and on whom the protagonist leads a full frontal attack in the following song, an attack that begins here, with the agitated and blistering guitar solo with which the track concludes.

Originally named after Rachel Carson's groundbreaking 1962 book *Silent Spring*, which helped to spawn the global environmental movement, the track appears to have been renamed "The Numbers," in order to accommodate the band's desired track sequence and preferred alphabetic ordering of the album's songs. The analogue emphasis occurs again, with the sounds of tape effect heard at the beginning, along with the track's domination by acoustic instruments, including piano, guitar, and percussion. The song's basis in the blues endows it with a confident sense of bravado, with which the singer makes reference to a type of guiding spirit that "shines its understanding" and reassuring light on humanity, in the guise of the smiling moon. His announcement that we're "not at the mercy of your chimeras and spells" reinforces this confidence, as does the "mmhm" vocal gesture that he makes, very much in the manner of the blues singer, immediately following his articulation of the phrase. Noting our oneness with the earth, it's significant that Yorke personifies it as a woman. But it's likewise significant that he affirms our future survival lies "inside us," dependent on our agency, and it's interesting that the album cover background lyrics to "Decks Dark" include the phrase "rag doll cloth people who . . . need reanimating."

In the second verse, he calls upon the people, whose power is evident in the threatening, dynamic string gestures that enter as the singer rails against our relative global inaction on climate change. This is conjured by the imagery of "rivers running dry" and "wings of butterflies," the latter being creatures of course presently threatened with extinction. Noting that the numbers, or the majority, don't make decisions in the realm of international politics, and that the system is thus "a lie," Yorke comments, in reference to the latter line, "painful cliche . . . but it's also true. . . . Why bother hiding it? It's a lie." The song concludes, nevertheless, with the suggestion that "we'll take back what is ours, one day at a time," and when asked on the BBC's *The First Time With . . .* in 2017 whether he had an optimistic outlook, Yorke responded in the affirmative, saying in reference to Donald Trump and British prime minister Theresa May, "You will be impeached shortly, mate. You are not a leader, love—and the people are going to see it very soon, love. One day at a time. You can't sustain this. It's not going to work. Good luck. One day at a time. We ain't stupid."

Dating back to 2008, the bossa nova–tinged "Present Tense" got its first public performance as part of Yorke's 2009 solo set at the UK's Latitude Festival. Speaking about the sadness or *saldaje* of Brazilian music, Ed O'Brien explained that it typically involves "a longing to be in a better and happier place," and dance, like other physical exercise, assists in this process, providing for the protagonist "a weapon of self-defence against the present." The strange echo effect used in the vocal suggests some kind of change of consciousness, as he promises not to get heavy but to "keep it light" and "keep it moving." Recalling the antihero of *The King of Limbs*, the protagonist affirms that he's "doing no harm"; rather, as his world "comes crashing down," he suggests he'll be dancing and "freaking out," and in a better place, "deaf, dumb, and blind" to all of his and the world's difficulties. In both repetitions of the chorus, in this relation, we hear a comforting shift to the major, which accompanies the words "In you I'm lost." And the song's final verse sees the protagonist forging forward in his perseverance, reinforced by the female background vocalists and careful not to fall "down a mine" of melancholy, concerned otherwise that "all this love will be in vain." He would appear to refer to the loving self-awareness he attained in "Desert Island Disk," but the song's conclusion in the minor leaves the listener uncertain of the protagonist's ongoing confidence.

With its first half already the title of a 1967 Yardbirds song cowritten by Jim McCarty and Jimmy Page, "Tinker Tailor Soldier Sailor Rich Man Poor Man Beggar Man Thief" takes its name from an English nursery rhyme, one typically used in children's games to decide who is "it." Given the character of Richard Anoyade's vignette for the song and the band's recent flirtation with James Bond, another notable popular culture reference to the rhyme occurs in John Le Carré's Cold War spy novel *Tinker Tailor Soldier Spy*, which uses the rhyme as code to identify a Soviet mole in the UK's MI6. In addition to the novel, the Swedish director Tomas Alfredson made a film adaptation in 2011 that may also have influenced Yorke, particularly as the main character and all the main intelligence recruits in the story are students from Oxford. The work refers to the U.S. intelligence agencies and the CIA in particular as "the cousins," while the best source of intelligence about the Soviet Union among the Secret Intelligence Services is code-named "Merlin," developed and sponsored under an operation appropriately codenamed "Witchcraft," bringing us full circle to the beginning of *A Moon Shaped Pool*. Partly the result of the electronic keyboard's dissonant chord progression, which doesn't function according to the laws of functional harmony, the song's creepiness and its reference to "the lonely and their prey" evoke a similar horror to the murderous protagonist of *OK Computer*'s "Climbing Up the Walls" who has "the smell of a local man whose got the loneliest feeling." It likewise recalls the antihero encountered in *The King of Limbs*, along with his associates, against all of whom "the shadows conspired." Wondering who is "it," in this light then, conjures the idea of who among them is next up to be eliminated.

One can assume that, at the end of the "Daydreaming" video, Yorke alone in his firelit cave might be reasonably considered one of the lonely. In this way, when "Tinker Tailor" begins with the lyric "all the holes," it conjures many such caves filled with isolated people, who "at once are coming alive, set free," but who are usually kept "out of sight, out of mind." They are the ones apparently in the first refrain who have to be kept at bay with our fires. But the second verse documents how, even the beasts, like birds and fishes, appear to flee the scene, with the approach of a seemingly monstrous creature, presumably a giant snake, "crawling out upon its belly." Recalling Yorke's firelit cave, and the sound of the menacing beast he encounters there, in the second repetition of the refrain, it's now apparently this creature that the listener's fires are meant to keep at bay. An association with the serpent or Satan, and the temptation to commit violence, adds special meaning to the last line of the refrain, which intones, "all you have to do is say yes." Referring again to "the lonely and their prey," he announces his presence and sings, to no one specifically, "come to me before it's too late."

Yorke tweeted an article in late 2014 by George Monbiot, with whom he was to do a joint interview with *La Monde*, ahead of the Paris conference in December 2015. Titled "The Age of Loneliness," Monbiot reported how a government study had found Britain to be the "loneliness" capital of Europe. The epidemic was increasing with notable speed, among both young adults and seniors, with two-fifths of the latter reporting that television functioned as their principal company. Monbiot connected this loneliness to the way British society was increasingly being structured, with company directors in the year 2014 making 120 times more than the average full-time employee (it was 47 times in 2000), and to a survey finding that wealth and fame were the sole ambitions of 40 percent of British children. The electronic sound effects, heard following the dramatic string arrangement at the song's conclusion, transfer us to the album's final track, and by emulating the sounds of a phonograph, they again return us to the album's analogue/digital theme. The faint sound of a slowed-down voice synthesizer is heard very faintly toward the end and seems akin to the character Dave putting HAL—the spaceship-controlling artificial intelligence that has turned against the astronauts—out of commission in *2001: A Space Odyssey*, a work similarly addressing the Cold War. Part of the reason "Tinker Tailor" is so haunting is that the song is unusually comprised only of major chords, and this effect is even more pronounced when the unsettling track also concludes on the major.

And with that, we arrive at the album's final offering, "True Love Waits," a song first performed live as far back as 1995 when the band was supporting *The Bends*, and their first attempt to record it came during the *Kid A/Amnesiac* sessions in 2000, though its title and some of its lyrics can be seen in Donwood's *OK Computer* artwork. During that period as well, the following appeared on the band's website, hinting apparently at the title's original reference to a Christian advocacy group that lobbies against having premarital sex:

> True love waits are you a virgin? every night we are haunted it paces up and down outside my room, it talks to me in its sleep. its in the tape going round and round. it stops and starts the tape machine. goes into record when it feels like it. just let it happen. just dont leave. dont leave. it waits patiently. mum left her 8 year old locked in for a week with lollipops and crisps. she had to work or forgot or

something. stanley says. you, like everyone else need to feel important.

Perhaps drawing some of its inspiration from the story of a mother
apparently abandoning her child at home for a week, it seems safe to
assume that the song was written around the time that Yorke and Rachel Owen first became an item. Although a live acoustic version is
found on the *I Might Be Wrong* EP, as previously noted, Nigel Godrich
was to say of the song to David Fricke of *Rolling Stone* in 2012, "We
tried to record it countless times, but it never worked. . . . To Thom's
credit, he needs to feel a song has validation, that it has a reason to exist
as a recording." As he went on to say, "We could do 'True Love Waits'
and make it sound like John Mayer. Nobody wants to do that."

The song sustains the loneliness theme, and its wrenching refrain
certainly acquires new meaning in the context of Yorke and Owen's
separation. One can imagine the first verse being the words of Owen
herself, as Yorke is set to leave for one of the agonizingly long tours
undertaken by the band to promote itself during the mid-1990s. The
second and third verses, in contrast, take the character of Yorke's reply,
and the song is characterized by an intimate sincerity and authenticity,
expressed in the analogue experience of hearing even the individual
hammers of the acoustic piano. Taking account of its major key, much
of the song's poignancy comes through the piano's repeated and accented emphasis on the dissonant note in the track's opening chord, which
simulates the pangs of separation, absence, and loneliness. When
young, we feel these pangs far more acutely, and I recall beholding my
seven-year-old nephew's emotional overwhelm when saying farewell to
family relatives visiting from another continent whom he had only just
met. I remember knowing the same gut wrench myself, in analogous
situations at a similar juncture in my own youthful development. We
soon recognize, as we age, of course, that we must begin to accustom
ourselves to such experience, as with the diminishing losses of Scott
Johnson, Nigel Godrich's father, and Rachel Owen.

The twentieth-century German poet Bertolt Brecht's observed that
singing during the dark times would be about the dark times, and it's
interesting, in this relation, that early in 2017 a data scientist, through
analysis of a number of parameters, including the song's Spotify valence
rating, determined "True Love Waits" to be Radiohead's saddest song.

In this regard, prior to Owen's death, one fan posted to reddit their best attempt to decipher the faint words upon which the lyrics of "Decks Darkness," as with all other songs, are superimposed on the special edition album sleeve. The following passage is relevant, its less discernible words expressed in bold:

> You are terminal and you are within me
> You will get your reward in heaven
> **If that is where you are heading**
> **Into my (cave?) there's** a wind blowing **(darkness?)**
> **Where I sit** alone and the fire's going out
> Only you can bring a spark to my fire.

Clearly, this passage reveals that the Radiohead singer was aware that his partner of nearly twenty-five years had already been diagnosed with terminal cancer, and the song's sadness is amplified exponentially, when known that it was recorded with this knowledge that his fire in the night was imminently to be extinguished. Having such awareness, of course, prompts a reread of "Daydreaming," where dreamers never learn to tame their extravagant hopes until they receive the diagnosis of a terminal illness, when all damage is done and it's too late because things are "beyond the point of no return." Death, the mighty reckoner, "goes beyond me" and "beyond you," and considering Yorke's above reference to "heaven," those whom they are happy to serve could very well be the divine, in anticipation of Rachel Owen's entry into the light.

11

LOOKING BACKWARD (2017–2018)

Ed O'Brien observed of our culture in 2017 to Kirsty Robinson that it had become completely spiritually bereft. What we lacked nowadays was connectedness and being with nature. Reflecting on his family's sojourn in Brazil, however, he enthusiastically reported that it was possible to have religious conversations among Brazilians. He estimated that 98 percent of white British musicians don't believe in God, and, of Richard Dawkins, perhaps the most prominent international voice promoting atheism during the early twenty-first century, the guitarist said, he "drives me round the bend." In this regard, he recounted spending the previous fifteen years discarding the "intellectual armor" with which he'd grown up. As he insisted, whether we refer to it as the Force or by some other name, there exists a "greater power" with which we have to engage. "The world needs kindness," O'Brien pointed out during the same conversation, commenting that his faith in humanity had been restored, through much of his recent experience. "Human beings are capable of extraordinary things," he said; "don't let anyone tell you not."

Notwithstanding, according to Adam Thorpe in 2016, Radiohead members have long been concerned about their age, and he reports that he overheard Thom Yorke say in 2003 that, not wanting to be like Mick Jagger, "still prancing about in his withered old age," he'd quit rock music when he was forty. Thorpe also records Phil Selway as saying, in reference to his 2015 solo performance at a festival in London's Victoria Park, "I looked around and realized I was the oldest participant, apart from Patti Smith." With the band's children now increasingly becoming teenagers and Selway's eldest son having turned eighteen in 2017, the band was now possessed of a retrospective impulse. "We're a little bit older," Selway was to say, in regard to the release of the band's twentieth-anniversary remastered version of *OK Computer OKNOTOK 1997 2017.* "I think we can afford to look back." An important aspect of this looking back involved dedicating the new collection to the memory of Rachel Owen, a mere six months after her passing.

In addition to the MP3 download, the boxed edition includes a hardcover art book, three twelve-inch vinyl records, a book of Yorke's notes from the period, and a sketchbook of his and Stanley Donwood's preparatory artwork. "It's been really, really, really mental going through it," said Yorke, in reference to these latter materials, which indicated the stresses of living on a tour bus for the better part of four consecutive years. "Going back into where my head was at—it's really bonkers," he said, adding that at the time he was basically "catatonic." But there was another element of these materials of which Yorke took note: "I was getting into the sense of information overload," he told Rolling Stone in May 2017. "Which is ironic, really, since it's so much worse now."

The special edition of the album includes as extra tracks the songs from *Airbag/How Am I Driving?* and the remaining B sides from that time, "Lull" and "How I Made My Millions." But it also includes three previously unreleased titles: "I Promise," "Man of War," and "Lift." While the first two were released as singles backed by music videos, the latter was released solely as a video. Also part of the boxed edition is an audiocassette, which includes session recordings, audio experiments, demos, and earlier versions of a handful of songs released on later albums ("The National Anthem," "Motion Picture Soundtrack," and "Nude"). If they run the cassette's final track on a ZX Spectrum computer, highly ambitious fans are rewarded with a "secret message," which appears on a black background printed in black text. Humorously, and perhaps ironically, it alludes to the backward-recorded message at the beginning of the song "Empty Spaces" from Pink Floyd's *The Wall* and makes reference to Syd Barrett: "Congratulations . . . you've found the secret message syd lives hmmmm. We should get out more."[1]

Another retrospective gesture took the form of the band releasing *Radiohead Complete*, a four-hundred-page songbook of lyrics and guitar parts for every song that the band had released, including singles and B sides. And 2017 also saw others looking back at the band. For the first time they became eligible for induction into the Rock and Roll Hall of Fame, though as one might expect, this was not a prospect that held tantamount interest for them. "I don't want to be rude about the Rock and Roll Hall of Fame because for a lot of people it means something," said O'Brien to Andy Greene of *Rolling Stone* on June 8, 2017, "but culturally I don't understand it. I think it might be a quintessential American thing." As he went on to say, "Brits are not very good at slapping ourselves on the back. It seems very show-biz and I'm not very show-biz," suggesting that he'd really rather be going to a gig or sitting at home in front of the fire. "I realized years ago that I didn't like award ceremonies. You walk in there and you feel self-conscious. It's just really uncomfortable. Wherever there is media there seem to be a real level of bullshit. It just feels non-authentic to us." As it turns out, O'Brien and the others didn't have to worry, since, though nominated, they were not chosen, losing out to Bon Jovi, Dire Straits, the Moody Blues, the Cars, and Nina Simone.

Another event that had the band looking to the past related to Scott Johnson. In 2013, charges had been laid in the catastrophic stage collapse that took the drum technician's life, but the trial was thrown out, because in the course of events, the judge was promoted from the provincial to the federal court in Canada, and the case was therefore no longer under his jurisdiction. Eventually, a mistrial was declared because the new judge took too long, according to new rules that had been passed down by the top court. The situation was devastating for Johnson's parents and the band, and in his effort to bring publicity to such a travesty of justice and to the need to get to the bottom of what happened that day in Toronto, Selway gave an interview with the Canadian Broadcasting System. In it he painfully revealed that he himself should ordinarily have been sitting where Johnson was killed, were it not for the fact of things being behind schedule that day. Selway spoke of the consequent "incredible weight" this held for him and that he could not just "let it lie." An inquest by Ontario's chief coroner into Johnson's death remains currently ongoing.

In March and April 2017, Radiohead toured the United States, including a couple of performances at Coachella. During the opening night, the band experienced technical difficulties during their first performance that resulted in their having to leave the stage multiple times.

"Can you actually hear me now?" Yorke asked, when things were finally fixed. "I'd like to tell you a joke, something to lighten the mood, but this is Radiohead so fuck it." The tour extended to Europe in June and July, and Yorke was to greet news of Donald Trump's withdrawal of the United States from the 2015 Paris Climate Agreement with a tweet that said "fucking clown." At their Glastonbury performance, similarly, he called for British prime minister Theresa May to "shut the door on the way out," and dementedly repeated the Tory election slogan "strong and stable" toward the end of the song "Myxomatosis." Later, the crowd rebuffed him, when he said, "A future worth having for our children, not one decided by useless politicians." As the band's audience were to do again, in a week and a half's time at a performance in Manchester, the crowd broke out into chants of "Oh, Jeremy Corbyn," who, two years before, had become the leader of Britain's Labour Party and was the favorite among young people to become the country's next prime minister.

The band found themselves rebuffed even more broadly, however, in relation to what was to be their final stop of the tour on July 19, a performance in Tel Aviv. Previous to this, the band had performed eight times in Israel, the last during the summer of 2000. But this was their first visit since Palestinian civil society groups had launched the Boycott, Divestment and Sanctions (BDS) movement in 2005, which urged an international cultural boycott of the Israeli state until it was to comply with international law in relation to the occupied territories. At their concert earlier in the year at the Greek Theater at Berkeley, a sizable banner was held up in protest against their willingness to perform in an "apartheid" state. After a number of alleged private communications, including from prominent BDS spokesperson Pink Floyd's Roger Waters (for whom Nigel Godrich had just produced his 2017 album *Is This the Life We Really Want?*), Artists for Palestine UK issued an open letter, asking the band not to break but to lend their support to the boycott, a cause that, in addition to that of Waters, had the support of Archbishop Desmond Tutu, Elvis Costello, Stephen Hawkings, Brian Eno, Ken Loach, Russell Brand, Richard Ashcroft, Naomi Klein, John Pilger, and Alice Walker, among others. At Glastonbury, a Radiohead 4 Palestine group was visible, and Palestinian flags were on display during the band's set, as was the case at Glasgow's TRSNMT festival, in response to which Yorke, while staring out into the audience, ahead of their performance of "Myxomatosis," murmured "some fucking people," while flipping his middle finger at the protesters.

It's ironic that Yorke appears to have been so highly scandalized by these actions, given his own propensity for publically calling others out in public, even sharing that his son was now working with him on behalf of Greenpeace. At the beginning of June 2017, after a long silence, Yorke finally gave a statement to Andy Greene of *Rolling Stone* in which he noted of the experience, "If you want me to be honest, yeah, it's *really* upsetting that artists I respect think we are not capable of making a moral decision ourselves after all these years. They talk *down* to us and I just find it *mind-boggling* that they think they have the right to do that. It's extraordinary." Yorke suggested that the kind of dialogue that his critics wanted to engage in was one of black and white, and he found it disrespectful "to assume that we're either being misinformed or that we're so retarded we can't make these decisions ourselves." Calling it "offensive" and "patronizing in the extreme," he added, "I just can't understand why going to play a rock show or going to lecture at a university [is a problem to them]."

Artists for Palestine UK released a statement reprinted by Winston Cook-Wilson in *Spin* magazine suggesting that Yorke's remarks appeared off-the-cuff and not a properly considered response, yet Israeli politicians and diplomatic missions predictably went on with enthusiasm to promote the group's stance, the Israeli government considering every major artist who appears in the nation a public relations victory. The group's statement suggested that any Palestinians who read Yorke's comments "will wonder if he knows anything at all about their dispossession and forced exile, and what it's like to live under military occupation." As they also noted, regarding Yorke's comments, "He doesn't mention the Palestinians other than to say guitarist Jonny Greenwood has 'Palestinian friends,'" adding to this, "A lot of us do, Thom. That doesn't mean we think it's okay to play a 40,000-strong stadium built on the ruins of a Palestinian village." Likewise problematic concerning Yorke's comments was that while he suggested Jonny Greenwood was the one "who knows most about these things," Greenwood has not apparently made any public comment outlining the nuances of the band's position. The Artists for Palestine UK signatories similarly pointed out that they didn't doubt the band's ability to make moral decisions; they simply considered the one they were making to be wrong. Radiohead Fans for Palestine, meanwhile, similarly issued an open letter on their blog, pointing out to Yorke that the calls to boycott originate from Palestinian citizens. "If you're going to justify your show in Tel Aviv, it is them you should be addressing," the letter said, also accusing the singer of avoiding the real point, "which is that you are playing on occupied land against the wishes of an oppressed people. And you're ignoring the voices of those people."

In his comments, Yorke also recommended that many people don't agree with the BDS movement, "including us," proposing that he didn't agree with its cultural ban at all, and neither did a long list of other people, including J. K. Rowling and Noam Chomsky. But when Artists for Palestine UK reached out to the latter, in order to ask the scholar to clarify his position, Chomsky provided the following statement that the group reprinted on its website: "I am opposed to any appearance in Israel that is used for nationalistic or other propaganda purposes to cover up its occupation and denial of Palestinian human rights. . . . While I have some tactical differences with the BDS movement," Chomsky continued, "I strongly support the actions and continue to participate in them."

To understand some of Yorke's reaction, it's helpful to know that the acts the band chose to open their show were Israeli-Arab and Muslim singer Nasreen Qadri, alongside Israeli musician Dudu Tassa, a descendant of Iraqi Jews who plays Arabic music and who also opened North American shows for the band. Likewise on the bill was Shye Ben Tzur, an Israeli musician who performs Sufi music, and who of course highly informs Greenwood's ongoing work with Junun. Clearly these choices were meant to represent cross-cultural understanding and dialogue, and it's evident that Yorke understands the BDS movement as energy that could be used more positively. "All of this creates divisive energy. You're not bringing people together," he remarked to *Rolling Stone* in "Thom Yorke Breaks Silence on Israel Controversy." "You're not encouraging dialogue or a sense of understanding. Now if you're talking about trying to make things progress in any society, if you create division, what do you get? You get fucking Theresa May. You get [Israeli prime minister Benjamin] Netanyahu, you get fucking Trump. That's divisive."

As Roger Waters was to respond to Yorke's comments, however, during an hourlong Facebook Live talk with the BDS movement, his comments reprinted by Daniel Kreps in *Rolling Stone*:

> My answer to people who say we should go there and sit around the campfire and sing songs: No, we shouldn't. We should observe the picket line. Anybody who's tempted to do that, like our friends in Radiohead, if only they would actually educate themselves. I know Thom Yorke's been whining about how he feels insulted, people are suggesting he doesn't know what's going on. . . . Well Thom, you shouldn't feel insulted because if you did know what's going on, you would have a conversation with [director] Ken Loach, who's been begging you to have a conversation, or with me, I begged you, Thom. I sent you a number of emails, begging you to have a conversation. As did Brian Eno; you ignored us all, you won't speak to anyone about anything. So it's that kind of isolationism that is extremely unhelpful to everybody.

It's not clear whether Yorke felt unable to address such enquiries in the immediate wake of his ex-wife's death, and there hasn't, for the moment, been any further discussion. In regard to how he alleges Yorke conducted himself, however, Waters humorously soon afterward referred to the Radiohead front man as "a self-absorbed, narcissistic, drippy, little prick." Just as humorous, of course, is the fact that many people would likely reserve the same epithet for describing the Pink Floyd cofounder.

After the Tel Aviv performance, in August, Yorke and Greenwood played a benefit show as a stripped-down duo at the Macerata Sferisterio, in the Italian region of Le Marche, which had recently been devastated by several earthquakes. The following month then saw the release of the band's collaboration with composer Hans Zimmer, with whom they redid the song "Bloom" from *The King of Limbs*. Retitled "Ocean (Bloom)," the track was recorded for the *Blue Planet II* prequel with the BBC Concert Orchestra, with Yorke providing new vocals. Interestingly, Yorke said that the *Blue Planet* series in part inspired not only the original song but also his very interest in ecological matters.

Following this, the band members went their separate ways to pursue their independent activities. That July Colin Greenwood made an appearance on BBC Radio 6 Music's *The Craig Charles Funk and Soul* and in April 2018 provided bass for a song on the debut EP of a twenty-one-year-old artist known as Tamino. The younger Greenwood, on the other hand, saw the vinyl release of his composition "Water" with the Australian Chamber Orchestra, while his latest soundtrack effort, another Paul Thomas Anderson film, *Phantom Thread*, saw its release in December. He'd likewise been busy toward the beginning of the year with some Junun live dates, alongside four special performances of his score for *There Will Be Blood*. These events saw Greenwood perform ondes martenot with the London Contemporary Orchestra at London's Royal Festival Hall and other venues, in Birmingham, Brighton, and Bristol. In the midst of all this, he was also in the process of scoring the soundtrack to Lynne Ramsay's thriller film *You Were Never Really Here*, released in the spring of 2018, while that summer saw the appearance, only as sheet music, of his 2015 two-movement composition for solo piano called "88 (No. 1)." The latter was inspired by the Canadian pianist Glenn Gould's treatment of Bach's Goldberg Variations, as was Greenwood's score for *Phantom Thread*.

In the meantime, Philip Selway released his own first soundtrack for the Polly Steele film *Let Me Go* in September 2017, backed a campaign to save a threatened Oxford music venue called The Cellar, and joined Ringo Starr in performing drums on "With a Little Help from My Friends" at the ex-Beatle's New York City Beacon Theatre concert in November. Ed O'Brien, in the intervening time, was busy collaborating with the Fender guitar company to release in November his own signature electric guitar, known as the EOB Sustainer Stratocaster. He also spent a couple of weeks writing with an acoustic guitar in Wales, as well as some time recording toward the end of the year and into the following, in anticipation of an intended 2018 release for his first solo album. O'Brien noted that the American poet Walt Whitman's famous poem "Leaves of Grass" had inspired much of this effort.

Yorke was as busy as ever, in February releasing a new song called "Why Can't We Get Along" for a Rag & Bone advertisement, and working on what became his own first soundtrack for the horror remake of *Suspiria*, released in late 2018. In December, he reissued his 2014 solo album *Tomorrow's Modern Boxes* on CD, vinyl, and streaming services via XL Recordings and played three American dates the same month with Nigel Godrich and the audiovisual artist Tarik Barri, whom he likewise did a number of European dates with in May and June 2018.

Yorke similarly collaborated with Barri on an original, new 360-degree AV surround-sound installation project, in association with Berlin's Institute for Sound and Music, designed for their Hexadome structure in the Martin-Gropius-Bau Museum.

In early 2018, it was discovered that all was not okay with Radiohead's website, which had a problem with leaking user data, in particular, every IP address to have visited the site between 2011 and 2013. Then, in March, the band settled a copyright dispute with Lana Del Rey, whose song "Get Free" allegedly owed something to Radiohead's "Creep." This was ironic, of course, since the band had themselves been sued for copyright infringement in relation to that song, and it owed something, in turn, to the Hollies' "Air That I Breathe." They reconvened in April for a tour of South American cities, and in July for a sixteen-date tour of the United States and Canada, with Greenwood's Junun as openers, which included their first Toronto performance in a decade.

It's never clear what the future holds with Radiohead, an entity that Jonny Greenwood in 2017 described to Greene in "Radiohead's Rhapsody in Gloom" as "just kind of an arrangement to form songs using whatever technology suits the song. And that technology can be a cello or it can be a laptop. It's all sort of machinery when looked at in the right way. That's how I think of it." There are certainly reports of new unrecorded songs from Yorke's recent solo performances, in addition to miscellaneous Radiohead songs of various vintages that have yet to be "committed to tape" or some other medium. Among these, we could include "I Froze Up," "Skirting on the Surface," "Cut a Hole," "Open the Floodgates," "Follow Me Around," "Come to Your Senses," and "Wake Me (Before They Come)."

The world likewise continues to appear ever more alarming with the direction being charted by Donald Trump, who recently attracted 250,000 demonstrators in London during his first trip to the UK. "Your glorious leader met our glorious leader," said Yorke, at one of Radiohead's four shows at New York's Madison Square Garden. "Made a fool of himself. Made a fool of the Queen. Made a fool of our country. Fuck him!" As the *Rolling Stone* commentator Rob Sheffield was to suggest, it's clear that things are definitely crazy when Thom Yorke empathizes with the House of Windsor. But such are the times, and we're left to wonder, at the moment, whether due process and the rule of law will help preserve American civilization, or whether its institutions aren't in the end up to the task. Let's hope they are and that O'Brien's expressed optimism was well founded, when he suggested in 2017 to Steve Lamacq on BBC Radio 6 that "people are waking up from the slumber . . . there is stuff to process, and to shout against, and to challenge." Let's hope as well that Radiohead is around for a long time yet, continuing to remind them.

NOTES

I. BECOMING RADIOHEAD

1. Other songs that appeared on this demo included the energetic "Nothing Touches Me," "Phillipa Chicken," and an earlier version of *Pablo Honey*'s "I Can't."

2. *Pablo Honey* did not include the single "Pop Is Dead," which made little impact when released two months after the album's release in April 1993. Along with live versions of previously released songs, "Pop Is Dead" included an acoustic version of "Banana Co.," a song that appears to express disdain for the general secrecy of certain multinational corporations.

3. "Creep" was released in a number of different formats, variously including also the songs "Yes I Am," along with an acoustic version of "Killer Cars," a later fully recorded version appearing in 1995.

2. TOWARD TECHNOLOGICAL APOCALYPSE

1. Patrick J. Kiger, "What Did the 1990s Mean?" *National Geographic*, accessed June 12, 2017, http://channel.nationalgeographic.com.

3. A SGT. PEPPER FOR THE "NET" GENERATION

1. "Radiohead: Played in Full," MTV, November 2001. Jonny Greenwood is also quoted as saying, "I think one album title and one computer voice do not make a concept album. That's a bit of a red herring."

2. In response to *Rolling Stone* magazine calling *OK Computer* "a stunning art-rock tour de force," the elder Greenwood replied in Martin Clarke's *Hysterical and Useless*, "What a ghastly thought. That makes it sound like Rick Wakeman and his Knights of the Round Table On Ice." In the Radiohead film released on Capital Video, *Meeting People Is Easy*, he can be heard saying, "we all hate progressive rock." Yorke, meanwhile, is quoted in *Hysterical and Useless* as saying, "We write pop songs. As time has gone on, we've gotten more into pushing our material as far as it can go. But there was no intention of it being 'art.'"

3. According to pollster Michael Adams in 2001, if Canadian citizens had been voting in that American election, Bush would have lost every Canadian province and territory, including Alberta.

4. BACK TO SAVE THE UNIVERSE, I'M YOUR SUPERHERO!

1. The electronic sound effects can be heard twice briefly between the 1:04 and 1:15 minute marks of the song, and more extensively after the 3:28 mark.

2. See chapter 11 of *Hitchhiker's Guide to the Galaxy*.

3. Note the hand-scrawled "street spirit" beside the scribbled-out "bulletproof" (another song from *The Bends*) superimposed upon the right-hand corner of the open book on the *OK Computer* CD booklet's back cover.

4. Though Yorke says of the songs comprising *OK Computer* that they are less personal than previous Radiohead songs, Jonny Greenwood expresses doubt, suggesting in Clarke's *Hysterical and Useless* that there remains "a large element of autobiography in there": "He confesses. He'd never admit that though. It's just like Mark E. Smith pretending none of his songs are about himself." Prior to *OK Computer*, Yorke had also commented in Jonathan Hale's *Radiohead: From a Great Height*, "I'm always losing my temper, and it's very rarely justified. I always feel myself doing it, but I can't stop it." Furthermore, when interviewer Phil Sutcliffe with *Q* magazine (October 1997) commented to him that there is so much anger on *OK Computer*, Yorke replied, "It's responding to incredibly hostile moments. Responding in kind. Which I

am wont to do." He might have added, in fact, that it's something that we're all "wont to do."

5. In this regard, Yorke once pointed out that he himself is wearing Nike shoes in the video for "Just."

6. Illustrating the moral superiority of nonviolence, Yorke was to say in Hale's *Radiohead: From a Great Height* of Tibet that "because the Tibetan struggle is a non-violent struggle, it shames the global community's ineffectiveness as a peace-keeping unit."

7. "Nothing scares me more than driving, I hate it with a fucking passion," says Yorke in James Doheny's *Radiohead: Karma Police.* "I hate it because it's the most dangerous thing you do in your life. Your average expensive German car gives you the feeling that you can't die. And that's a fraud. Really, when you think about it, every time you get home you should run down the street screaming 'I'm back! I'm alive!'" The car appears in earlier tracks by Radiohead including the songs "Stupid Car" and "Killer Cars," the former apparently about a car accident that Yorke survived in 1987.

8. The Beatles are also conjured through the chorus's quotation of a harmonic turnaround from the verse section of the song "Sexy Sadie" (C–D–G–F#). In this regard, *The Beatles* (1968)—unofficially known as "the White Album"—was quite influential for Radiohead during this time.

9. The image of the recently diffused automated teller machine (ATM) is appropriate, the "hole in wall" being a colloquial British usage based on the particular "hole-in-the-wall" brand of the British banking firm Barclays. That the protagonist still performs "favours for favours" would appear to illustrate his mercantile approach to moral life.

10. Yorke reported that the number of people they encountered in their work likened that which politicians come into contact with, and he even began to joke with people that he met, "I trust I can rely on your vote."

11. In *Hysterical and Useless*, Yorke alternatively put it, "Some people don't dare to sleep with the window open, because they're afraid that the monsters that they see in their imagination will come inside. This song is about the monster in the closet."

12. Radiohead's merchandising arm W.A.S.T.E. derives its name from the underground mail system in Pynchon's novel *The Crying of Lot 49* (1966).

5. THE MEDIA FALLOUT OF *OK COMPUTER*

1. For an alternative account of this process, see M. Hansen, "Deforming Rock: Radiohead's Plunge into the Sonic Continuum," in *The Music and Art of Radiohead*, ed. Joseph Tate, 118–38 (Burlington, VT: Ashgate, 2005).

2. The film shows the band members doing numerous interviews, photo shoots, and long lists of radio promos. During a session of the latter, bassist Colin Greenwood is heard to remark, "I hate this."

3. One finds in fact a great deal of symbolic similarity between *Dark Side of the Moon*'s "On the Run" and the cover of *OK Computer*, including the downed airplane. Both amount to representations of the accelerated conditions of life in contemporary culture. Among other thematic similarities between the two albums, one could also refer to their mutual explorations of paranoia and madness. See B. Schleifer, "Eclipsing: The Influence of *The Dark Side of the Moon* on the Next Generation's Music through Radiohead's *OK Computer*," in *"Speak to Me": The Legacy of Pink Floyd's The Dark Side of the Moon*, ed. R. Reisling, 208–17 (Hampshire, UK: Ashgate, 2005).

4. Compare with the following from Roger Waters as noted in Nicholas Schaffner's *Saucerful of Secrets*: "At that point all our ambitions were realized. When you're fifteen and you think, 'Right, I'm gonna start a group,' the pinnacle that you see (apart from very vague thoughts about rather smart bachelor flats and not having to get up till four in the afternoon) . . . is the Big Album. The number one in *Billboard*. And once you've done that, a lot of your ambitions have been achieved. . . . Yes, it does feel wonderful for a month or something . . . and then you begin to start coping with [the realization] that it's not going to make any difference really to how you feel about anything, and—it doesn't work. It doesn't mean changes. If you're a happy person, you were before and you will be afterwards, and if you're not, you weren't before and you won't be afterwards. And that kind of thing doesn't make a blind bit of difference to how you feel about anything. But even though you know that, it still takes you a long time to assimilate it."

5. Yorke, explains O'Brien to *Access Mag*, "is the lead singer, he's the primary songwriter in the band, so you've always got leaders, and he's the leader of the band." In my book *Roger Waters and Pink Floyd: The Concept Albums* (Madison, NJ: Fairleigh Dickinson University Press, 2015), I posit that Roger Waters was the creative leader of Pink Floyd.

6. In *Meeting People Is Easy*, Yorke remarks that performing for 40,000 people at the Glastonbury festival in June 1997 "wasn't a human feeling" and that he had "never felt like that." This experience became common during the *OK Computer* tour, which led to reservations about future touring. In retrospect Yorke said to G. Yago on VH1, "To me, it was a long series of having to deal with these ghosts in my cupboard and they were all coming out one by one. The touring thing especially. I really didn't think that I could deal with it . . . at all. I just didn't think I could cope. And I can't really explain to you why. Other than, as Ed was saying, at the end of doing *OK Computer*, and we were doing these really stupidly big gigs. Uhm. It was like, I dunno. Like there

was suddenly 40,000 people in here °taps head°, and I'd left." The song "How to Disappear Completely" from *Kid A* (2000), a title "allegedly snatched from a book on dismantling and reconstructing identities," as Brent Sirota noted in *Pitchfork*, documents the prelude to a similar experience the same month at a concert in Dublin. Compare this response with Waters's satirization of "stadium rock" in Pink Floyd's *The Wall* (1979).

7. I would surmise that the practice of including lyrics was resumed because Yorke's crisis period, by the time of *Hail to the Thief*, had been successfully navigated.

8. "On previous records," Colin Greenwood mentions on BBC's *Mixing It* with Robert Sandall and Mark Russell, "we've had copies of the words while we were working them out live in our rehearsal room, but on [*Kid A*] Thom had a long period of difficulty finding outlets for expression. So it didn't even get to the stage where we had copies of the words to look at because he wasn't sure what he wanted to say with them anyway."

9. "[Yorke] didn't stop there either," according to James Doheny in *Radiohead: Karma Police*; he "grafted the reverse phonetics onto some wholly new, forward-going words so well that if you didn't know otherwise you would think the first verse was simply running backwards as part of the original track."

10. The vocoder is an electronic device that synthesizes speech, and the *ondes martenot* referred to below is an electronic instrument that Maurice Martenot invented and that the French composer Olivier Messiaen most famously employed.

11. Yorke suggests that the model for "Pyramid Song" is "Freedom" by Charles Mingus, whose influence is also heard in "The National Anthem," specifically in its horn arrangement. "We were influenced," said Yorke to Greg Kot of *CD NOW*, "so much by [pioneering German electronic bands] Can and Kraftwerk, and Faust, and [avant-garde classical composers Olivier] Messiaen and [Krzysztof] Penderecki, and the 13th Floor Elevators, and all this electronic malarkey, it is difficult to still justify just being a rock band, and that's it. I think toleration and absolutely no musical or technological restriction is going to change the way we feel about music, but I still love electric guitars, and drums, and singing."

12. First made possible by sound recording technologies (as Yorke's mention above of the tape machine suggests), it's easy to forget that this was an unprecedented experience in the musical life of human beings prior to the late nineteenth century.

13. According to Yorke in Nick Kent's "Happy Now?" "He's got all this mad shit that's got nothing to do with the electric guitar. He joined the band when he was 14 and he was already a multi-instrumentalist even then. He can play keyboards and write string arrangements. He can even read music. Actually

they all can now, except for me. Bit scary, that. Everything he picks up he can make music on. It's totally logical that he should be trying other things." As Yorke reported to Kot of *CD NOW*, "There is a restriction about people defending their own musical patch, which just gets a bit daft after a while. It wasn't really the point. I think everybody was surprisingly cool with not being involved necessarily directly in certain tracks."

14. The biases of digital technologies, that is, their potential for precision, have led to an increased effort to make "perfect" music. The Autotuner represents a primary example of this. Rhythmically, moreover, one ensemblist will often play slightly ahead of the beat, while his or her fellows may play just behind the beat, creating an interesting groove. The tendency, however, is for this idiosyncratic "feel" to be expunged from recorded performances in favor of the exactitude achievable through digital manipulation.

15. This activity is often designated as "internet viral marketing."

16. At the end of an interview in August 2001, Thom asked the host, "Do you think anybody will listen to that? It was a bit technical. I just can't imagine it on a modern rock station" and proceeded to howl with laughter, 99.1 WHFS (http://www.whfs.com).

17. Pink Floyd had considered performing *The Wall* in a similar manner by employing Mark Fisher's "Slug" tent, but the idea was abandoned due to the problems at the time of licensing temporary sites on which to use it.

6. CRAZY, MAYBE?

1. Definitely ahead of their time, the group went on to establish Sandbag, a company that offered the expertise of W.A.S.T.E. to others, and that then got its own warehousing and distribution arm, Quicksand Distribution, and an American subsidiary, Eleventy Five, whose business is unclear.

2. In regard to the *Kid A/Amnesiac* sessions, O'Brien was to say, as Mac Randall notes in *Exit Music*, "I've never smoked so much weed in my life. It was a way to get through the chaos." In Trevor Baker's *Thom Yorke: Radiohead and Trading Solo*, Yorke is quoted as saying, "I love getting stoned."

3. Yorke puzzlingly suggested at the same time, "They are separate because they cannot run in a straight line with each other. They cancel each other out as overall finished things."

4. This new technological power was, perhaps, to culminate on April 12, 2003, in what were perhaps the largest ever simultaneous worldwide mass protests, which took place against the Anglo-American invasion of Iraq.

5. That money creation is inherent in the modern conception of political sovereignty is apparent in the fact that "[Benjamin] Franklin cited restrictions

upon paper money as one of the main reasons for the alienation of the American provinces from the mother country," and therefore, though it's seldom observed by historians, as James Ferguson points out in *The Power of the Purse*, the colonists' rights to create their own money was among the primary reasons for the American War of Independence. In this respect, insofar as they diminish the degree of control that states have on their monetary policy, the contemporary movement toward establishing regional currencies—as with the "Euro" and the proposed North American "Amero"—are similar vexations of political sovereignty. In the latter case, however, it is one that is being brought into effect with minimal public debate, and driven primarily by actors such as the U.S. Council on Foreign Relations.

8. GOING SOLO

1. In late 2008, according to the *New Musical Express*, the band joined a pressure group known as the Featured Artists' Coalition, which argues that bands should maintain the copyright to their music by leasing it to record labels and that its members should be consulted with regard to how their music is used, how it is sold, and who receives the money—wanting performers' rights to be brought into line with those of songwriters.

2. Interestingly, this all parallels the band's lack of progress during the initial rehearsals and recordings for the album, and in interviews Yorke likened not having a record deal to the old cartoons that had the coyote chasing the roadrunner, then running off a cliff, but not falling until he looked down.

3. In the song "Skip Divided" from *The Eraser*, the protagonist flaps around and dive-bombs "frantically around your light," swooping around the person's head and blinded by their "daylight."

10. FORGING FORWARD (2013–2016)

1. Radiohead formed Xurbia Xendless Ltd. prior to self-releasing *In Rainbows* and formed Ticker Tape Ltd. in order to distribute *The King Of Limbs*. The band has apparently formed some twenty entities since the early 1990s.

11. LOOKING BACKWARD (2017–2018)

1. See my book *Roger Waters and Pink Floyd: The Concept Albums* (Madison, NJ: Fairleigh Dickinson University Press, 2015).

FURTHER READING

Abramovich, Alex. "The Anti-Christs: Radiohead Defies Rock's Own, Personal Jesus Myth." *Slate*, June 8, 2001. Accessed July 25, 2018. http://www.slate.com.

Access Mag. "Interview with Ed." *Access Mag* (year end issue), December 2000–January 2001. Accessed March 7, 2002. http://www.accessmag.com.

Adams, Douglas. *The Hitchhiker's Guide to the Galaxy*. London: Pan Books, 2009.

Adams, Michael. "Reflections on an Ethical Society." *IDEAS*, CBC Radio, Toronto, 2001.

Adams, Tim. "Thom Yorke: 'If I Can't Enjoy This Now, When Do I Start?'" *Observer*, February 23, 2013. Accessed July 25, 2018. https://www.theguardian.com.

Amore, Roy, and Julia Ching. "The Buddhist Tradition." In *World Religions: Eastern Traditions*, ed. W. Oxtoby, 198–315. Don Mills, Ontario: Oxford University Press, 2002.

Artists for Palestine UK. "Chomsky Clarifies Position on the Cultural Boycott of Israel." *Artists for Palestine UK Website*, October 12, 2017. Accessed December 1, 2018. https://artistsforpalestine.org.uk.

Baker, Trevor. *Thom Yorke: Radiohead and Trading Solo*. Shropshire, UK: Independent Music Press, 2009.

Baldwin, Alex. "Interview with Thom." *Here's the Thing*, WNYC, April 1, 2013. Accessed July 25, 2018. https://www.wnycstudios.org.

Barber, Benjamin. *A Passion for Democracy*. Princeton, NJ: Princeton University Press, 1998.

Barlow, Eve. "From Panic Attack to Solace: The Arc of a Radiohead Concert." *LA Weekly*, August 4, 2016. Accessed July 25, 2018. http://www.laweekly.com.

Bartleet, Larry. "What Thom Yorke Thinks About Corbyn, YouTube, His Last Album, and Old Radiohead Songs: His Italian Interview Translated." *NME*, December 1, 2015. Accessed July 25, 2018. https://www.nme.com.

BBC. "Interview with Thom." *The First Time With . . .* , BBC Radio 6 Music, June 11, 2017. Accessed July 25, 2018. https://www.youtube.com.

Bhattacharya, Shaoni. "Global Suicide Toll Exceeds War and Murder." *New Scientist*, September 2004. Accessed July 25, 2018. http://www.newscientist.com.

Binelli, Mark. "The Future according to Radiohead: How Radiohead Ditched the Record Business and Still Toed the Charts." *Rolling Stone*, February 2008, 1045. Accessed July 25, 2018. http://www.rollingstone.com.

Bittanti, Matteo. "Art Game: Radiohead's 'PolyFauna.'" *Game Scenes*, February 11, 2014. Accessed July 25, 2018. http://www.gamescenes.org.

Blum, Justin. "Exxon Posts Record Profit Net Is Highest Ever for a U.S. Company." *Washington Post*, January 31, 2006. https://www.washingtonpost.com.

Borow, Zev. "The Difference Engine." *Spin*, November 2000, 110–20.

Brennan, Anthony. "The Journey from 'Wherefore Are Thou Romeo? to 'Where Is My Romeo?': The Structure of *Romeo and Juliet*." In *Shakespeare's Dramatic Structures*, 52–69. London: Routledge, 1986/1988.

Burke, Kenneth. *Counter-Statement*. Berkeley: University of California Press, 1953/1968.

Byrne, David. "David Byrne and Thom Yorke on the Real Value of Music." *Wired* 16, no. 1, December 18, 2007. Accessed July 25, 2018. http://www.wired.com.

Capitol Records. "Radiohead Biography." Accessed July 25, 2018. http://capitolrecords.com.

Carson, Paula, and Helen Walters. "Radiohead: Modified Organisms." *Creative Review*, October 2000. Accessed July 25, 2018. https://citizeninsane.eu.

Cayley, David. "The Scapegoat: Rene Girard's Anthropology of Violence and Religion." *Ideas*, CBC Radio (Toronto), March 5–9, 2001.

Clarke, Martin. *Radiohead: Hysterical and Useless*. London: Plexus, 2000.

Coke Babie. "Interview with Thom Yorke." Coke Babie, 1997. http://cokebabie.tripod.com.

Cook-Wilson, Winston. "Artists, Activists Challenge Thom Yorke's Defense of Radiohead's Israel Concert." *Spin*, June 13, 2017. Accessed July 18, 2018. https://www.spin.com.

Crystal, Graef. *In Search of Excess: The Overcompensation of American Executives*. New York: Norton, 1991.

Dalton, Stephen. "How to Disappear Completely." *Uncut*, August 2001, 42–47.

Daly, Rhian. "Thom Yorke Tops List of Most Legally Downloaded Artists on BitTorrent in 2014." *NME*, December 25, 2014. Accessed July 25, 2018. http://www.nme.com.

Davies, Mark. "Trade Campaign Hoping for 'Delia Effect.'" *BBC News*, June 24, 2003. Accessed July 25, 2018. http://news.bbc.co.uk.

Dazed and Confused. "Splitting Atoms." February 2013. Accessed July 25, 2018. https://citizeninsane.eu.

Deibert, Ronald J. *Black Code: Inside the Battle for Cyberspace*. Toronto: McLelland & Stewart, 2013.

Del Signore, John. "A Conversation with Jonny Greenwood." Gothamist, October 10, 2007. Accessed July 25, 2018. http://gothamist.com.

Dewey, John. *Freedom and Culture*. New York: Capricorn Books, 1963.

Dickinson, Emily. *The Poems of Emily Dickinson: Variorum Edition*. Edited by Ralph W. Franklin. Cambridge, MA: Belknap Press of Harvard University Press, 1998.

Doheny, James. *Radiohead: Karma Police*. London: Carlton Books, 2002.

Donwood, Stanley. *Dead Children Playing*. London: Verso, 2015.

Doyle, Alister. "UN Urges World to Slow Extinctions: Three Each Hour." *Truthout*, May 23, 2007. Accessed July 25, 2018. http://www.truthout.org.

Draper, Brian. "Interview with Thom Yorke, October 11th, 2004." Connecting with Culture, 2005. Accessed July 25, 2018. http://www.licc.org.uk.

Eisenhower, Dwight. *Public Papers of the Presidents*. Office of the Federal Register, National Archives and Records Administration, 1960.

Ellul, Jacques. *Propaganda: The Formation of Men's Attitudes*. New York: Vintage, 1965.

———. *The Technological Society*. New York: Vintage, 1964.

Fanning, Dave. "Here's Looking at You, Kid." *Hot Press* 29, no. 19 (October 11, 2000): 28.

Ferguson, James. *The Power of the Purse: A History of American Public Finance, 1776–1790*. Chapel Hill: University of North Carolina Press, 1961.

Fisk, Phil. "Thom Yorke—In Pictures." *Guardian*, February 23, 2013. Accessed July 20, 2018. https://www.theguardian.com.

FM Reactor. "Interview with Ed." March 16, 2012. Accessed July 25, 2018. https://www.youtube.com.

Footman, Tim. *Radiohead: A Visual Documentary*. New Malden, UK: Chrome Dreams, 2002.

———. *Radiohead: Welcome to the Machine; OK Computer and the Death of the Classic Album*. New Malden, UK: Chrome Dreams, 2007.

Forbes, B., and G. Reisch. *Radiohead and Philosophy: Fitter Happier More Deductive*. Chicago: Open Court, 2009.

Fricke, David. "Bitter Prophet: Radiohead's Thom Yorke Lifts the Veil on Thief." *Rolling Stone*, June 3, 2003. Accessed July 25, 2018. http://www.rollingstone.com.

———. "Bitter Prophet: Thom Yorke on 'Hail to the Thief.'" *Rolling Stone*, June 26, 2003. Accessed December 4, 2018. http://www.rollingstone.com.

———. "Radiohead Reconnect." *Rolling Stone*, April 26, 2012. Accessed July 25, 2018. https://www.rollingstone.com.

———. "Radiohead Reloaded." *Rolling Stone*, October 27, 2011. Accessed July 25, 2018. https://citizeninsane.eu.

Fromm, Erich. *The Sane Society*. Greenwich, CT: Fawcett, 1970.

Gabriella. "Radiohead: They're Not So Angst-Ridden Once You Get to Know Them." *NY-Rock*, December 2000. Accessed August 16, 2005. http://www.nyrock.com.

Gandhi, Mohandas. *The Essential Gandhi*. Edited by L. Fischer. New York: Random House, 1962.

Garner, Marty. "Weird Fission: Thom Yorke Detonates Atoms for Peace." *Filter*, March 2013. Accessed July 25, 2018. https://citizeninsane.eu.

Gee, Grant, dir. *Meeting People Is Easy*. DVD. London: Parlophone, 1998.

Gibsone, Harriet. "Thom Yorke Opens Up to Radiohead Fan Daniel Craig in Celebrity Interview." *Guardian*, July 15, 2013. Accessed July 25, 2018. https://www.theguardian.com..

Girard, René. "The Plague in Literature and Myth." In *"To Double Business Bound": Essays on Literature, Mimesis, and Anthropology*, 136–54. Baltimore: Johns Hopkins University Press, 1978.

———. *The Scapegoat*. Baltimore: Johns Hopkins University Press, 1986.

Greene, Andy. "19 Things We Learned Hanging Out with Radiohead." *Rolling Stone*, June 8, 2017. Accessed July 25, 2018. https://www.rollingstone.com.

———. "Radiohead's OK Computer: An Oral History." *Rolling Stone*, June 16, 2017. Accessed July 25, 2018. http://www.rollingstone.com.

———. "Radiohead's Rhapsody in Gloom: 'OK Computer' 20 Years Later." *Rolling Stone*, May 31, 2017. Accessed July 25, 2018. https://www.rollingstone.com.

Griffiths, Dai. *OK Computer*. New York: Continuum, 2004.

Grossman, Karl. *Weapons in Space*. New York: Seven Stories Press, 2001.

Guardian. "Radiohead's 'Sixth Man' Reveals the Secrets behind Their Covers." November 22, 2006. https://www.theguardian.com.

"*Hail to the Thief* release party." Citizen Insane, June 10, 2003. Accessed July 25, 2018. http://citizeninsane.eu.

Hainge, Greg. "To(rt)uring the Minotaur: Radiohead, Pop, Unnatural Couplings, and Mainstream Subversion." In *The Music and Art of Radiohead*, edited by Joseph Tate, 62–84. Burlington, VT: Ashgate, 2005.

Hale, Jonathan. *Radiohead: From a Great Height*. Toronto: ECW Press, 1999.

Hansen, M. "Deforming Rock: Radiohead's Plunge into the Sonic Continuum." In *The Music and Art of Radiohead*, edited by Joseph Tate, 118–38. Burlington, VT: Ashgate, 2005.

Hardy, Thomas. *Jude the Obscure*. London: Penguin Classics, 1896/1985.

Harrison, Andrew. "Radiohead: The Escape Artists." *Word*, May 7, 2008. Accessed July 25, 2018. http://www.wordmagazine.co.uk.

Held, Barbara. "The Tyranny of the Positive Attitude in America." *Journal of Clinical Psychology* 58, no. 9 (2002): 965–69.

Hill, Jamie. "A Chat with Philip Selway from Radiohead." *Ocelot*, November 2011. Accessed July 25, 2018. https://citizeninsane.eu.

Ignatieff, Michael. "The Narcissism of Minor Difference." In *Clash of Identities: Media, Manipulation, and Politics of the Self*, edited by James Littleton. Toronto: Prentice Hall, 1996.

Ingham, Tim. "Thom Yorke Just Compared YouTube to Nazi Germany." *Music Business Worldwide*, November 30, 2015. Accessed July 25, 2018. https://www.musicbusinessworldwide.com.

Johnson, Nathaniel. "Swine of the Times." *Harper's Magazine*, May, 2006. Accessed November 28, 2018. https://harpers.org.

Johnston, Amy E. Boyle. "Ray Bradbury: Fahrenheit 451 Misinterpreted." *LA Weekly*, May 30, 2007. Accessed July 25, 2018. http://www.laweekly.com.

Jones, Lucy. "Hail to the Thief Is 10: Revisiting Radiohead's Underrated Masterpiece." *NME*, June 7, 2013. Accessed July 25, 2018. http://www.nme.com.

Kamer, Gijsbert. "Interview with Thom Yorke." *Lola-da-musica*, Dutch TV (VPRO), October 19, 2000.

Kemp, Mark. "OK Computer." *Rolling Stone*, July 10, 1997. Accessed November 28, 2018. http://www.rollingstone.com.

Kennedy, John. "Interview with Ed." *XFM "X-Posure,"* June 2017. Accessed July 25, 2018. https://www.youtube.com.

———. "Interview with Thom and Ed." *XFM "X-Posure,"* January 3, 2008. Accessed July 25, 2018. http://citizeninsane.eu.

———. "Thom Yorke on 'Hail to the Thief.'" XFM Uploaded, 2003. Accessed July 25, 2018. http://www.xfm.co.uk.

Kent, Nick. "Happy Now?" *Mojo*, June 2001. Accessed July 25, 2018. http://www.followmearound.com.

———. "Ghost in the Machine." *Mojo*, August 2006. Accessed July 25, 2018. https://citizeninsane.eu.

Klein, Naomi. *No Logo: Taking Aim at the Brand Bullies*. Toronto: Vintage Canada, 2000.

———. Excerpt from *HUMO*. October 2001. Accessed November 28, 2018. http://radiohead1.tripod.com/news/october.htm.

Klosterman, Chuck. "Fitter Happier: Radiohead Return." *Spin*, 2003. Accessed July 25, 2018. http://www.spin.com.

Kot, Greg. "Alluring Otherworldliness: It's Difficult Justifying Being a Rock Band." *Chicago Tribune*, July 31, 2001, 1.

———. "Radiohead: Making Records Is Easy." *CD NOW*, June 2001. Accessed July 25, 2018. http://www.geocities.com.

Kreps, Daniel. "Roger Waters Criticizes 'Whining' Thom Yorke Over Radiohead's Israel Gig." *Rolling Stone*, July 16, 2017. Accessed July 25, 2018. https://www.rollingstone.com.

Kuttner, Robert. *Everything for Sale: The Virtues and Limits of Markets*. Chicago: University of Chicago Press, 1999.

Lamacq, Steve. "Interview with Ed and Phil." *BBC Radio 6 Music*, June 2017. Accessed July 25, 2018. https://www.youtube.com.

———. "Interview with Thom, Ed, and Colin." *Evening Session*, BBC Radio 1, May 29, 2001. Accessed July 25, 2018. https://www.youtube.com.

Letts, M. T. "'How to Disappear Completely': Radiohead and the Resistant Concept Album." PhD diss., University of Texas at Austin, 2005.

Lin, Marvin. *33 1/3 Kid A*. New York: Continuum, 2010.

McGovern, Kyle. "Radiohead Start Work on a New Album This Summer." *Spin*, February 13, 2013. Accessed July 25, 2018. https://www.spin.com.

McLean, Craig. "All Messed Up." *Observer*, June 18, 2006. Accessed July 25, 2018. http://www.guardian.co.uk.

———. "Caught in the Flash." *Observer*, December 9, 2007. Accessed July 25, 2018. https://www.theguardian.com.

———. "Radiohead: How They Took On 2001. And Won." *Face*, January 2002. Accessed July 25, 2018. https://citizeninsane.eu.

———. "Rainbow Warriors: Radiohead Interview." *Living Scotsman.com*, June 22, 2008. Accessed July 25, 2018. http://living.scotsman.com.

———. "Thom Yorke: 'It's Not My Job to Do Business with Politicians.'" *Observer*, June 17, 2006. https://www.theguardian.com.

McLuhan, Eric. *Electric Language: Understanding the Present*. Toronto: Stoddart, 1998.

McLuhan, Marshall. "Culture without Literacy." *Explorations* 1 (1953): 117–27.

———. *The Gutenberg Galaxy: The Making of Typographic Man*. Toronto: University of Toronto Press, 1962.

———. *The Medium and the Light: Reflections on Religion*. Toronto: Stoddart, 1999.

———. "New Media as Political Forms." *Explorations* 3 (1955): 120–26.

———. *Understanding Media: The Extensions of Man.* Cambridge, MA: MIT Press, 1994/ 1964.

McLuhan, Marshall, and Quentin Fiore. *War and Peace in the Global Village.* New York: Bantam, 1968.

Meyrowitz, Joshua. *No Sense of Place: The Impact of Electronic Media on Social Behavior.* Oxford: Oxford University Press, 1986.

Mincher, Chris. "Radiohead's Thom Yorke and Ed O'Brien." A.V. Club, July 1, 2008. Accessed July 25, 2018. http://www.avclub.com.

Minsker, Evan. "Colin Greenwood Working with Children's Radio Foundation, Shares Updates From South Africa." *Pitchfork,* January 26, 2013. Accessed July 4, 2018. https:// pitchfork.com.

Monster Children. "The Untold Stories behind Radiohead's Album Covers." November 8, 2017. Accessed July 25, 2018. https://www.monsterchildren.com.

Moon, Tom. "Radiohead: Companion to Kid A Sessions." *Philadelphia Inquirer,* June 3, 2001, H8.

Moran, Caitlin. "Everything Was Just Fear." *Select,* July 1997. Accessed November 28, 2018. https://citizeninsane.eu.

MTV. Colin Greenwood interview. July 1997. Accessed November 28, 2018. http://colin-greenwood-interviews.blogspot.com.

———. "Interview with Thom." April 30, 2008. Accessed July 25, 2018. https://citizeninsane.eu.

Music Ally. "Exclusive: Warner Chappell Reveals Radiohead's 'In Rainbows' Pot of Gold." October 15, 2008. Accessed July 25, 2018. http://musically.com.

National Public Radio (NPR). "Interview with Thom and Ed." *All Things Considered,* October 6, 2011. Accessed July 25, 2018. https://www.youtube.com.

Nicks, Denver. "Thom Yorke Releases Experimental Solo Project as Radiohead Confirms New Album." *Time,* September 26, 2014. Accessed July 25, 2018. http://time.com.

NME. "Bright Yorke." January 31, 2001. Accessed July 25, 2018. http://www.nme.com.

———. "Radiohead and Kaiser Chiefs Push for New Music Rights." October 4, 2008. Accessed July 25, 2018. http://www.nme.com.

———. "Radiohead Ask Fans to Reconsider How They Get to Gigs." May 2, 2008. Accessed July 25, 2018. http://www.nme.com.

———. "Radiohead Defend Their Carbon Footprint to Fans." January 3, 2008. Accessed July 25, 2018. http://www.nme.com.

———. "Radiohead Reveal How Successful 'In Rainbows' Download Really Was." October 15, 2008. Accessed July 25, 2018. http://www.nme.com.

———. "Radiohead Reveal Terrifying New Album." April 3, 2006. Accessed July 25, 2018. http://www.nme.com.

———. "Radiohead Slam George Bush on U.S. TV." April 24, 2008. Accessed July 25, 2018. http://www.nme.com.

———. "Radiohead's Eco-Friendly Tour Secrets Revealed." May 23, 2008. Accessed July 25, 2018. http://www.nme.com.

———. "Radiohead's Thom Yorke Rubbishes Suggestion That Music's Future Is on the Internet." January 2, 2008. Accessed July 25, 2018. http://www.nme.com.

———. "Rainbow Warriors." December 8, 2007. Accessed July 25, 2018. https://citizeninsane.eu.

———. "Thom for Peace, Love, and Understanding." December 11, 2001. Accessed July 25, 2018. http://www.nme.com.

———. "Thom Yorke and Rachel Owen Announce Separation." August 15, 2015. Accessed July 2, 2018. http://www.nme.com.

———. "Thom Yorke Leads Protest Over Bush Visit." November 19, 2003. Accessed July 25, 2018. http://www.nme.com.

———. "Thom Yorke Leads 'Star Wars' Protest." September 27, 2004. Accessed July 25, 2018. http://www.nme.com.

Occupy TV. "3D and Thom Yorke." November 12, 2008. Accessed July 25, 2018. https:// www.youtube.com.

Official *Hail to the Thief* interview CD. April 2003. Accessed July 25, 2018. https://www.youtube.com.

Oldham, James. "Radiohead." *New Musical Express* (Christmas double issue) 23, no. 30 (December 2000).

Oliveros, P. "Invisible Jukebox." *Wire*, July 2001, 209.

Ong, Walter. *Orality and Literacy*. London: Routledge, 1982.

Orwell, George. *Nineteen Eighty-Four*. New York: Penguin, 1949.

Pareles, John. "On 'OK Computer,' Radiohead Saw the Future: Ours." *New York Times*, June 21 , 2017. Accessed July 25, 2018. https://www.nytimes.com.

———. "Pay What You Want for This Article." *New York Times*, December 9, 2007. Accessed July 25, 2018. https://www.nytimes.com.

———. "With Radiohead, and Alone, the Sweet Malaise of Thom Yorke." *New York Times*, July 2, 2006. Accessed July 25, 2018. http://www.nytimes.com.

Patterson, Sylvia. "Let's Try to Set the Record Straight." *NME*, May 19, 2001. Accessed July 25, 2018. https://citizeninsane.eu.

Paytress, Mark. "Chasing Rainbows." *Mojo*, February 2008. Accessed July 25, 2018. https://citizeninsane.eu.

———. *Radiohead: The Complete Guide to Their Music*. London: Omnibus, 2005.

Postman, Neil. *Amusing Ourselves to Death: Public Discourse in the Age of Show Business*. New York: Penguin, 1985.

———. *Technopoly: The Surrender of Culture to Technology*. New York: Vintage, 1993.

Powell, Andrew. *Living Buddhism*. Berkeley: University of California Press, 1995.

Powers, Anne. "A Conversation with . . . Thom Yorke: Free Agent." *Los Angeles Times*, June 28, 2006. Accessed July 25, 2018. https://citizeninsane.eu.

Pricco, Evan. "A Stanley Donwood Interview." *Juxtapoz*, September 2, 2010. Accessed July 25, 2018. https://web.archive.org.

Price, Nancy. "Interview: Radiohead (Part 2)." *Consumable*, September 15, 1997. Accessed July 25, 2018. http://www.westnet.com.

Pynchon, Thomas. "Is It O.K. to Be a Luddite?" *New York Times Book Review*, October 28, 1984, 40–41.

Pytlik, Mark. "Radiohead: The King of Limbs Album Review." *Pitchfork*, February 24, 2011. Accessed July 25, 2018. https://pitchfork.com.

Radiohead Fans for Palestine. "A Reply to Thom Yorke's Comments in Rolling Stone." *Radiohead Don't Play Israel* (blog), June 2, 2017. Accessed Dec. 1, 2018. https://radioheaddontplayisrael.blogspot.com.

"Radio-Unfriendly Unit Shifters." *Melody Maker* 71 (October 1, 1994): 48–49.

Raftery, Brian. "Bent Out of Shape." *Spin*, August 2006. Accessed July 25, 2018. https://citizeninsane.eu.

Randall, Mac. *Exit Music: The Radiohead Story*. London: Omnibus, 2012.

———. "Radiohead Get the Details." *Musician*, no. 226 (September 1997): 46–53.

Reuters. "Human Being or Human Folly?" *Wired News*, March 9, 2001. Accessed July 25, 2018. http://www.wirednews.com.

Reynolds, Simon. "Walking on Thin Ice." *Wire*, no. 209 (July 2001): 26–33.

Rivera, Adam. "Radiohead Unpackt." 2001. Accessed June 1, 2013. http://www.radioheadunpackt.com/okc13.html.

Robinson, John. "It's Clear and Pretty—but I Think People Won't Get It." *NME*, May 3, 2003. Accessed July 25, 2018. https://citizeninsane.eu.

Robinson, Kirsty. "Interview with Ed." *Saints of Somewhere*, June 2017. Accessed July 25, 2018. https://www.youtube.com.

Roffman, Michael. "Atoms for Peace, Thom Yorke's Side Project, Isolated and Lost on Amok." *Time*, February 28, 2013. Accessed July 25, 2018. http://entertainment.time.com.

Rolling Stone. "Thom Yorke Breaks Silence on Israel Controversy." June 2, 2017. Accessed July 25, 2018. https://www.rollingstone.com.

Rose, Phil. "René Girard as Media Ecologist." In *Valuation and Media Ecology: Ethics, Morals, and Laws*, edited by C. Anton, 91–122. Cresskill, NJ: Hampton, 2010.

————. *Roger Waters and Pink Floyd: The Concept Albums*. Madison, NJ: Fairleigh Dickinson University Press, 2015.

Sagan, Carl. *The Demon-Haunted World: Science as a Candle in the Dark*. New York: Ballantine, 1997.

Sandall, Robert, and Mark Russell. "Interview with Jonny and Colin." *Mixing It*, BBC Radio 3, January 20, 2001. Accessed July 25, 2018. https://citizeninsane.eu.

Schaffner, Nicholas. *Saucerful of Secrets: The Pink Floyd Odyssey*. New York: Harmony Books, 1991.

Schleifer, B. "Eclipsing: The Influence of *The Dark Side of the Moon* on the Next Generation's Music through Radiohead's *OK Computer*." In *"Speak to Me": The Legacy of Pink Floyd's The Dark Side of the Moon*, edited by R. Reisling, 208–17. Hampshire, UK: Ashgate, 2005.

Schneiderman, Davis. "'We Got Heads on Sticks/You Got Ventriloquists': Radiohead and the Improbability of Resistance." In *The Music and Art of Radiohead*, edited by Joseph Tate, 15–37. Burlington, VT: Ashgate, 2005.

Severs, John. "Into the Woods: Radiohead's In-House Artist Captures Britain's Hidden Forest Walks." *Independent*, October 4, 2013. Accessed July 25, 2018. https://www.independent.co.uk.

————. "Radiohead: The King of Limbs—Artist Stanley Donwood Talks about His Newspaper Visuals." *Pitchfork*, May 2, 2011. Accessed July 25, 2018. https://pitchfork.com.

Sheffield, Rob. "Radiohead's Summer 2018 U.S. Tour Is a Career-Capping Triumph." *Rolling Stone*, July 16, 2018. Accessed July 25, 2018. https://www.rollingstone.com.

Sinclair, David. "Q&A: Thom Yorke." *Rolling Stone*, December 25, 1997, 90.

Sirota, Brent. "The Ministry of Information: Journey to the Center of Kid A." *Pitchfork*, October 3, 2000. Accessed March 7, 2002. http://www.pitchfork.com.

Smith, A. "Sound and Fury." *Observer*, October 1, 2000. Accessed September 17, 2001. http://observer.guardian.co.uk.

Somerville, Margaret. "Reflections on an Ethical Society." *Ideas*, CBC Radio (Toronto), 2001.

Sood, Akhil. "Jonny Greenwood Is the Controller: Typewriters and Washing Machines." *Sunday Guardian*, February 21, 2015. Accessed July 25, 2018. http://www.sunday-guardian.com.

Steele, Sam. "Grand Control to Major Thom." *Vox*, July 1997. Accessed July 25, 2018. https://citizeninsane.eu.

Stevenson, Jane. "Radiohead of State: Brit Band's New Album a Bush Bash." *Toronto Sun*, June 3, 2003.

Sullivan, James. "Thom Yorke Loosens Up." *San Francisco Chronicle*, June 24, 2001. Accessed November 28, 2018. https://www.sfgate.com.

Sutcliffe, Phil. "Death Is All Around." *Q*, October 1997. Accessed July 25, 2018. http://www.followmearound.com.

Sweet, Jay. "Dancing in the Dark." *Paste*, August 2006. Accessed July 25, 2018. https://citizeninsane.eu.

Then It Must Be True. "Interview with Eric Gorfain." September 2001. Accessed July 25, 2018. http://thenitmustbetrue.com.

Thomas-Hansard, Artemis. "Thom Yorke Had the Best Response to Radiohead's Coachella Sound Issues." *LA Weekly*, April 15, 2017. Accessed July 25, 2018. http://www.laweekly.com.

Thompson, Ben. "There Was a Really Cool Momentum." *Mojo*, March 2013. Accessed July 25, 2018. https://citizeninsane.eu.

Thorpe, Adam. "In a Room with Radiohead." *Times Literary Supplement*, May 18, 2016. Accessed July 25, 2018. https://www.the-tls.co.uk.

Times (London). "Bush Was 'Tired of Swatting Flies' and Targeted al Qaeda." April 8, 2004. Accessed July 14, 2018. https://www.thetimes.co.uk.

Toronto Star. "Interview with Thom Yorke." June 8, 2003. https://www.thestar.com.

Van Aelst, Peter, and Stefaan Walgrave. "New Media, New Movements? The Role of the Internet in Shaping the 'Anti-Globalization' Movement." *Information, Communication and Society* 5, no. 4 (2002): 465–93.

Vulliamy, Ed. "How Radiohead Took America by Stealth." *Observer*, August 19, 2001. Accessed October 25, 2001. http://observer.guardian.co.uk.

Walker, Tim. "Thom Yorke: Why He's Glad to Have Made Such a Big Noise." *Independent*, January 3, 2008. Accessed July 25, 2018. http://www.independent.co.uk.

Washington Post. "Are CEOs Worth Their Salaries?" October 2, 2002. https://www.washingtonpost.com.

Wiederhorn, Jon. "Radiohead: A New Life; Interview with Thom." MTV, June 19, 2003. Accessed July 25, 2018. http://www.mtv.com.

Wieseltier, Leon. "On Love and Death: Part II." *Ideas*, CBC Radio (Toronto), 2001.

Williams, Eliza. "Stanley Donwood and the Tempest." *Creative Review*, January 3, 2017. Accessed July 25, 2018. https://web.archive.org.

Wolf, Maryanne. *Proust and the Squid: The Story and Science of the Reading Brain.* New York: HarperCollins, 2007.

Yago, G. "Radiohead: Played in Full." VH1, July 18, 2001. Accessed April 1, 2002. http://www.vh1.com.

Yorke, Thom. "Losing the Faith." *Guardian*, September 8, 2003. Accessed July 25, 2018. https://www.theguardian.com.

———. "Thom Yorke: Why I'm a Climate Optimist." *Observer*, March 20, 2008. Accessed July 25, 2018. http://www.guardian.co.uk.

Zoric, Lorin. "Fitter, Happier, More Productive." *Juice Magazine*, October 2000. Accessed July 25, 2018. http://www.followmearound.com.

FURTHER LISTENING

RADIOHEAD

Pablo Honey (Parlophone, 1993)
The Bends (Parlophone, 1995)
OK Computer (Parlophone, 1997)
Kid A (Parlophone, 2000)
Amnesiac (Parlophone, 2001)
I Might Be Wrong: Live Recordings (2001)
Hail to the Thief (Parlophone, 2003)
In Rainbows (XL Recordings, 2007)
Radiohead Box Set (Parlophone, 2007)
Radiohead: The Best Of (Parlophone, 2008)
The King of Limbs (XL Recordings, 2011)
TKOL RMX (XL Recordings, 2011)
A Moon Shaped Pool (XL Recordings, 2016)
OK Computer OKNOTOK 1997 2017 (XL Recordings, 2017)

RADIOHEAD EPS

Drill (Parlophone, 1992)
Itch (Parlophone, 1994)
My Iron Lung (1994)
No Surprises/Running from Demons (Parlophone, 1997)
Airbag/How Am I Driving? (Parlophone, 1998)

Com Lag (2plus2isfive) (Parlophone, 2004)

JONNY GREENWOOD ALBUMS

Junun (with Shye Ben Tzur and the Rajasthan Express; Nonesuch Records, 2015)

JONNY GREENWOOD SOUNDTRACKS

Bodysong (Parlophone, 2003)
There Will Be Blood (Nonesuch Records, 2004)
Norwegian Wood (Nonesuch Records, 2007)
We Need to Talk About Kevin (Nonesuch Records, 2011)
The Master (Nonesuch Records, 2012)
Inherent Vice (Nonesuch Records, 2014)
Phantom Thread (Nonesuch Records, 2017)
You Were Never Really Here (Nonesuch Records, 2017)

JONNY GREENWOOD CONCERT WORKS

2004   *smear* for two ondes martenots and chamber ensemble of nine players

2004   *Piano for Children* for piano and orchestra (withdrawn)

2005   *Popcorn Superhet Receiver* for string orchestra

2007   *There Will Be Blood* live film version

2010   *Doghouse* for string trio and orchestra

2011   *48 Responses to Polymorphia* for 48 solo strings, all doubling optional pacay bean shakers

2011   *Suite from "Noruwei no Mori" (Norwegian Wood)* for orchestra

2012   *Suite from "There Will Be Blood"* for string orchestra

2014   *Water* for two flutes, upright piano, chamber organ, two tanpura, and string orchestra

PHIL SELWAY SOLO ALBUMS

Familial (Bella Union, 2010)
Weatherhouse (Bella Union, 2014)

PHIL SELWAY EPS

Running Blind (Bella Union, 2011)

PHIL SELWAY SOUNDTRACKS

Let Me Go (Bella Union, 2017)

THOM YORKE SOLO ALBUMS

The Eraser (XL Recordings, 2006)
The Eraser Rmxs (XL Recordings, 2009)
Amok (with Atoms for Peace; XL Recordings, 2013)
Tomorrow's Modern Boxes (self-released, 2014)

THOM YORKE EPS

Spitting Feathers (XL Recordings, 2007)

INDEX

ABOUT THE AUTHOR

Phil Rose (PhD) has published numerous articles on various topics related to media ecology and is author of the book *Roger Waters and Pink Floyd: The Concept Albums* (2015), a project for which he extensively interviewed the former creative leader of the classic group. He is likewise the author of *Radiohead and the Global Movement for Change: "Pragmatism Not Idealism"* (2016) and editor of a collection dedicated to the thought of cultural critic Neil Postman titled *Confronting Technopoly: Charting a Course toward Human Survival* (2017). A past president of the Media Ecology Association, he has taught at a number of Canadian universities and is current chair of the Silvan Tomkins Institute.